Zoom

by Phil Simon
Author of *Slack For Dummies*

Kansas City, MO Public Library
0000187934328

W9-BKI-473

Zoom For Dummies®

Published by: **John Wiley & Sons, Inc.**, 111 River Street, Hoboken, NJ 07030-5774, www.wiley.com

Copyright © 2020 by John Wiley & Sons, Inc., Hoboken, New Jersey

Published simultaneously in Canada

No part of this publication may be reproduced, stored in a retrieval system or transmitted in any form or by any means, electronic, mechanical, photocopying, recording, scanning or otherwise, except as permitted under Sections 107 or 108 of the 1976 United States Copyright Act, without the prior written permission of the Publisher. Requests to the Publisher for permission should be addressed to the Permissions Department, John Wiley & Sons, Inc., 111 River Street, Hoboken, NJ 07030, (201) 748-6011, fax (201) 748-6008, or online at http://www.wiley.com/go/permissions.

Trademarks: Wiley, For Dummies, the Dummies Man logo, Dummies.com, Making Everything Easier, and related trade dress are trademarks or registered trademarks of John Wiley & Sons, Inc. and may not be used without written permission. Zoom is a trademark of Zoom Video Communications, Inc. All other trademarks are the property of their respective owners. John Wiley & Sons, Inc. is not associated with any product or vendor mentioned in this book.

LIMIT OF LIABILITY/DISCLAIMER OF WARRANTY: THE PUBLISHER AND THE AUTHOR MAKE NO REPRESENTATIONS OR WARRANTIES WITH RESPECT TO THE ACCURACY OR COMPLETENESS OF THE CONTENTS OF THIS WORK AND SPECIFICALLY DISCLAIM ALL WARRANTIES, INCLUDING WITHOUT LIMITATION WARRANTIES OF FITNESS FOR A PARTICULAR PURPOSE. NO WARRANTY MAY BE CREATED OR EXTENDED BY SALES OR PROMOTIONAL MATERIALS. THE ADVICE AND STRATEGIES CONTAINED HEREIN MAY NOT BE SUITABLE FOR EVERY SITUATION. THIS WORK IS SOLD WITH THE UNDERSTANDING THAT THE PUBLISHER IS NOT ENGAGED IN RENDERING LEGAL, ACCOUNTING, OR OTHER PROFESSIONAL SERVICES. IF PROFESSIONAL ASSISTANCE IS REQUIRED, THE SERVICES OF A COMPETENT PROFESSIONAL PERSON SHOULD BE SOUGHT. NEITHER THE PUBLISHER NOR THE AUTHOR SHALL BE LIABLE FOR DAMAGES ARISING HEREFROM. THE FACT THAT AN ORGANIZATION OR WEBSITE IS REFERRED TO IN THIS WORK AS A CITATION AND/OR A POTENTIAL SOURCE OF FURTHER INFORMATION DOES NOT MEAN THAT THE AUTHOR OR THE PUBLISHER ENDORSES THE INFORMATION THE ORGANIZATION OR WEBSITE MAY PROVIDE OR RECOMMENDATIONS IT MAY MAKE. FURTHER, READERS SHOULD BE AWARE THAT INTERNET WEBSITES LISTED IN THIS WORK MAY HAVE CHANGED OR DISAPPEARED BETWEEN WHEN THIS WORK WAS WRITTEN AND WHEN IT IS READ.

For general information on our other products and services, please contact our Customer Care Department within the U.S. at 877-762-2974, outside the U.S. at 317-572-3993, or fax 317-572-4002. For technical support, please visit https://hub.wiley.com/community/support/dummies.

Wiley publishes in a variety of print and electronic formats and by print-on-demand. Some material included with standard print versions of this book may not be included in e-books or in print-on-demand. If this book refers to media such as a CD or DVD that is not included in the version you purchased, you may download this material at http://booksupport.wiley.com. For more information about Wiley products, visit www.wiley.com.

Library of Congress Control Number: 2020941202

ISBN 978-1-119-74214-2 (pbk); ISBN 978-1-119-74216-6 (ePDF); ISBN 978-1-119-74215-9 (epub)

Manufactured in the United States of America

SKY10020063_072420

Contents at a Glance

Table of Contents

Introduction

D epending on your age, you may take today's powerful communication technologies for granted. (I have done it myself.) Trust me, however: Not that long ago, communicating with others was a dramatically different experience.

As recently as the early 1990s, the most pervasive methods for exchanging messages included instruments of which you may have never heard: landlines, intra-office memos, typewriters, and Telex and fax machines. For personal correspondence, handwritten letters were commonplace, not relics of a bygone era.

The following statistic illustrates the extent to which communication has changed over the last 30-plus years.

On January 24, 2001, the Federal Communications Commission (FCC) released a study on the telecommunications industry. Remarkably, the FCC found that the average per-minute rate for interstate calls in 1984 was roughly 17 cents. (Read the study yourself at bit.ly/fcc-zoom.)

Say that you lived in northern New Jersey in 1984, as I did at the time. You called your friend in New York and talked for an hour. You could expect to pay $10 for the privilege. And forget about international calls. Back then, talking to someone in another country was prohibitively expensive. (And you think that long-distance relationships are hard now?) Even worse, the quality and reliability of audio calls usually left more than a bit to be desired. As for video calls, they were pipe dreams back then.

Fast forward to today. Put mildly, we're not in Kansas anymore.

Communication has undergone a veritable sea change. Thank the usual suspects: increasingly powerful computers, the Internet, the World Wide Web, email, Moore's Law, social networks, smartphones with their über-addictive apps, the explosion of affordable broadband connections, improvements from telecommunications carriers, ambitious entrepreneurs, and cloud computing.

The most recent addition to this formidable list is Zoom. Its suite of tools allows hundreds of millions of people to communicate and collaborate easily, affordably, and reliably with others no matter where they are. Both professionally and personally, Zoom allows people to stay in touch with each other, especially during pandemics and stay-at-home orders.

Zoom's products help teachers conduct virtual classes with their students. Pilates and yoga instructors use Zoom in similar ways. Rock bands jam via Zoom, including Marillion — one of my very favorites. Rabbis and priests rely upon Zoom to connect with their congregations from their homes. Journalists conduct interviews with it. In the corporate world, Zoom helps salespeople close deals, host untold numbers of employee- and customer- training sessions, and allow executives to address their troops from distant locations.

No, Zoom doesn't solve every conceivable communication problem. No software program can. Still, when used properly, Zoom promotes simple and effective communication — and more than 300 hundred million people have taken notice.

About This Book

Against this backdrop arrives *Zoom For Dummies* — the most extensive guide on how to use this powerful, flexible, affordable, and user-friendly suite of communication and collaboration tools. It provides an in-depth overview of Zoom's most valuable features   some of which even experienced users may have overlooked. The book you're holding goes beyond merely demonstrating how to install, configure, and customize Zoom's flagship Meetings & Chat product, though. It also offers practical tips on how individual users, groups, and even entire firms can get the most out of Zoom's tools. Finally and perhaps most important, I describe how to secure Zoom from prying eyes.

As with all titles in the *For Dummies* series, you'll find the book's organization and flow straightforward and intuitive. My tone is conversational, and I drop the occasional joke. (Whether or not it ultimately lands is your call to make.) Ideally, you'll have fun while concurrently learning how to use an increasingly important, popular, and useful set of tools. I certainly enjoyed writing it.

Foolish Assumptions

I wrote *Zoom For Dummies* with a number of different cohorts in mind:

>> People who want to adopt a contemporary videoconferencing tool.

- People who generally want to know more about Zoom's different products and how they work. Perhaps they have subscribed to one (usually, Meetings & Chat) and want to learn more about the others.

- Employees at companies that have already experimented with or purchased Zoom but haven't explored most of its powerful features.

- Organization decision-makers who believe that their employees can collaborate and communicate better and be more productive. (Make no mistake: They are right.)

REMEMBER

The target audience for *Zoom For Dummies* is everyday users, not application developers. To be sure, I mention a few resources for people who want to know more about creating third-party apps. Coders looking for a text on how to build Zoom apps, however, will have to go elsewhere.

Zoom For Dummies presumes zero prior use or even knowledge of Zoom's suite of tools. Zilch. Fret not if you're not exactly tech-savvy. You'll be fine. Perhaps you just want to understand more about what this "Zoom thing" does and how you can do it. In fact, even if you have used Zoom's tools, reading this book will teach you a great deal.

Congratulations. You've found the right book.

I do, however, make a few assumptions. Specifically:

- You are curious about how you can use Zoom to communicate with your colleagues, partners, customers, vendors, and/or friends.

- You know how to use a proper computer, whether it's a Mac or PC.

- You can navigate a mobile device, such as a smartphone or a tablet.

- At some point in your life, you've accessed the Internet via a web browser.

I'm a firm believer in truth in advertising. By way of background, my editor and I wanted to keep this book at a reasonable length and cost. Accomplishing this objective forced me to make some conscious decisions about its content that I want you know from the get-go.

First, the book that you're holding is no 700-page opus. *Moby Dick* it is not. At the same time, though, it certainly isn't slim. *Zoom For Dummies* does not include step-by-step directions to configure and tweak every setting or feature for a single Zoom service, never mind all of them. Please understand this choice going in. Such a task is simply impractical. Even if it were, Zoom adds new features on a regular basis and, on occasion, changes and retires existing ones. All software companies do today. Way it goes. . .

At a high level, *Zoom For Dummies* highlights

>> Its essential and frequently used features

>> Some relatively obscure functionality that people should use or, at the very least, ought to know about

In some cases, I describe a feature without spending valuable space on how to actually do it because Zoom makes it self-explanatory.

Second and along these lines, I have intentionally written all the instructions in this book in a device-agnostic manner. In other words, I demonstrate how to do things in Zoom by using its desktop client and, in some necessary cases, via a web browser.

No, I'm not living in the past. (Well, I am with my tastes in music and movies, but I digress.) I know full well that mobile devices arrived in earnest a long time ago. At times, I mention in passing how you can perform a specific Zoom task on a smartphone or tablet. Due to space considerations, however, I simply cannot replicate how to execute each Zoom action on all iOS and Android versions and devices. Minor differences persist.

Even if I somehow managed to pull off that remarkable feat in the following pages, odds are that you'd ignore large chunks of *Zoom For Dummies*. Very few folks use every mainstream operating system or OS. People typically pick one side or the other. As Mr. Spock says in the 1982 film *The Wrath of Khan*, "Logic clearly dictates that the needs of the many outweigh the needs of the few."

Fear not, young Jedi. (Apologies to sci-fi geeks for putting *Star Wars* and *Star Trek* references so close together.) The vast majority of users find Zoom to be remarkably intuitive. You'll soon be able to naturally perform many of Zoom's key functions. In the event that accomplishing something on your phone or tablet vexes you, the support portion of Zoom's website contains detailed instructions on how to do whatever you want on every OS.

Icons Used in This Book

Zoom For Dummies highlights key information in the margins. You'll find small pictures that indicate the following:

TIP

This icon identifies shortcuts and/or tricks that should save you some time.

WARNING

Be careful whenever you see this icon.

TECHNICAL STUFF

This icon highlights technical information that may or may not interest you. If not, then feel free to skip it.

REMEMBER

You'll want to keep these key points in mind as you work in Zoom. This icon emphasizes those points.

Beyond the Book

In addition to the book that you're reading right now, you can also access a free Zoom Cheat Sheet. It's full of pointers and shortcuts on how to immediately start using Meetings & Chat. Access it by visiting www.dummies.com and typing "Zoom For Dummies Cheat Sheet" in the Search box.

Where to Go from Here

If you like, you can start reading this book on page one and continue to the end. The option is yours. *Zoom For Dummies* isn't a novel or play. If you've already dabbled with Zoom's powerful suite of communication tools, then you can jump around to the sections that pique your interest. I've written it in that vein.

If you're only considering hopping on the Zoom train or have only heard about it, then begin with the first three chapters. From there, you'll want to read in a relatively linear manner.

Regardless of where you ultimately start reading, you'll find it helpful to create a new, free Zoom account or log into your existing one at www.zoom.us. You should also download the Zoom desktop client for your computer. Over the years, I have taught myself plenty of new programming languages, applications, and technologies. I have found that getting my hands dirty and doing the exercises myself to be invaluable.

Thank You

Thank you for buying *Zoom For Dummies*. I hope that you find it useful, informative, and even a little entertaining. Throughout the book, I demonstrate Zoom's many potential benefits and how to take advantage of them.

I deliberately qualified the previous statement with the word "potential." Zoom's tools have never been an elixir. They don't let Zoom's customers magically solve all of their communication-related challenges.

Zoom will never be such a tool, nor will any technology or app for that matter. Despite being able to use Zoom, many employees will invariably revert to incessant email threads; these folks will use Zoom intermittently, if at all. In the process, they will fail to recognize its considerable advantages. As with any new tool, Zoom's ultimate individual, group, and organizational success hinges upon many factors. At the top of my list are opening your mind and setting realistic expectations for what it can and can't do.

Good luck on your journey for better communication and collaboration. Let me know if I can help.

Phil Simon | *www.philsimon.com*

June 30, 2020

1

Staying Connected with Zoom

IN THIS PART . . .

Find out about Zoom and the core technologies behind it.

Discover how Zoom became the gold standard for videoconferencing.

Get to know Zoom's robust suite of collaboration and communication tools.

Chapter **1**

Communicating and Collaborating Better with Zoom

What is Zoom anyway? Where did it come from? Was it the result of long-term planning, a eureka moment, or a happy accident? Is Zoom only for large organizations, or can smaller ones benefit from it? And what business problems does Zoom solve, anyway?

This chapter answers these questions in spades. Further, it provides some background information about Zoom, the technologies behind it, and its main competition.

Introducing Zoom

Zoom provides a suite of simple, affordable, powerful, secure, and interoperable communication and collaboration tools. As of this writing, the company's self-purposed mission is to make video communications frictionless.

As you see in this book, Zoom has accomplished its mission in spades. Zoom's management and investors bet the company on the belief that it could build a better mousetrap. With it, people could accomplish more than they could without it. Again, you can check that box. That gamble has paid off handsomely. It has vastly exceeded its early aspirations.

Discovering Zoom's origins

In August 1997, Eric Yuan began working as a software engineer at Webex — one of the first enterprise-videoconferencing companies. Yuan grew his team from ten engineers to more than 800 across the globe. To paraphrase Ron Burgundy of *Anchorman* fame, Webex became kind of a big deal. On March 15, 2007, Cisco Systems acquired the company in a deal worth $3.2 billion.

At Cisco, Yuan rose to the level of VP of Engineering — a key role at a tech juggernaut. As part of his job, he spent a good chunk of his time talking to Webex enterprise customers about the videoconferencing program. To put it bluntly, many businesses disliked Webex's complexity and general clunkiness. (Apropos of nothing, I felt the same way back then.)

After a few years, Yuan began to doubt whether Cisco would be able to improve Webex as much as its customers were demanding. To boot, other software vendors were starting to catch up. Yuan questioned whether Cisco's management would invest the requisite time and resources required to build a new, better generation of videoconferencing products — one that could easily scale up and down as needed thanks to the rise of cloud computing.

Yuan wasn't guessing; he exactly knew what enterprise customers needed. He envisioned a single, modern app that would seamlessly work on any device: laptop, computer, tablet, and smartphone. Because of his background, Yuan realized that minor tweaks to Webex's legacy code base would not suffice. Rather, undertaking such an endeavor would require a ground-up product rebuild.

Yuan knew that transforming Webex at Cisco would require him to fight many bruising internal battles. After several relatively enjoyable post-acquisition years, the politicking was starting to wear Yuan down. As he told NBC in August 2019, "Every day, when I woke up, I was not very happy. I even did not want to go to the office to work." (Visit `cnb.cx/zfd-123` to read the article.)

Yuan predictably left Cisco in June 2011 and took 40 talented engineers with him. Later that month, he founded Zoom Video Communications, Inc. He wanted to refine a concept that he first conceived during the 1990s as a college student in China. Back then, Yuan had to commute ten hours to his then-girlfriend, now his wife. (Read the entire interview at `bit.ly/zfd-eric`.)

The company launched its flagship Meetings & Chat service in January 2013. Its target customers remained the same from Yuan's Webex and Cisco days: other businesses. By May 2013, more than 1 million people used Zoom products. In March 2019, Zoom officially filed to go public on the NASDAQ. April 18, 2019, marked its first day of trading.

Understanding what Zoom does

Zoom's tools help individuals, formal and informal groups, departments, and even entire organizations communicate and collaborate better. In this way, Zoom falls under the umbrella of technologies often labeled as *Unified Communications* (UC). The term first gained popularity in the mid-1990s. (I'm happy to report that I was there.) In a nutshell, UC describes a collection of integrated, enterprise-grade communication services. Specific examples include

>> **Instant messaging (IM):** Also known as *chat*.

>> **Presence information:** Status indicators that conveys one's availability to communicate.

>> **Voice:** This bucket includes calls or, more precisely, Internet Protocol (IP) telephony.

>> **Audio, web, and video conferencing:** The ability to hold different types of calls with large groups of people.

>> **Desktop sharing:** The ability to instantly see what your peer is doing.

>> **Data sharing:** Interactive whiteboards, annotation, and the like.

>> **Unified messaging:** Integrated voicemail, email, and fax.

You may not have heard of UC before now. Again, though, it's not exactly new. In fact, the idea of using the web to do things such as make audio and video calls is almost as old as the web itself.

The following sidebar explains a bit of history behind some of UC's technical underpinnings. Make no mistake: These pillars remain critical today even if they run seamlessly in the background. Feel free to skip the nearby sidebar, however, if you consider it too much information — or TMI, as the kids say today.

A BRIEF PRIMER ON COMMUNICATING OVER THE INTERNET

You probably have not heard of ARPANET, but you almost certainly use the technology behind it every day.

In the 1960s, the Cold War between the United States and the former Soviet Union was simmering. The two powers nearly destroyed each other during the 1962 Cuban Missile Crisis. Things got very real. In the aftermath of the near debacle, government officials began to wonder how citizens would communicate with each other in the event of a nuclear conflict and tens of millions of deaths.

Against this backdrop, the U.S. Department of Defense launched the Advanced Research Projects Agency. The agency began work on a decentralized network that would, at a high level, address that very question. Launched in 1969, ARPANET represented the first network of its kind. Back then, communication networks were primitive, especially by today's standards. (If Netflix had existed back then, you would not have had any luck streaming 4K videos.)

But how would that network actually work?

Packets

Circuit-based networks are centralized in nature. Examples include traditional telephone systems. In the event of a nuclear war, one strategic missile would render the entire network inoperable. What's more, they involve a great deal of manual intervention. That's why switchboard operators manually patched through calls to recipients beginning in 1878. Brass tacks: The ARPA folks knew that a circuit-based network ultimately wouldn't meet their objectives.

Remember that even the most powerful networks of the time could not transmit even modest amounts of information in one big chunk. To overcome this obstacle, ARPANET engineers and scientists relied upon a concept called *packet switching*. Developed by American computer scientist Paul Baran in the early 1960s, the basic idea involved automatically breaking down data sent over digital networks into their smallest possible components: packets. The network would disseminate these packets without any human intervention. For more on this arcane yet fascinating subject, check out Katie Hafner's 1998 book *Where Wizards Stay Up Late: The Origins of the Internet* (Simon & Schuster).

To this end, APRANET was downright revolutionary. It represented the first wide-area packet-switching network. Ever. Even though today's telecommunications networks are far more robust than they were 50 years ago, packet switching remains a core tenet of today's Internet. And so are protocols.

Protocols

Think of protocols as common languages that allow devices, networks, computers, and servers to communicate with each other. For example, all websites begin with *http*. That's no coincidence. The acronym stands for *Hypertext Transfer Protocol*. Among other things, http defines how the web formats and transmits messages, images, web pages, and much more. Email also relies upon several essential protocols.

As it relates to some of Zoom's suite of services, two protocols are especially important:

- **H.323** provides multimedia communication standards for equipment, computers, and services across packet-based networks. It specifies precisely how to transmit real-time video, audio, and data. H.323 is popular with IP-based videoconferencing, Voice over Internet Protocol (VoIP), and Internet telephony.

- **Session Initiation Protocol** (SIP) initiates, maintains, and terminates real-time sessions. Typical applications include voice, video, and messaging.

Bottom line: Without packets and protocols, you wouldn't be able to send an email or view a web page, much less make audio or video calls from your devices.

Reviewing the numbers behind Zoom's rapid ascent

Zoom has been a popular enterprise tool since its inception. Case in point: In December 2019, 10 million people regularly used Zoom's tools. Most CEOs only dream about this level of success. Along the way, Zoom has landed many prominent customers, including

» The Nasdaq stock market

» Ridesharing behemoth Uber

» Delta Airlines

» Harvard University

» High-end audio vendor Sonos

Of course, the preceding list consists of large organizations and/or multibillion dollar companies. You may be thinking that Zoom lies outside of the reach of your local law firm, dentist's office, or web-design shop.

And you'd be spectacularly wrong.

For a variety of reasons that I cover later in this chapter, Zoom has long appealed to the smallest of startups and mid-sized businesses. (See the section "Reaping the Benefits of Zoom's Tools.")

Case in point: My friend Andrew Botwin runs a successful executive coaching shop. His company is the very definition of a small business. Like me, he gladly pays a modest annual fee for Zoom's Pro Meetings & Chat plan. (Chapter 2 covers Zoom's specific offerings, plans, and prices, in far more detail.) As Botwin told me, "Zoom allows me to conduct meetings with an in-person type of feel. It also lets me easily share my computer screen with my clients."

Zoom's industry penetration runs the gamut: healthcare, retail, higher education, manufacturing, finance, nonprofit — you name it. As for employer age, companies both young and old have jumped on the Zoom bandwagon. For years, thousands of businesses have regularly used Zoom's tools to communicate and collaborate with their employees, customers, prospects, and partners.

TIP

To read more about how a wide array of companies uses Zoom in innovative ways, go to `bit.ly/zm-cust`.

All of this is to say that, as a company, Zoom was doing extraordinarily well before a global pandemic shook the world to its core.

Assessing how COVID-19 changed Zoom's trajectory

Starting in early February 2020, the company's floodgates began to blow open. In a matter of weeks, oodles of businesses from mom-and-pop stores to large enterprises started getting Zoom religion. Examples of rapid Zoom adoption abounded during this unprecedented time. Here's one of them.

On March 19, 2020, California governor Gavin Newsom issued a stay-at-home order for his state's citizens. As a result, thousands of California-based businesses needed to adapt to a new world — and fast. One such shop was Reeder Music Academy based in Danville, California. Within a week, the 28-employee company migrated roughly 70 percent of its classes online using — you guessed it —Meetings & Chat. Thousands of small businesses in just one state would have immediately shuttered were it not for affordable videoconferencing tools such as Zoom.

A VERY BRIEF HISTORY OF CORONAVIRUS

In late 2019, tens of thousands of Chinese citizens mysteriously contracted a severe respiratory illness and started dying. People with heart disease, diabetes, obesity, and generally weak immune systems were particularly susceptible to contracting it. Ultimately dubbed coronavirus, the outbreak quickly escalated to nightmarish proportions and every country in the world. On March 11, 2020, the World Health Organization did the inevitable and declared COVID-19 a global pandemic.

Since that time and as of this writing, the numbers have been nothing short of grim: According to Johns Hopkins University, more than 500,000 people have died across the globe. More than five million others became infected but have since recovered. Epidemiologists almost unanimously agree that a second wave is coming in the fall of 2020.

When coronavirus hit the United States in earnest, it evoked images of the 1918 Spanish flu. To minimize the carnage and stress on their healthcare systems, state governments — some far more reluctantly than others — issued stay-at-home orders.

COVID-19 did not just leave more than 100,000 dead bodies in its wake. It wrought psychological, social, and economic devastation as well. With respect to the latter, tens of millions of Americans lost their jobs. U.S. unemployment spiked to nearly 15 percent in April 2020. Most workplaces, parks, restaurants, schools, retail stores, and places of worship closed. Musicians postponed concerts, comedians canceled shows, and professional sports as the world knows them ceased to exist.

Against this backdrop, hundreds of millions people needed to find new, virtual ways to work and, more than that, recapture some semblance of normalcy. In each case, Zoom was the most popular choice.

And Zoom adoption quickly spread to decidedly non-corporate environments. As but one example during the height of frenzy, teachers from more than 90,000 schools across 20 countries began educating their students from their homes via Meetings & Chat. Beyond professional reasons, people needed a way to connect with their family and friends. Again, Zoom answered the bell.

To say that Zoom's user numbers exploded over a three-month period would be the acme of understatement. By the end of March 2020, more than 200 million people participated in both free and paid Zoom meetings every day. (Industry types refer to this number as *daily active users*, or DAUs.) By way of comparison, just four months earlier, Zoom had averaged approximately 10 million DAUs. The 2,000 percent increase was downright stupefying.

And Zoom's user growth didn't stop there.

During its first fiscal quarter of 2020 (ending on April 30), Zoom reported that its DAUs had climbed to 300 million — a 50 percent jump from only a month earlier. Many of those users decided to become proper customers. Company revenue in that quarter grew by an eye-popping 169 percent. Analyst Richard Valera of the asset-management firm Needham called the results "incredible." (Read more about Zoom's most recent financial results at on.wsj.com/2Y0RJjz.)

Fast-forward a few weeks. As of July 1, 2020, Zoom's market capitalization exceeded a staggering $73 billion. If you had bought Zoom stock just a few months earlier, you'd be ecstatic.

It wasn't all puppy dogs and ice cream for Zoom, though. On the flip side, its viral consumer growth has led to some unexpected issues and a slew of bad press. (I cover those legitimate concerns in Chapter 9.) For now, however, rest assured: Zoom's management has taken its unforeseen challenges very seriously.

Reviewing Zoom's industry awards and recognition

Beyond Zoom's outrageous growth, the company has garnered plenty of recognition and even won some prestigious industry awards. Highlights include

» **Leader in Gartner 2019 Magic Quadrant for Meeting Solutions:** You may not be familiar with the world of enterprise software. Trust me, though, vendors expend an enormous amount of energy trying to land in the vaunted Magic Quadrant.

» **2019 Inc. 5000 list of America's fastest-growing private companies:** Employers that make this list are doing something right.

» **Glassdoor Second Best Place to Work in 2019:** Employees tend to like working at Zoom. This accolade and its attendant publicity help the company attract, retain, and motivate highly skilled workers.

MY ZOOM BONA FIDES

As a reader, it's fair to ask about my experience using the tool about which I am writing.

By way of background, I've been using videoconferencing tools for two decades. (I'm no spring chicken anymore.) Over the years and in no particular order, I've played with Skype, Webex, Join.me, and Adobe Connect. Thanks to Zoom, though, I have largely said *adios* to those applications. (I return to them later in this chapter in the section "Main competitors.")

For the last few years, I've used Zoom primarily for individual and group videoconferencing, screen-sharing, and webinars. What's more, because I wear a number of different hats, I've become a convert on a several levels. First, as an independent writer, speaker, trainer, and advisor, I frequently hold Zoom meetings with my clients and prospects when in-person meetings just aren't possible. Second, during my days as a college professor, I engaged with my students on a near-daily basis via Zoom — and Slack as well, to be fair. (If you're not familiar with Slack, check out my book *Slack For Dummies*.)

That's not to say that I don't enjoy real-world interactions. I most certainly do. Again, though, physical meetings aren't always possible, especially with online students halfway across the globe.

Analyzing Zoom's competitive landscape

When it comes to videoconferencing apps right now, Zoom is unequivocally the prettiest girl at the ball. To be fair, though, it's hardly the only one.

Before continuing, a disclaimer is in order: Contending that one tool is inherently and objectively "better" than another is silly. (Try telling a long-time Samsung user that she's missing out on the far cooler iPhone. See how that goes.) So much hinges on personal preferences. For example, say that you're a die-hard fan of BlueJeans. In this case, no one will convince you that you ought to use Zoom — and that includes yours truly.

Still, consider the following two types of software vendors:

>> **Group A:** Large companies that dabble in many fields. Examples here include Microsoft, Oracle, Adobe, SAP, and Amazon.

>> **Group B:** Smaller outfits that specialize in one specific type of application. Examples here include Zoom, Slack, and BlueJeans.

Generally speaking, the Davids in Group B have historically tended to more quickly innovate and respond to their customers than the Goliaths in Group A. This claim is especially valid over the past 15 years. Precisely because of their laser focus, boutique firms often produce better wares than their larger brethren do. Scrappy upstarts are almost always better at keeping their eyes on the prize.

Main competitors

Table 1-1 provides a list of Zoom's main contemporary rivals.

TABLE 1-1   Mainstream Videoconferencing Tools

Name	Description
Cisco Webex	Born in early 1995, Webex was one of the first web-based videoconferencing tools. Fast-forward to March 2007. Cisco acquired it for $3.2 billion. Over the years, plenty of products have surpassed Webex in terms of popularity and functionality. At the risk of being a bit harsh, asking sometime to join you via Webex today is tantamount to sending an email from an America Online (AOL) address. It may still technically work, but you probably won't score many points with others by suggesting that they use it for your upcoming videoconference.
Vonage	Founded by Jeff Pulver in 1998, the company was one of the pioneers of Voice over Internet Protocol (VoIP) and exceptionally popular back in the days of landlines. Fun fact: I worked on a consulting project at its headquarters in the mid-2000s.
RingCentral	Born in 1999, the company remains among the UC leaders in terms of revenue and subscriber seats. Now publicly traded, its market capitalization is roughly $24 billion as of early June 2020.
Skype (consumer version)	Initially released way back in August 2003, at one point nearly 700 million people used the service. After acquisitions first by eBay and then by Microsoft, Skype has lost some steam. Plenty of observers and former employees say that the company squandered its opportunities. (For more on this subject, see cnb.cx/zoom2-ps.)
Skype for Business	Formerly known as Lync, Microsoft rebranded it as *Skype as Business*. (Yes, the regular consumer-grade version of Skype is alive and well.) Much like Google, Microsoft supports a bevy of related collaboration tools.
Amazon Chime	Amazon launched its foray into the crowded space in July 2017. Chime lets users meet, chat, and place business calls inside and outside your organization.
BlueJeans Meetings	BlueJeans started in 2009 and offers similar services to Zoom. Remarkably, in its first 75 days, the company landed 4,000 subscribers from 500 firms. Not too shabby.
GoToMeeting	Initially released in July 2004, the tool has evolved over the years and still sports a loyal user base. At one point, I paid for it.

Name	Description
Zoho Meeting	The company released its offering in 2017. It serves as part of its suite of productivity tools.
Join.Me	Now owned by parent company LogMeIn, Join.Me still sports some prominent customers. I used it for a long time before switching to Zoom.
Fuze	Formerly known as ThinkingPhones, the videoconferencing company also focuses on enterprise customers.
Google Meet	To paraphrase the iconic *Simpsons'* character Troy McClure, you may remember this tool as an original feature of Google's ill-fated social network Google+. Hangouts became a standalone product in 2013. At that time, Google also started integrating features from Google+ Messenger and Google Talk into Hangouts. If all of these related products seem to overlap and strike you as a tad confusing, trust your judgment. In this way, Google resembles its rival Microsoft.
UberConference	Founded in 2012, the tool sports a clean, elegant design.
Facebook Messenger Rooms	Launched in May 2020, Messenger Rooms lets people join Facebook group video calls even if they abstain from using the social network, as I do.
Intermedia AnyMeeting	AnyMeeting launched in 2011 and survived as an independent entity until September 2017 when Intermedia gobbled it up and rebranded it.
Adobe Connect	Adobe Connect is the umbrella term for former Macromedia products that the company acquired and rebranded. The linages of these products trace back to the early 2000s.

For a useful chart that compares many of these tools, visit `bit.ly/vc-compare`.

Say that your organization suddenly adopts Zoom. If you've used any of the tools listed in Table 1-1, odds are that most employees will pick up Zoom relatively quickly.

Slack and Microsoft Teams

Table 1-1 intentionally omits two prominent collaboration tools: Slack and Microsoft Teams. To be sure, both applications allow users to hold video calls. I should know because I regularly use them. Still, it's misleading to call Slack and Microsoft Teams videoconferencing tools.

Sure, Slack and Teams both let users hold multiperson videoconferences and share their screens. If you think that that's the sum total of what those programs can do, though, then you're sorely mistaken. You're severely underestimating what they can do. It's like using your smartphone only to make phone calls or your Lexus convertible for the sole purpose of holding your coffee flask, to paraphrase one of my favorite jokes by the erudite comedian Gary Gulman.

Why today's breed of videoconferencing tools crushes its ancestors

It's important to remember that many popular, first-generation VoIP and video-conferencing tools have disappeared. (For an interesting read on the history of the technology, see `bit.ly/vcz-hist`.) Today's major players benefit from many advantages that their predecessors lacked:

>> **Better broadband availability:** Not that long ago, most people dialed up via modems and were lucky to connect to the Internet at 56k per second. In large part, you can thank better pipes in the form of fiber-optic cables.

>> **More robust networks:** Cellular network technology is a far cry today from 20 years ago. This trend will only intensify as carriers, such as AT&T and Verizon, start rolling out 5G.

>> **Far cheaper data-storage costs:** Companies such as Zoom can store a virtually unlimited number of 400-megabyte (MB) customer videos because it's inexpensive to do so. It wasn't always that way.

>> **Smartphones:** iPhones and Androids destroy BlackBerrys. There. I said it.

>> **Application programming interface (APIs):** These powerful tools allow developers to easily stitch together different applications. I explain more about this concept in Chapter 7.

>> **The widespread availability of cloud computing:** Companies can spin up new services in a fraction of the time required during the late 1990s.

>> **Machine learning and artificial intelligence:** Software is constantly improving its speech-recognition and transcription capabilities. Yeah, Siri remains pretty dumb, but it's getting smarter all the time.

>> **Powerful repositories of open-source software:** Code repositories help developers build all sorts of cool things — including videoconferencing. For some free alternatives, check out `https://red.ht/2Jqyjxz`.

For these reasons, contemporary videoconferencing applications such as Zoom represent a quantum leap over first-generation ones. It's not even close.

It's no coincidence that Zoom's suite of tools works so well and reliably. In large part, Zoom's rock-solid performance stems from how its bright founder and engineers deliberately chose to build it. In other words, Zoom embraced powerful and contemporary technologies from the get-go — not as an afterthought. Because of its greenfield approach and intelligent design, Zoom's offerings remarkably support a raft of concurrent users without a degradation in quality. For more information on this subject, see the nearby sidebar "Looking under Zoom's hood."

LOOKING UNDER ZOOM'S HOOD

Zoom works so well because it made intelligent choices about specific technologies and design:

- **A distributed architecture:** Early videoconferencing vendors built their wares in a relatively centralized and resource-intensive manner. For example, say that you were in New York in 2005 calling a coworker in the same building with one of those legacy tools. Your app may have to route the call through a data center all the way in Ireland. By contrast and like many newer tech companies today, Zoom has embraced a distributed configuration. This deliberate design choice means that the app automatically directs users to the nearest of the 13 data centers in its vast network. (The company continually invests in its data centers.) As a result, Zoom provides its customers with greater reliability and reduced call latency.

- **Multimedia routing:** Early videoconferencing systems tended to use Multipoint Control Unit (MCU), a resource-intensive streaming method that restricts call quality and scalability. For its part, Zoom uses a more contemporary and efficient streaming method called *multimedia routing*.

- **Multi-bitrate encoding:** Zoom recognizes that one size doesn't fit all. Calling your friends from home via your laptop and your ultra-high-speed Internet connection is a far cry from using your smartphone on your carrier's data plan. Zoom automatically adjusts your call quality based on the capabilities of your hardware devices and Internet Service Provider (ISP).

- **Application-layer service quality:** Zoom wisely built a layer into its technology stack specifically to optimize video, audio, and screen-sharing. At a high level and similar to multi-bitrate encoding, this layer accounts for users' different devices and bandwidth levels.

- **Intelligent use of data and metadata:** Zoom is able to route data on its network more efficiently than legacy videoconferencing tools could. There's plenty to unpack here, but a key point is that Zoom makes extensive use of call metadata. (*Metadata* is simply data about data.) For example, Zoom knows the device and location of all call participants.

- **Cloud computing:** Zoom relies heavily on cloud computing to deliver the goods. For hosting, Zoom engages industry leader Amazon Web Services (AWS). More than 1 million AWS customers know that they can easily and automatically scale up in the face of rapid and unexpected spikes in demand — in other words, precisely during events such as COVID-19.

(continued)

(continued)

Consider the following two scenarios:

- **Scenario A:** You're making a videocall to your friend on your Android phone with your AT&T data plan in a remote area.
- **Scenario B:** An executive hosts a multiperson videoconference via her laptop in corporate headquarters with extensive bandwidth through its ISP.

In those scenarios, Zoom will automatically allocate more resources to the call in scenario B.

TECHNICAL STUFF

Visit `bit.ly/zm-stack` for more on the specific technologies that Zoom uses to make the magic happen.

Zoom's current market share

Where does Zoom rank in comparison to its competitors?

It's a fair question to ask. After all, you don't want to invest in a niche tool that may quickly disappear.

The answer is a little complicated.

In April 2019, Tom Eagle of the respected firm Gartner Research told the website CIO Dive that Zoom is "displacing some of these other giant vendors." Zoom's rise has carved out market share from Microsoft, Cisco, and some of the other established behemoths listed earlier in this chapter in Table 1-1. (Visit `bit.ly/ciodive-z` to read the piece.) Back then, estimates of Zoom's market share ranged from about 15 to 20 percent.

Of course, answering that question amid the rapid adoption taking place is now virtually impossible. Blame COVID-19 for that difficulty, among many others. Still, it's inarguable that Zoom's market share has grown over the past year. How much is anyone's guess, but the increase is probably substantial.

Exhibit A: In March 2020, Academy Award-winning actress Reese Witherspoon of *Legally Blonde* fame conducted a highly unscientific Twitter poll on individuals' preferred work-from-home (WFH) tool. Figure 1-1 displays the results.

It doesn't take a survey expert to poke holes in Witherspoon's informal methodology — not that she's a scientist. The results, however, offer additional evidence that Zoom's ascension is sudden and real. The natural question is why.

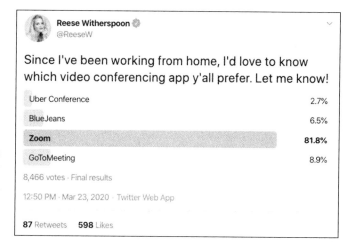

Reese Witherspoon @
@ReeseW

Since I've been working from home, I'd love to know
which video conferencing app y'all prefer. Let me know!

Uber Conference	2.7%
BlueJeans	6.5%
Zoom	**81.8%**
GoToMeeting	8.9%

8,466 votes · Final results

12:50 PM · Mar 23, 2020 · Twitter Web App

87 Retweets   **598** Likes

FIGURE 1-1:
Reese
Witherspoon's
informal Twitter
poll on video-
conferencing
usage.

TIP

Every year, videoconferencing hardware maker Owl Labs creates a slick and informative report on the state of the industry. The 2019 version of the survey includes responses from more than 1,000 U.S.-based professionals. (You can access it by visiting `bit.ly/zoomowl`.) Short version: The vast majority of Zoom's customers love using it.

Reaping the Benefits of Zoom's Tools

Zoom's suite of tools isn't hurting for powerful features. In other words, it allows both employers and their employees to communicate and collaborate better in a number of ways.

The company sells a number of related, but distinct, offerings. (See Chapter 2 for more on this topic.) In this section, though, I focus on the overall benefits of Zoom's products and services. As such, the following benefits don't apply universally to all of Zoom's solutions, much less equally. For example, you can't call others via Zoom Video Webinars. For its part, Zoom Phone does not let you hold webinars. On a general level, though, the advantages that I list hold up reasonably well when viewing the entire Zoom suite.

Zoom solves some of today's key communications problems

I'll start with the elephant in the room: Zoom helps people communicate and collaborate far better than when they rely upon text-based messages alone. Specifically,

Zoom and its ilk provide key context to everyday communications, thus minimizing the chance for misunderstandings and outright blunders.

That statement may seem obvious and impersonal. It may even invoke a "Duh!" I'll bet, though, that at some point you sent a colleague, manager, or friend an email or text message that confused her. I'll also wager that someone has befuddled you with a vexing email as well. As I wrote in my 2015 book *Message Not Received: Why Business Communication Is Broken and How to Fix It* (Wiley), stripping out essential context is a fundamental limitation of text-based communication. Put differently, when it comes sending to asynchronous messages to others, the fleas come with the dog.

When people actually engage in real-world conversations, they dramatically increase the odds that they are truly communicating. They allow others to immediately ask questions — and vice versa. Remember, the word *communicate* means "to make common." It is often hard to achieve that elusive goal exclusively via text messages.

Zoom makes people more productive

Say that you're experiencing a problem on your computer. For example, a program or your operating system is acting funky, to use a technical term. You write a long email to the vendor's technical support team detailing the problem. Maybe you even include all the relevant information.

Still, the support rep doesn't seem to get it. He responds, and the two of you go back and forth over the course of days or, heaven forbid, weeks. Your frustration level rises. Drink in hand, you start venting on social media.

Odds are that the rep isn't incompetent or evil. He's just not picking up what you're putting down. If only you had a way to show him exactly what's happening in a synchronous manner, then he could try to solve your problem.

Again, thanks to Zoom, you most certainly do. I have used it and its predecessors hundreds of times to share my screen and quickly diagnose technical issues. Other times, I have simply wanted to get someone's real-time input on a book chapter, blog post, or slide for one of my presentations.

NONVERBAL CUES MATTER . . . JUST NOT AS MUCH AS YOU MAY THINK

You may have heard the oft-cited statistic that roughly 90 percent of communication is nonverbal.

The infamous number stems from *Silent Messages*, a 1971 book by Albert Mehrabian (Wadsworth Pub. Co). The text represented the culmination of Mehrabian's research into human communication patterns with his colleagues at the University of California, Los Angeles. Mehrabian looked at the language that salespeople used and whether prospects understood them. At a high level, he found two things.

- People often communicate in inconsistent or contradictory ways. (No shocker there.)

- In one study, Mehrabian asked his subjects to quantify how much of the salespersons' credibility stemmed from their use of single, spoken words. In the aggregate, that number was a mere 7 percent.

This statistic begs the question: What about the other 93 percent?

The answers are gestures and tonality. Collectively and in certain contexts, these two attributes can accurately convey meaning and emotions far more than the words themselves.

As it often happens, however, the mass media widely circulated that 7 percent figure without the requisite context. Many people started taking that number as gospel. (I have been guilty of it as well.)

A good deal of subsequent research has debunked the 7 percent myth. For example, in 2007, David Lapakko of Augsburg College published a study called "Communication is 93% Nonverbal: An Urban Legend Proliferates."

Tone of voice and body and facial expressions certainly matter, but probably not to the extent that most people think.

Zoom just works

Zoom's Meetings & Chat and Video Webinars services are especially easy to set up, use, and manage. If you know how to operate a computer, tablet, or smartphone, then you can be up and running in minutes. For their part, Zoom Rooms and Zoom Phone require some assembly to proceed. In all cases, though, you don't need to be a coder, a techie, or a hardware expert to use Zoom's most popular services.

Zoom's tools work well on computers, tablets, and smartphones. That's not to say that you can perform every task on every type of device. For example, Meetings & Chat allows up to 49 people to concurrently their video feeds in a 7-x-7 grid. (See `bit.ly/zm-ag` for a cool animated gif of this grid in action.) If you think that you'll be able to clearly see those 49 images on your smartphone, think again. Also, showing all those individuals' screens will tax your laptop's central processing unit (CPU) and slow down your machine. Put simply, your computer and its operating system may not be up to the task. Ditto if you're concurrently running ten demanding software programs in the background.

TECHNICAL STUFF

Your device's CPU is its main processor. It is the electronic circuitry that executes instructions of computer programs. Without a CPU, your computer is effectively a useless, expensive, and heavy paperweight.

These disclaimers aside, though, Zoom's tools generally just work. If you're of a certain age, then you may remember when mainstream videoconferencing applications were downright janky.

Zoom is affordable

Say that you're excited to start using Zoom, but the accountant in you wonders how much it costs.

The answer depends on the specific plan that you choose. (Chapter 2 covers Zoom's different plans and products in far more detail.) Enterprises with tens of thousands of employees will certainly pony up more than your indie record store owner will.

Not sure about what Zoom can do for you? Fine. Give it a spin for free. For now, suffice it to say that your employer need not spend tens of thousands of dollars on Zoom. What's more, it doesn't need to lock itself into expensive and rigid multi-year deals. Upgrade, downgrade, leave, and return whenever you like. In terms of contracts, think Netflix, not AT&T or Verizon.

Zoom is flexible and interoperable

In the past, videoconferencing and collaboration tools didn't always play nicely with one another. For example, Webex may have worked well for Walter, a Windows 7 user running Internet Explorer. His colleague Donnie, however, wasn't so lucky using his Mac to run the Mojave operating system and Safari as his web browser. In the past, many conference calls and webinars reverted to a comedy of errors not unlike the one portrayed in this classic YouTube video: `bit.ly/cc2-zoom`. Half an hour after the scheduled start time, a dozen people were still restarting their computers and finagling with their devices' audio and video settings.

Fortunately, and as Zoom users know, those days are gone.

Zoom runs on anything. The company has built a flexible and interoperable solution for meetings, phone, webinars, and chat. Say that you're holding a webinar from your desktop application. Fifty people attend, but they connect in different ways and on different types of devices. Some want to watch via their web browser. Others are on different smartphones and tablets. The attendees also run the gamut: Windows, Android, iOS, MacOS, and even Linux.

It gets even better.

Zoom works seamlessly with more than 200 other third-party apps. (I cover this subject in Chapter 7.) Here are a few examples:

>> You use Microsoft Outlook and want to easily add a Zoom meeting to an existing event. You also want to prevent people from calling you when you're busy. Check.

>> Like millions of progressive-minded folks, you're a passionate fan of the collaboration tool Slack. As such, you want to automatically launch Zoom calls from the Slack desktop client. Check.

>> Your company uses Salesforce as its customer-relationship management (CRM) system. You want to start an instant Zoom meeting from a Salesforce event, lead, or contact page. Check.

>> A college professor wants to hold virtual office hours with her students in Canvas, her university's learning management system (LMS). Check.

I could go on for hours. Brass tacks: Zoom plays nicely with the other arrows in your quiver.

Zoom stays in its lane

A man's got to know his limitations.

— Clint Eastwood as "Dirty" Harry Callahan, *Magnum Force*

On a related note, Zoom doesn't attempt to replace essential productivity tools that billions of people have used for years. Zoom enhances other applications and systems; it does not supplant them.

Even Zoom power users continue to rely upon email and other communication tools on a daily basis. Because of Zoom, though, they don't use those tools quite as much as they did before. For example, you may decide to chat with a colleague via text or voice over Zoom rather than exchange a series of emails in Outlook or Gmail. (Kudos for seeing the light.) Slack users can call each other without Zoom. Those who want to grant others control of their screens, however, will have to use Zoom or another tool. (Slack does not include this functionality.)

Zoom doesn't try to be all things to all people. It won't act as your spreadsheet, word-processing program, or CRM system. Zoom will, however, augment these applications. (I revisit this subject in Chapter 12.)

Zoom lets people rediscover their humanity

To state the obvious, Zoom's customers realize significant benefits from using it. Why else would they pony up for monthly and annual subscriptions? Fair enough, but foolish is the soul who believes that Zoom is a suite of apps that only busi-nessfolks can use. In fact, untold numbers of people frequently use Zoom products for decidedly nonprofessional purposes. (Chapter 17 includes some of them.)

I'm a perfect example.

In early March 2020, I was practicing social distancing like billions people across the globe. I enjoy my space and downtime as much as the next guy. Still, after a few weeks, I craved some human interaction. I held a few virtual happy hours via Meetings & Chat with five of my college friends. No, it wasn't the same as getting beers with them in person and playing hoops, but it was certainly more fun than our normal, audio-only call.

Chapter **2**

Getting to Know Zoom's Suite of Communication Tools

Z oom's tools let small and even enormous groups of people improve how they communicate. What's more, Zoom's offerings are flexible, powerful, affordable, and intuitive.

Of course, in order for you and your colleagues to reap the benefits of using Zoom's services, you must first understand them. Purchasing the wrong product altogether — or the right one but the wrong plan — will frustrate you and cost you time and money.

This chapter provides a high-level overview of each Zoom subscription. I cover the features, costs, and limitations of each core Zoom service.

Zoom's Core Services

Many people new to Zoom think of it exclusively as a communications or video-conferencing app. That belief is understandable, because Zoom has exploded in popularity. At the same time, though, it is not at all accurate.

As of this writing, Zoom's suite of videoconferencing tools consists of four core products and services. Two of them will run on just about any contemporary computing device — with or without a webcam — within a matter of minutes. In other words, they require neither special hardware nor elaborate setup.

The ready-to-go tools include

>> Zoom Meetings & Chat

>> Zoom Video Webinars

Zoom's two other services are more intricate in nature. In order to work, they require a bit more setup and, in all likelihood, special hardware. That is, you won't be up and running in a few minutes. Put differently, the following two Zoom services fall into the some-assembly-is-required bucket:

>> Zoom Rooms

>> Zoom Phone

Regardless of the time and resources needed to get started, all Zoom products share some similarities, including the underlying technology behind them. What's more, in their own way, each helps the company achieve its lofty mission of "improving the quality and effectiveness of communications forever."

Put all of Zoom's services together, and you arrive at Figure 2-1.

REMEMBER

An individual or large enterprise need not purchase or subscribe to every Zoom product in Figure 2-1. Each one works quite nicely on its own. To be sure, some organizations have gone all-in on Zoom and gladly subscribe to all of its services. I suspect that the vast majority of Zoom's customers, however, opt for only a few of them.

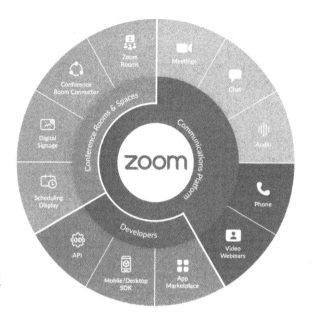

FIGURE 2-1:
Zoom's suite of
tools.

Ready to Go

This section details the two Zoom offerings that require no special hardware or elaborate setup: Meetings & Chat and Video Webinars. If you've purchased your computer, smartphone, or tablet in the last five years, odds are that you'll be up and running with each of these services within a few minutes.

Zoom Meetings & Chat

Zoom has named its most popular service Meetings & Chat. (The nomenclature on Zoom's website is a bit inconsistent.) Regardless of its moniker, the product allows users to hold high-definition (HD) audio and video calls and send text messages. As such, Meetings & Chat is ideal for the following types of work-related meetings and interactions:

>> Simple one-to-one chat sessions

>> Online training sessions

>> Company announcements

>> Calls to technical support to diagnose user's issue, especially with screen-sharing

>> And many more

SEARCH BEFORE GOOGLE

People of a certain age remember the web's first search engines. If you don't remember, then I'll cut to the chase: They weren't very good.

For example, in 1996, I was interning at Data General, a now defunct hardware manufacturer based out of Westborough, MA. During my lunch hour or periods of boredom, I would use Yahoo!, AlltheWeb, AskJeeves, and other early search engines to find information. I wanted to read the latest updates on NBA free agent signings.

And my searches would usually fail.

Then, in 1998, along came Google.

Search was never the same.

As many subsequent books have covered, cofounders Larry Page and Sergey Brin created a tool that didn't make search 10 percent better. Google made search ten times better.

Big difference.

I can't say that Meetings & Chat has made videoconferencing ten times better than its antecedents. (Some of them remain functional.) At the same time, though, Meetings & Chat represents a significant leap forward on a number of key levels, including call quality, ease of use, and reliability.

If concept of making audio and video calls over the Internet seems old hat to you, trust your instincts. (Chapter 1 covers many of Zoom's predecessors in this field.) In other words, it's not that Meetings & Chat does something fundamentally different than its predecessors did; it's that Meetings & Chat does the same thing much better. Think of it as souped-up version of Skype. As the nearby sidebar "Search before Google" illustrates, Zoom finds itself in illustrious company in this regard.

Main features and benefits

Meetings & Chat is a robust offering that provides its users with an arsenal of potent bells and whistles.

BUILT-IN COLLABORATION TOOLS

Many tools let users share their screens with others. Meetings & Chat takes this a step further. Multiple participants can concurrently share their screens, co-annotate their screens, and more. Ultimately, all these features provide for more interactive meetings.

DEVICE AGNOSTICISM

In the past, mainstream videoconferencing tools tended to work well only on certain types of computers running specific operating systems.

Not Zoom.

Meetings & Chat lets you start and join meetings and collaborate across any device.

WARNING

That's not to say, though, that you can perform every task on every type of device.

SCHEDULING MADE EASY

Meetings & Chat integrates with popular calendar applications, such as Microsoft Outlook, Gmail, and iCal. As a result, you won't have to waste time synchronizing multiple applications. Third-party apps, covered in Chapter 7, make this integration even tighter.

HOLDING SECURE MEETINGS

No application is entirely safe from prying eyes, but Zoom has invested a great deal of resources in making Meetings & Chat as bulletproof as possible. To this end, the product

- » Encrypts all meetings
- » Offers role-based user security
- » Lets users protect their meetings with passwords
- » Allows hosts to create waiting rooms for participants
- » Lets users place attendees on hold

Chapter 9 has plenty more to say about security and privacy.

RECORDING, STORING, AND TRANSCRIBING MEETINGS

Many previous videoconferencing tools required a third-party plugin or app to record meetings. Not Meetings & Chat. Depending on your plan, Zoom lets you

- » Record and save your meetings locally or to the cloud
- » Download searchable transcripts that improve in quality all the time

SENDING MESSAGES AND FILES

Sometimes you might not be in the mood for a video call. Maybe you haven't put your face on yet or your house is a mess.

No bother.

As the second half of its name suggests, Meetings & Chat lets you communicate via text. That is, you can chat with groups of people just like you would with WhatsApp, Slack, and many more apps. You can search that history and upload files for others to view. Even better, Zoom maintains this archive for a decade.

Oh, and if you want to move your conversation from text to voice, that's easy to do as well.

Plans and costs

For Meetings, Zoom offers one free Meetings & Chat plan and three paid ones.

BASIC

Zoom's Basic plan for Meetings & Chat offers a great deal of functionality at zero cost. No, you can't take advantage of every Zoom bell and whistle. Still, the starter plan lets you do quite a bit. Here are some highlights:

- » Host meetings with up to 100 participants for a maximum of 40 minutes each. (Note that Zoom has waived this limit for teachers struggling to hold remote classes with their students in the wake of COVID-19.)
- » Host an unlimited number of meetings
- » Chat with groups and send files
- » Split your meeting into separate breakout rooms
- » Brainstorm and take notes with a virtual whiteboard
- » Share single or multiple screens with meeting attendees
- » Call into a meeting via a phone

I cover more of these features in Chapter 4.

When it comes to upgrading Meetings & Chat, as of this writing, Zoom offers the following paid plans:

- » Pro
- » Business

>> Enterprise

>> Enterprise Plus

>> Education

Throughout the text, I collectively refer to these options as *premium plans*.

TIP

Date before you get married. As with any software plan or subscription, kick the tires first before making a long-term commitment.

PRO

Zoom's first step up from the Basic plan is its Pro plan. The latter delivers all the options of the Basic plan plus a bunch more. Here are some of its highlights:

>> Hold meetings for up to 24 hours.

>> Run a variety of reports on member usage.

>> Delegate your meetings. You can let someone else set up your meetings for you. (Note that your delegate also needs to subscribe to a Pro plan or above.)

>> Create and distribute a personal meeting ID (PMI).

>> Store up to a ridiculous one gigabyte (GB) of files in the cloud.

>> Grant different rights to different people (a.k.a. *user management*).

>> Control what other people in your organization can do. For example, you can enable and disable the others' ability to record calls, encryption, chat, and notifications.

For the Pro plan, Zoom charges $14.99 (USD) per month per host when billed monthly or $149.90 (USD) when billed annually.

BUSINESS

Zoom's next offering is its Business plan. This plan delivers all the options of the Pro plan plus a bunch more. Highlights here include

>> Host meetings with up to 300 participants.

>> Receive dedicated phone support.

>> Access the Zoom Dashboard. Administrators on the account can view information ranging from overall usage to live in-meeting data.

>> Create a vanity web address. Say that I ran a record store called Phil's Records. I could direct people to *philsrecords.zoom.us*.

>> Automatically add users to your account via email-address domains.

>> Automatically generate call transcripts.

For the Business plan, Zoom charges $19.99 (USD) per month when billed monthly or $166.58 (USD) when billed annually.

ENTERPRISE

Zoom's next Meetings offering delivers all the options of the Business plan plus the following:

>> Host meetings and webinars with up to 500 participants.

>> Receive unlimited file storage.

>> Work with a dedicated customer-success manager.

>> Talk to Zoom execs about its product roadmap and future direction.

>> Receive discounts on other Zoom products.

The Enterprise plan costs $19.99 (USD) per month per host when billed monthly. What's more, an organization needs to commit to a minimum of 50 hosts or soft-ware licenses. For a proper quote, you'll have to contact Zoom's sales staff. All else being equal, more licenses translates into a bigger bill — although I would expect the per-license fee to drop. (I have learned a few things about enterprise software in my years.)

ENTERPRISE PLUS

Zoom's most expensive and robust Meetings offering delivers all the options of the Enterprise plan at a per-user discount. It allows you to host meetings and webinars with up to 1,000 participants.

The Enterprise Plus plan requires

>> A minimum of 2,500 licenses

>> A two-year minimum commitment

To receive a proper quote for this plan, you'll have to contact Zoom.

Zoom also offers specialized plans for organizations that must abide by specific legislation:

>> **Zoom for Education:** For more information, see `bit.ly/zfd-ed`.

>> **Zoom for Telehealth:** For more information, see `bit.ly/zfd-th`.

In both cases, you'll have to contact a Zoom sales rep to receive a proper quote.

Add-ons

Zoom realizes that one size does not fit all. To this end, it allows its customers to significantly customize their individual plans. Specific add-ons to its Meetings subscription include the following:

>> **Webinars:** I cover this topic in both the next section and in Chapter 8.

>> **Zoom Rooms:** See the section "Zoom Rooms," later in this chapter, for a brief introduction. Chapter 10 devotes much more space to it.

>> **Large meetings:** This feature allows users to attend Zoom meetings with 500 or 1,000 participants, depending on the customer's license. Owners or admins of Pro accounts can simply can add this feature to the monthly or annual tab.

>> **Audio conferencing options:** Perhaps you want to make it easy for your employees, customers, and prospects to talk to you — especially the international ones. To these ends, Zoom allows you to pay for toll-free numbers, fee-based toll numbers, and dedicated dial-in numbers.

>> **Cloud recording:** If your storage needs exceed those that Zoom offers under your current plan, then you can upgrade as needed. That is, you don't need to purchase a more expensive plan solely because you need to upgrade a single feature.

Zoom Video Webinars

Zoom's offering here lets even the least tech-savvy person hold full-featured, intuitive, and engaging webinars. Webinar hosts can easily manage and administer the meetings thanks to Zoom's useful controls. As for size, you won't be lacking. As of this writing, up to 100 people can actively participate and 10,000 people can attend a single webinar.

Main features and benefits

Here are some of the most powerful and useful features of Zoom Webinars.

>> **Recording:** Zoom lets users easily and automatically record events for later publishing and viewing.

- **» Broadcasting to popular third-party sites:** Unless you live in a bubble, you're probably aware that untold millions of people view live-streamed videos on Facebook Live and YouTube Live every day. Fortunately, Zoom lets webinar hosts concurrently broadcast their events to those sites. Doing so often gooses user interest and engagement.

- **» Reporting:** Say that your organization sells widgets. To this end, it wants to use Zoom Webinars as a sales tool. Zoom lets users easily run reports on webinar registrants, attendees, polls, attendee engagement, and more. This information helps individuals qualify leads for their companies.

- **» Integrating with other enterprise systems:** Many organizations use webinars for lead-generation purposes. That is, by demonstrating the product or service, they hope to convert interested prospects into paying customers. To this extent, they need to easily integrate webinar-attendee data with popular marketing and customer-relationship management (CRM) applications, such as Marketo and Salesforce. Zoom makes this a breeze.

- **» Ensuring security:** Zoom safeguards all attendee log-in and webinar session data. As of this writing, version 5.1.1 of Meetings & Chat provides 256-bit Advanced Encryption Standard (AES). (Chapter 9 goes far deeper into this subject.)

Plans and costs

Zoom's plans are remarkably flexible: You don't need to pay for licenses that you don't need. (Trust me: Years ago, companies often wasted bundles on unused software seats.)

Unfortunately, the company's flexibility admittedly makes understanding the pricing for Zoom Video Webinars a tad confusing in the following regard: Zoom does not offer its webinars subscription on a standalone basis. (Zoom Rooms — discussed in the next section — is the only exception to this rule.)

To subscribe to the webinar plan, you'll first need to sign up for one of the premium Meetings & Chat plans listed in Table 2-1. In this sense, webinars represent an add-on to the core Meetings & Chat subscription. What's more, Zoom charges by the *host*. In this case, a host is a webinar emcee. More hosts means a larger monthly and annual tab. Ditto for increasing the cap on webinar participants.

Table 2-1 displays the Zoom Video Webinar offerings as well as their costs as of this writing.

TABLE 2-1   Zoom Webinar Add-On Pricing Information

Plan Name	Host Minimum	Monthly Cost (USD) per Host	Annual Cost (USD) per Host
Pro	1	$40	$400
Business	10	$199.90	$1,999
Education	20	n/a	$1,800
Zoom Rooms	1	$40	$400

Note that Zoom does not provide add-on pricing for webinars for its Enterprise and Enterprise Plus offering. In this way, webinars resemble the Meetings & Chat product. You'll have to contact Zoom's sales folks and negotiate a deal.

Chapter 8 covers Zoom Video Webinars in far more detail.

Some Assembly Required

This section details Zoom's two enterprise-grade services: Zoom Rooms and Zoom Phone. Unlike the subscriptions in the previous section, the ones in this section may involve purchasing special hardware and some effort configuring it. Put differently, these tools require more than just an individual device, such as a MacBook Air, Microsoft Surface Pro 7, or a contemporary smartphone.

TECHNICAL STUFF

Note that your organization may not need to shell out beaucoup bucks to take advantage of Zoom's offerings in this section. Your employer's IT folks may be able to configure its existing video displays, speakers, and the like.

WARNING

Zoom's hardware-intensive services cannot perform miracles. Say that your company is located in an area with notoriously weak and spotty Internet connectivity. In this case, it's imperative to temper your performance expectations.

Zoom Rooms

Meetings & Chat and Video Webinars allow you to hold robust video-based meetings. Say that you're in Timbuktu, your boss Pete is in Montreal, and your client Ian is in Colombia. The three of you can meet online, but you won't feel as if you're in the same room.

But what if you and Pete are in the same physical location? Yep, I'm talking about an actual, brick-and-mortar room. What if you wanted to enter a souped-up conference room and share it with Mark in London, Steve H. in Gaza, and Steve R. in Warsaw, Poland? (These are the names of the insanely talented members of Marillion, one of my very favorite bands, but I digress.) Collectively, you want to do more than host a simple teleconference from your homes or hotel rooms with basic screen-sharing and video feeds.

And what if employees at your firm regularly needed to conduct these types of high-end meetings from the same physical locations? That is, you want to fit a bunch of conference rooms with affordable hardware and software that really make an impression with your colleagues and prospects. Alternatively, what if your company routinely conducts remote training classes with new hires? In these cases, Meetings & Chat may not be sufficient for your needs.

Welcome to Zoom Rooms, a way of taking Meetings & Chat up a notch.

Main features and benefits

Zoom Rooms transforms normal conference rooms into something more powerful, interactive, and collaborative. I like to think of Zoom Rooms as Meetings & Chat on steroids. That is, with Zoom Rooms, you can do many of the same things as Meetings & Chat, but the former is a far more robust product.

RECORDING YOUR MEETINGS

Just like with Meetings & Chat, Zoom Rooms lets users easily record what takes place in your company's conference and training rooms and with its virtual guests.

MAKING MAINTENANCE EASY

Many IT departments and employees struggle to maintain their companies' legacy audio/visual systems. Compared to many of its predecessors, Zoom Rooms requires very little software and hardware maintenance.

WHITEBOARDING AND ANNOTATING

Do you often brainstorm with others during meetings? Do you consider yourself a visual learner or thinker? Say that you're trying to nail that new product launch or find the best way to solve a vexing technical problem. Annotating a computer screen just doesn't cut it for you. You need something more.

Zoom Rooms allows for far more interactive whiteboarding than Meetings & Chat does. Meeting participates can

>> Concurrently annotate across all devices and Zoom Rooms without everyone sharing the same virtual dry erase marker

- » Concurrently use up to 12 whiteboards
- » Can save and distribute their collaborative whiteboarding sessions

WIRELESSLY SHARING CONTENT

Users can easily and concurrently share multiple desktops in the room. Meeting attendees and hosts can take advantage of a variety of simple wireless sharing options.

INTEGRATING WITH EXISTING A/V SYSTEMS

Say that your employer already installed an expensive audio/visual (A/V) system in its conference rooms. Depending on its current configuration, it may well be able to integrate those devices with Zoom Rooms. That is, your company may not need to trash its current setup.

MAKING SCHEDULING EASY

To reserve a room for a given time and date, employees can simply tap on a physical screen outside of a Zoom Room. From there, they can also view the scheduled meetings for that room. (Yes, they can do the same through Zoom software no matter where they are.)

GUARANTEEING SYSTEM UPTIME

The company guarantees its Zoom Room customers system uptime of 99.99 percent. I did the math. This provision means that, in a given year, Zoom Rooms will go offline for a maximum of about nine hours.

To be fair, the 99.99 number is certainly impressive, but not unique. That level has been fairly common in the tech world for years. For example, cloud-computing juggernauts Amazon Web Services (AWS), Microsoft Azure, and Google all guarantee similar uptime percentages in the end-user license agreements (EULAs). Ditto for the collaboration tool Slack.

Plans and costs

Subscribing to Zoom Rooms does not require the purchase of another Zoom product. That is, it's a standalone solution, although you can certainly add on to it.

Zoom Rooms costs $49 (USD) per month per room. Organizations that want so save a few bucks can opt for the annual plan: $499 per month per room.

Note that there's no practical limit to the number of meeting participants under this plan. If you can cram 2,112 in a room for a single training session, have at it. Zoom won't be monitoring your meetings. (Chapter 9 covers security and privacy in far more detail.)

Supercharging Zoom Rooms

Depending on your organization's needs and its current videoconferencing hardware, it may want to consider two complementary products:

>> Zoom Conference Room Connectors

>> Zoom Rooms for Touch

Both work in conjunction with Zoom Rooms.

ZOOM CONFERENCE ROOM CONNECTORS

Say that you work at Gray Matter Technologies (GMT). Five years ago, it purchased and deployed expensive telecommunications equipment. I'm talking about regular, speaker, and even video-enabled phones. Also assume that GMT contracted Cisco, Polycom, Lifesize, or another popular vendor. The implementation went fairly smoothly.

Today, those devices still function, but users wish that they could do more with them. Depending on their age, you find them a bit long in the tooth. The software isn't very intuitive and employees sometimes employees complain about audio call quality Video feeds are sometimes choppy. Finally, you cannot easily record conference calls, much less store them.

But your A/V system still technically works.

You try making the case to GMT's chief technology officer (CTO), Elliot. He agrees with you, but he simply cannot justify the cost of replacing all of its videoconferencing hardware.

What to do?

Thanks to Conference Room Connectors, GMT can have its cake and eat it, too.

Companies can purchase Zoom Conference Room Connectors — devices that let their employees make Zoom video calls using their organization's existing conference-room hardware. Put differently, this fresh coat of paint allows employees to take advantage of Zoom's intuitive user interface (UI) while moving their existing, on-premises videoconferencing systems to the cloud.

TECHNICAL STUFF

If you want to know more about the core technologies behind Zoom competitors, see Chapter 1.

ZOOM ROOMS FOR TOUCH

I'll bet that you've become accustomed to touchscreens over the past 12 years. In fact, you may chuckle when you see someone with a BlackBerry or an old-school flip phone. Odds are, though, that you don't touch your television or large computer monitor.

Zoom Rooms for Touch takes the core Zoom Room product to the next level. It turns a Zoom Room into an app the size of a television. Specific features include being able to do the following:

>> Instantly collaborate with others and share content over remarkably fluid video.

>> Brainstorm with your entire team on a massive digital video screen.

>> Easily share your screen and whiteboard with meeting participants.

Chapter 10 provides more information on Zoom Rooms, the hardware required to run them, and their add-ons.

Zoom Phone

Got a landline?

Fifteen years ago, you almost certainly did.

Data provider Statista reports that, in 2004, you could find a landline in nearly 93 percent of U.S. households. As of 2018, that number had declined to 41.7 percent. (See the chart yourself at `bit.ly/2004-zoom`.) Brass tacks: At home, hundreds of millions across the globe have dropped their landlines altogether.

At work, however, it may well be a different story. Traditional desk-based phones haven't gone the way of the Dodo just yet. After all, do you want to give your personal cellphone number to every Tom, Dick, and Harry? I'm talking about customers, colleagues, vendors, and partners. Plus, what about call centers? Millions of businesses still need to provide traditional desks and company-owned phones to their employees. Many organizations have discovered their answer in the form of Zoom Phone.

Main features and benefits

Zoom's final offering as of this writing is Zoom Phone — a high-tech version of a traditional business phone system. Its slick software and technical underpinnings (again, cloud computing) make it a vast improvement of early VoIP efforts.

>> **Centralized management:** Administrators can quickly provision and manage users. Zoom Phone dashboards allow administrators to easily view key information on the calls that employees are making. What's more, the visualizations allow for quick identification of call performance. As a result, the company can quickly identify any network-related quality issues before they mushroom.

>> **Security and reliability:** The company has taken great pains to ensure that users' Zoom Phone calls are both secure and clear.

>> **Traditional phone features:** You may not leave voicemails for your friends and family, but the feature remains important in many corporate settings. Ditto for call recording. Zoom Phone offers both of these essential features.

>> **Call routing:** Zoom Phone allows organizations to quickly and intelligently route queued calls to available agents and assistants. Without this essential functionality, modern day call centers would cease to exist.

Plans and costs

Like Video Webinars, Zoom Phone is an add-on to its core Meetings & Chat plan. Table 2-2 displays the available types of Zoom Phone plans and their costs.

Chapter 11 covers Zoom Phone in far more depth.

TABLE 2-2   **Zoom Phone Options**

Plan	Locations	Cost (USD)
Unlimited Calling	U.S. and Canada	$15 per month per license
Metered Calling (ideal for infrequently used phones)	U.S. and Canada	$10 per month per license
Additional Phone Numbers	U.S. and Canada	$5 per month per number
Toll-Free Phone Numbers	U.S. and Canada	$5 per month per number
Metered calling options for calls placed outside of your designated calling plan	All	Variable

2

Communicating and Collaborating in Zoom

IN THIS PART . . .

Download and install the Zoom desktop client.

Set up Zoom and hold individual and group meetings.

Learn how to record calls, share your screen, and perform other essential functions.

Discover advanced calling, chatting, and scheduling features.

Chapter **3**

Setting Up Zoom

Z oom allows people to easily hold high-quality videoconferences with their colleagues, partners, customers, families, friends, or students. You may be jumping at the bit to start one.

I understand your excitement, but hold the phone. It's essential to first cover a few foundational topics. Case in point: Before you can host a meeting, you need to take care of a few things.

This chapter explains the necessary housekeeping that you'll have to perform in order to start using Zoom in earnest. Don't worry. You'll be up and running with Meetings & Chat shortly.

Taking Your First Steps

The world is data-driven. Rare is the company today that doesn't want to collect basic information about its users and customers. To this end, in order for you to host a Zoom meeting, you'll have to first create an account.

REMEMBER

Zoom labels all audio and video calls with others as *meetings*. This term may seem a bit formal to you. Still, I use it consistently throughout the book to avoid confusion with Zoom's other offerings.

Creating a new Zoom account

Like many apps and web-based services today, Zoom requires users to establish accounts online if they want to host meetings.

REMEMBER

Someone in your organization may have already created a Zoom account for you. That is, management may have already subscribed to one of Zoom's premium plans and registered you. In this case, you don't need to create a new account; you'll just log in with your existing email address and password. If you're not sure, just check with your employer's IT department.

To create a new Zoom account, follow these steps:

1. **Go to the Zoom web portal at** `https://www.zoom.us`.

2. **In the upper right-hand corner of the website, click on the orange Sign up, it's free button.**

   From here, Zoom provides you with three sign-up options via

   - An email address
   - Google
   - Facebook

   If you select the second or third option, then Zoom makes you authenticate your new account through that service. At a high level, you are granting Zoom permission to access some of the data that you have provided to Facebook or Google.

   Admittedly, this practice is quite common. For example, for years Spotify has allowed people sign up for new accounts with Facebook. When they do, new users don't need to provide Spotify with their names, dates of birth, email addresses, and the like. Facebook already stores this information about its users — and plenty more, depending on how much they share on the social network.

   Say that that thought terrifies you or you don't use those popular services. Simply select the first option and continue.

   The following instructions assume that you're signing up for Zoom with your email address, and not via Facebook or Google.

3. **Enter your email address and click on the Sign-Up button.**

   Zoom informs you that an email confirmation is on its way (see Figure 3-1).

We've sent an email to ⬛⬛⬛⬛@gmail.com.
Click the confirmation link in that email to begin using Zoom.

if you did not receive the email,

Resend another email

FIGURE 3-1:
Zoom browser
message.

WARNING

To minimize spam and the impact of bad actors, Zoom blocks certain domains from registering new accounts. For example, Zoom rejected `heliyar802@ mailboxt.com` because people often use that domain to create disposable email addresses. (Chapter 9 dives much deeper into security and privacy.)

4. **Check your inbox and open the Zoom-authentication email.**

The message resembles Figure 3-2.

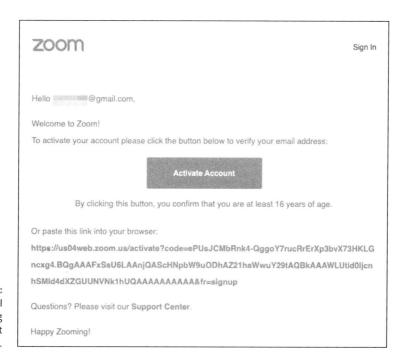

zoom   Sign In

Hello ⬛⬛⬛⬛@gmail.com,

Welcome to Zoom!

To activate your account please click the button below to verify your email address:

Activate Account

By clicking this button, you confirm that you are at least 16 years of age.

Or paste this link into your browser:

https://us04web.zoom.us/activate?code=ePUsJCMbRnk4-QggoY7rucRrErXp3bvX73HKLG
ncxg4.BQgAAAFxSsU6LAAnjQAScHNpbW9uODhAZ21haWwuY29tAQBkAAAWLUtid0ljcn
hSMld4dXZGUUNVNk1hUQAAAAAAAAA&fr=signup

Questions? Please visit our Support Center.

Happy Zooming!

FIGURE 3-2:
Zoom email
requesting
account
authentication.

5. **Open the email and click on the blue Activate Account button.**

   Zoom takes you to a new window or tab in your default web browser, as Figure 3-3 displays.

FIGURE 3-3:
Completing your
Zoom account.

6. **Complete your Zoom account by entering the required information.**

   Zoom requires you to enter your first and last name. What's more, you'll need to create and confirm your password. When you click on the password field, Zoom prompts you with guidelines about what it can and cannot contain. For example, setting your password as *starwars* won't fly. Try again, young Skywalker.

7. **Click on the orange Continue button.**

   The Don't Zoom Alone screen appears.

8. **(Optional) Invite your friends, family, and/or colleagues by typing in their email addresses.**

   Skip this step if you like by clicking on the button in the lower left-hand corner of the page. Zoom ultimately directs you to a page that lists your personal Zoom web page or URL, such as the one that Figure 3-4 displays.

    URL stands for *Uniform Resource Locator*. Many people equate this term to *web address*, although technically speaking that's incorrect.

   TECHNICAL STUFF

9. **Check your inbox again.**

   Zoom has sent you an email confirming your account and listing the features of your current plan, as Figure 3-5 displays. (Chapter 2 explains more about Zoom's different plans.)

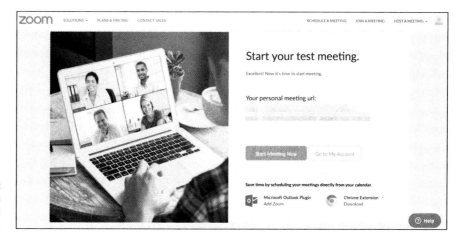

FIGURE 3-4:
Zoom page with personal meeting URL.

FIGURE 3-5:
Zoom email confirming new account.

Congratulations. Your Zoom account is now active.

You're now halfway home. To take advantage of the powerful features in Meetings & Chat, however, you'll want to install its desktop client. (For instructions, see the section "Downloading and installing the Zoom desktop client," later in this chapter.)

REMEMBER

Just like with many services today, you can create Zoom different accounts with different email addresses. In fact, you may want to create a personal Zoom account independent of your work account to separate church and state.

Modifying your Zoom plan

At some point, your business may expand, contract, or change. For example, maybe the sales folks begin to offer webinars and other customer-information sessions. Fortunately, Zoom allows its customers to easily upgrade, downgrade, cancel, and add on to their plans.

WARNING

Your current Zoom role may prevent you from upgrading yourself or your organization to a more robust plan. (For more on roles, see the section "Creating new user roles," later in this chapter.)

Upgrading from the Basic to the Pro plan

Say that you kicked the tires on Zoom's Basic Meetings & Chat plan. You're impressed and want to take it to the next level. Follow these directions to upgrade to the Pro plan:

1. **In the Zoom web portal, under the Personal header, click on Profile.**

2. **Scroll down until you see the User Type section.**

    Zoom displays your current plan. In this example, it's the Basic one.

3. **Click on the Upgrade link to display a new page.**

4. **Click on the orange Upgrade Account button.**

    A table that describes Zoom's different plans and features appears.

5. **Click on the button of the plan to which you want to upgrade.**

    In this case, it's the Pro plan.

6. **Select the number of meeting hosts that you want to purchase.**

    Zoom's default is one. More hosts results in a larger bill.

7. **Select the length of your subscription.**

    Zoom defaults to annual (with a discount), but you can easily select monthly, if that's your preference.

8. **(Optional) Select your desired add-ons.**

    For more information on these options, see Chapter 2.

9. **Click on the Continue button at the bottom the page.**

10. **On the page that appears, enter your contact information and payment method.**

11. **Confirm that you're not a robot and agree to the Privacy Policy and Terms of Services by selecting the appropriate checkboxes.**

12. **Click on the blue Upgrade Now button.**

    Zoom displays an order summary.

13. **Look over the summary to ensure that you're subscribing to your desired plan and for the desired time period; if you're happy with what you see in the summary, then click on the orange Confirm button.**

    Zoom displays a message confirming that you've upgraded your plan, as shown in Figure 3-6.

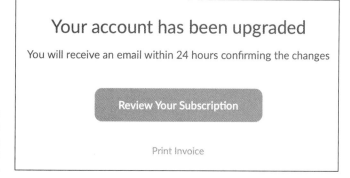

Your account has been upgraded

You will receive an email within 24 hours confirming the changes

Review Your Subscription

Print Invoice

FIGURE 3-6:
Zoom message
confirming
upgrade from
Basic to Pro plan.

REMEMBER

Note that your specific upgrade steps may vary slightly based upon

>> Your organization's existing plan

>> The length of its current subscription

>> Whether or not it had already upgraded

Canceling and making other changes to your existing plan

If you decide to cancel, change, or add on to your existing Meetings & Chat plan, follow these directions:

1. **In the Zoom web portal, under the Admin header, click on Account Management.**

2. **Click on Billing to display your current plans and add-ons.**

Zoom displays your current plans and add-ons. Figure 3-7 displays my Zoom account dashboard.

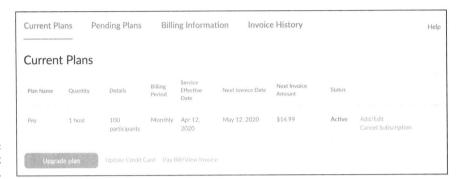

FIGURE 3-7:
Zoom account
dashboard.

3. **Make your desired changes.**

From the Zoom dashboard, you can

- Downgrade your Zoom plan.

- Cancel your Zoom Meetings & Chat subscription.

- Update your credit card.

- Pay your bill.

- View your invoices.

- Add new features to your existing Zoom Meetings & Chat subscription.

Downloading and installing the Zoom desktop client

To be sure, Zoom users and customers can participate in meetings no matter where they are as long as they can connect to the Internet. Again, Meetings & Chat runs on anything: smartphone, tablet, laptop, and desktop.

Still, to take advantage of all of Zoom's robust functionality, you'll want to install the Zoom desktop client. Fortunately, if your computer runs MacOS, Windows, or even Ubuntu/Linux, Zoom has you covered.

TECHNICAL STUFF

A *desktop client* is an application running on a desktop computer. Although purists will probably furrow their brows, I use the terms *desktop client* and *computer app* interchangeably. By the way, you can run that desktop client on your laptop.

To install the Zoom desktop client on your computer, follow these steps:

1. **In the Zoom web portal, hover over the word Resources in the top right-hand corner.**

   A drop-down list appears.

2. **Select Download Zoom Client from the drop-down list.**

   Zoom takes you to its Download Center, shown in Figure 3-8.

FIGURE 3-8:
Zoom Download Center.

3. **Click on the Download button.**

   Depending on your browser and how you've configured its settings, you may receive a warning that you're about to download a file. If you do, then proceed.

4. **Save this file to your computer.**

   The specific location is generally a matter of personal preference, but it's wise to follow these common conventions:

   - For PC/Windows users: C:\Program Files
   - For Mac users: *Hard-drive name*\Applications

   Remember where you save this file.

5. **Once the download completes, locate the file.**

The specific type of file hinges upon your computer's operating system. As of this writing, here are the filenames and extensions:

- **For PC/Windows users:** An executable file or with an .exe extension called ZoomInstaller.exe.

- **For Mac users:** An installer package archive file with a .pkg extension named zoomusInstaller.pkg.

Remember where you saved this file. You're going to need it for the next step.

6. **Double-click on the file to launch Zoom's installation wizard.**

The exact steps that you follow depend upon your computer's operating system. If you've ever installed a new program on your computer before, then you'll recognize the steps required.

7. **Complete the steps in the wizard.**

Once you do, then the Zoom desktop client is installed. You can easily host audio and videoconferencing calls with people on any device across the globe.

TIP

If you want to access Zoom directly via your web browser of choice, you're in luck. Just visit `bit.ly/zoom-brows` and install the extension for Chrome, Firefox, or another browser. Note, however, that using Zoom via a browser means that you won't be able to do everything that you can on the desktop client.

Signing in to the Zoom desktop client

After you sign up for a Zoom account and download and install the desktop client on your computer (see preceding section), you can sign in to the Zoom desktop client:

1. **Launch the Zoom desktop client.**

Zoom displays the window shown in Figure 3-9.

Note two things here: Zoom remembers who you are after you successfully log in. Second, Figure 3-9 displays an option that I have not mentioned yet: *single sign-on* or SSO. If you'd like to know more about it, then read the nearby sidebar "Making life simple with SSO." For the purposes of the simple directions, however, you can ignore it.

2. **Enter your email address and password.**

3. **Click on the blue Sign In button.**

Zoom takes you to the main screen.

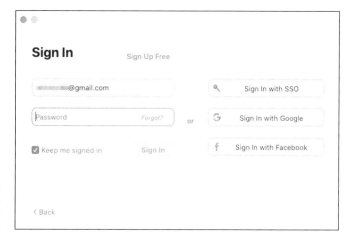

FIGURE 3-9:
Logging in to
the Zoom
desktop client.

Completing your Zoom profile

At a bare minimum, you'll want to add a profile picture so that your colleagues and/or friends will recognize you.

MAKING LIFE SIMPLE WITH SSO

Madrigal Electromotive is an international conglomerate with tens of thousands of employees. Those workers need to access a wide variety of applications, web services, and internal systems. They include

- Company email
- Productivity apps, such as Google Drive and Microsoft Office 365
- A slew of internal enterprise systems
- Collaboration applications, such as Slack and Zoom

If you think that managing all of these employees' usernames and passwords can be confusing, trust your judgment. In this vein, Madrigal has deployed SSO. Now, employees can sign into all of these services using the same username and password. From the IT department's perspective, SSO streamlines user administration and saves it mounds of headaches.

To set your profile photo, follow these steps:

1. **In the Zoom web portal, under the Personal header, click on Profile.**

2. **Click on Change, which is below the person icon next to your name.**

   The Change Picture window appears.

3. **Click on the Upload button in the lower left-hand corner.**

   Zoom warns you that the maximum file size is 2MB.

4. **Choose the photo that you want to upload from your computer.**

5. **(Optional) Crop the photo.**

6. **Click on the blue Save button.**

REMEMBER

From time to time, you may want to modify your Zoom profile. For example, perhaps you changed jobs or locations within your company. Zoom lets you make plenty of additional, self-explanatory edits in this part of its web portal. Note, however, that your role may limit the changes that you can make to your profile and account. (See the section "Discussing the Importance of Zoom Roles," later in this chapter, for more information.)

Getting to know the Zoom UI

After you create your account and install the Zoom desktop client, you can explore Zoom's user interface (UI). Figure 3-10 displays the screen that appears when you log in to Zoom. Keep in mind that Figure 3-10 displays the UI for Zoom Meetings & Chat, not for its other offerings.

FIGURE 3-10:
Zoom Meetings & Chat user interface.

Think of the UI as a dashboard from which you can launch meetings, join existing meetings, tweak your settings, and do much more. After installing the Zoom app, the following icons and elements (from left to right) appear at the top of the screen:

- » **Home:** Clicking on Home always takes you back to this main screen. Think of Home as the equivalent of the home page in your favorite web browser.

- » **Chat:** In Chat, you can start new text-based individual and group chats. You can also access your previous ones.

- » **Meetings:** In Meetings, you can find information on your previous and future meetings and view recording meetings, among other things.

- » **Contacts:** You can access your directory of Zoom contacts and create *channels*, or containers for group-based text messages and file exchanges.

- » **Search bar:** You can search for messages, files, and contacts that exist within Zoom.

- » **Your Zoom Meetings & Chat profile:** You can set your status, edit your profile, check for app upgrades, and more.

- » **Settings icon:** You can control settings, such as video, audio, chat, and screen-sharing for Zoom meetings.

The following four icons adorn the left-hand side of the screen:

- » **New Meeting:** Start and host a new Zoom meeting.

- » **Join:** Join an existing Zoom meeting — that is, one that another host has initiated.

- » **Schedule:** Set up a future meeting and configure its settings.

- » **Share Screen:** Share your screen with other meeting participants.

I unpack these features and settings in Chapters 4 and 5. For now, suffice it to say that you'll frequently return to the home screen of Zoom's desktop client. In other words, you won't just set it and forget it.

Reviewing Zoom Account Management

Think about your colleagues for a moment. How many of them are relatively new to your group or organization? How many have been there for a decade or more?

Zoom understands that organizations are living, breathing things. Things change. Maybe the president hires a new VP of finance and five programmers. Conversely, Travis's bad behavior finally caught up with him, and management has shown him the door. Your cross-town rival poaches a few of your rock stars.

Fortunately, Zoom makes account management a breeze.

REMEMBER

You must belong to a premium plan to add users to your Zoom account. (For more information on Zoom's different plans, see Chapter 2.)

WARNING

If you're on the Zoom's Basic plan, then the rest of this chapter covers functionality unavailable to you. Still, I'd encourage you to carefully read the rest of this chapter. At some point, you or your organization may upgrade from the Basic plan to one of Zoom's premium offerings. To this end, failure to understand the features on these Zoom plans can result in excess charges, lost data, security issues, and a bevy of other troubles.

Adding new users to your Zoom account

It's a cinch in Zoom to create new user accounts for your employees, partners, vendors, and customers. In fact, you can add new Zoom users to your account for anyone in the world, even if those folks don't work for your organization, by follow these steps:

1. **In the Zoom web portal, under the Admin header, click on User Management.**

2. **Click on Users to see a list of your organization's current Zoom users.**

3. **On the right-hand side of the page, click on the Add Users button.**

   The Add Users window appears, as shown in Figure 3-11.

4. **Enter the email addresses for any users you want to add, using commas to separate their email addresses.**

5. **Select the type of user(s) that you're adding.**

   Your choices are

   - **Basic:** Zoom lets these users ride for free, but they aren't able to access any of your plan's premium features.

   - **Licensed:** Zoom's default option results in account charges, the extent to which hinge upon your organization's plan.

   - **On-Prem:** These users can host meetings with unlimited minutes only if they use a Zoom Meeting Connector. (Chapter 11 discusses Zoom Phone in much more depth.)

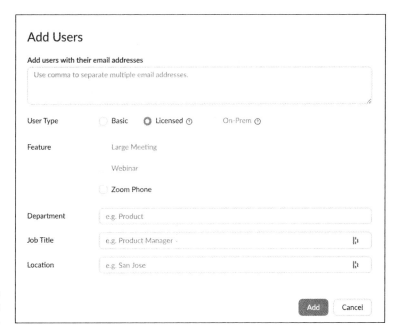

FIGURE 3-11:
Zoom prompt to
add new users.

WARNING

Pay attention here. Some people have neglected to check this option only to find unexpected charges at the end of their billing cycles.

6. **Select the features that you want to assign to the user(s).**

   Note that Zoom restricts you based upon your existing plan. For example, if you're currently not paying for webinars, then Zoom forbids you from adding a user with the ability to host them. In this case, you have to subscribe to webinars as an add-on first.

7. **(Optional) Enter the new user's department, job title, and/or location.**

8. **Click on the blue Add button at the bottom of the screen.**

   Zoom displays a temporary message at the top of the screen that lets you know the user(s) have been added.

Deactivating existing accounts

Say that John has stepped on a bunch of shattered glass and has to take a two-month medical leave. (He wasn't wearing shoes. It's a long story.) Here's how you can deactivate his Zoom account.

1. **In the Zoom web portal, under the Admin header, click on User Management.**

2. **Click on Users to see a list of your organization's current Zoom users.**

3. **On the left-hand side of the page, select the checkbox to the left of the name of the person whom you want to deactivate.**

4. **On the right-hand side of the page, click on the three horizontal dots that correspond to his name.**

   Zoom displays three options:

   - Deactivate
   - Delete
   - Unlink

5. **Choose Deactivate from the menu that appears.**

   Zoom asks you to confirm the deactivation. The user will no longer be able to access any Zoom service.

6. **Click on the blue Deactivate button.**

REMEMBER

A few months later, John has healed and wants to return to work. Reactivate him by following the same steps with one exception: You'll choose Activate in Step 5.

Deleting existing users from your Zoom account

Sometimes deactivating an employee's user account is insufficient. Perhaps an employee did something unconscionable, such as stole company secrets. Maybe an employee passed away.

In either case, you want to permanently eliminate the person's Zoom account. Follow these steps:

1. **Follow Steps 1 through 4 in the "Deactivating existing accounts" section, earlier in this chapter.**

2. **Choose Delete.**

   Zoom displays a window asking whether you want to transfer the data associated with the current user's account. This step is optional, but your choices are

   - All upcoming meetings
   - All upcoming webinars
   - All cloud recording files

3. **Select your desired data transfer options by selecting the appropriate checkboxes, entering an email address when prompted.**

   Zoom assigns all of the current user's data to the account associated with the email address that you enter here.

4. **If you selected data transfer options in the preceding step, then click on the Transfer Data, Then Delete button; otherwise, click on the Delete Now Without Data Transfer button.**

   Either way, you need to click on a red button to proceed with the account deletion. Zoom displays a message at the top of the screen indicating that it has processed the account deletion. That account no longer appears in the list of users.

   This step is permanent. There is no CTRL+Z.

WARNING

Unlinking users from your Zoom account

Zoom offers one final option for managing accounts, one slightly less draconian than deletion. By unlinking an account from the mother organization, the account continues to exist — just under a different, unaffiliated email address. Think of it as a divorce.

Follow these steps to remove a user account from your organization in Zoom:

1. **Follow Steps 1 through 4 in the "Deactivating existing accounts" section, earlier in this chapter.**

2. **Choose Unlink.**

   Zoom displays a window asking whether you want to transfer the data associated with the current user's account. This step is optional, but your choices are

   - All upcoming meetings

   - All upcoming webinars

   - All cloud recording files

3. **Select your desired data transfer options by selecting the appropriate checkboxes, entering an email address when prompted.**

   Zoom assigns all of the current user's data to the account associated with the email address that you enter here.

4. **If you selected data transfer options in the preceding step, then click on the Transfer Data, Then Unlink button; otherwise, click on the Unlink Now Without Data Transfer button.**

   Either way, you need to click on a red button to proceed to unlink the account.

WARNING

Note that the email address must correspond to an active and existing Zoom account in your organization.

Zoom displays a message at the top of the screen indicating that it has unlinked the account. That user account no longer appears in your Zoom web portal.

TIP

You can do even more with Zoom's robust account management functionality. See `bit.ly/zm-acct-x` for loads of additional information on this topic.

Unlocking the power of Zoom user groups

Zoom offers customers on premium plans a particularly valuable and timesaving feature: user groups. At a high level, user groups grant admins and owners the ability to manage user settings at the group level. In other words, they can concurrently change or lock the settings for multiple users. If that seems a bit abstract, then consider one of the many potential applications of user groups.

The fictitious Octavarium University has subscribed to Zoom's Education plan for years. To build camaraderie and minimize misunderstandings, the school encourages its employees to enable their video when holding remote meetings. (See Chapter 4 for more information on this subject.)

At the same time, its administrators are justifiably concerned about student privacy, especially during the pandemic. They want to ensure that students don't join their professors' Zoom meetings with their video automatically enabled. In other words, undergraduates can activate their webcams if they want, but the choice should ultimately be theirs to make.

Jordan is Octavarium's Zoom admin. To make this change for all university professors, he follows this three-step process:

1. **Create a new user group.**
2. **Populate the user group.**
3. **Apply the relevant Zoom account setting for that user group.**

TIP

You can also restrict apps to specific user groups. Chapter 7 covers Zoom's third-party apps in more detail.

Creating a new user group

You first create a specific Zoom user group for professors by following these directions:

1. **In the Zoom web portal, under the Admin header, click on User Management.**

2. **Click on Group Management.**

3. **On the right-hand side of the page, click on the white Add Group button.**

4. **From the prompt, enter the name of the user group.**

   In this case, he calls it Professors.

5. **(Optional) Enter a description of the group.**

6. **Click on the blue Add button.**

   Zoom displays a brief message in green at the top of the screen that the group is created.

Populating a user group

Jordan has created a new user group, but by itself it is useless. In order to customize users' settings, he needs to place existing Zoom members into these groups — specifically, all of Octavarium's college professors.

You can populate a user group by following these directions:

1. **In the Zoom web portal, under the Admin header, click on User Management.**

2. **Click on Group Management.**

3. **On the right-hand side of the page, click on the name of the group to which you want to add members.**

   In this case, it's the Professors user group.

4. **On the right-hand side of the page, click on the white Add Members button.**

5. **From the prompt, select as many users as you want by entering part of their email addresses into the text box.**

6. **Click on the blue Add button.**

   Zoom confirms that you successfully added the group members.

Now that Jordan has both created the user group and added professors to it, he can now apply a specific change to all Octavarium professors in one fell swoop. At a high level, Zoom's options fall into three buckets:

>> **Meeting:** Chapter 4 delves into Zoom's robust meeting options.

>> **Recording:** Chapter 4 delves into this subject as well.

>> **Telephone:** Zoom Phone is the subject of Chapter 11.

Changing a user group

Jordan is almost finished. He wants to allow group members to join meetings without enabling video:

1. **In the Zoom web portal, under the Admin header, click on User Management.**

2. **Click on Group Management.**

3. **On the right-hand side of the page, click on the name of the group whose settings you want to change.**

4. **Find the setting that you'd like to tweak for this group.**

   In this example, Jordan wants to ensure that students can join meetings without enabling their video.

5. **Click on the Meeting tab on the right-hand side of the page to enable members to join meetings without enabling videos.**

6. **Next to Participants video, slide the blue toggle button left.**

   It turns gray, indicating that it's now off.

   Zoom displays a brief message in green at the top of the screen that confirms that the settings have been updated.

7. **As an added safety measure, click on the gray lock icon to the right of the toggle button so that no one can override this setting.**

   Zoom displays the same confirmation message at the top of the screen. Voilà! Now Octavarium students can join Zoom meetings with their professors via audio only if they desire.

I have just scratched the surface on what user groups can do. Chapter 9 covers this meaty topic in the context of Zoom's privacy and security settings, many of which owners and admins can easily apply via user groups.

For much more information on user groups, see `bit.ly/zfd-groups`.

TIP

Discussing the Importance of Zoom Roles

Zoom relies heavily upon user roles. In this way, Zoom resembles most powerful systems and applications. The basic premise behind roles is straightforward: In any organizations, users' needs and responsibilities will differ. As such, they require the ability to perform certain actions. Just as important, certain users should not be able to do specific things. It's not hard to imagine the chaos that would result if everyone in Zoom could perform every task.

Like users (the topic of the previous section), Zoom roles apply only to its premium plans: Pro, Business, Enterprise, Enterprise Pro, and Education. If your organization is currently a member of Zoom's Basic plan, then it will have to upgrade to take advantage of the considerable flexibility and functionality that roles provide.

REMEMBER

Reviewing Zoom's default roles

Zoom ships with three default user roles:

>> **Owner:** This role grants full privileges to access and manage the organization's Zoom account. No one outranks the owner. For example, an owner can invite others to the Zoom account and downgrade, upgrade, or cancel a Zoom subscription altogether.

>> **Admin:** While an admin technically sits underneath an owner, their privileges run the gamut. They can perform a number of essential tasks, both for themselves and others. For example, an admin can add, remove, and edit users.

>> **Member:** Members operate largely within the boundaries that owners and admins have set for them. Many times, they can change their individual settings, but they generally cannot alter Zoom settings that affect others in the organization.

Creating new user roles

If the roles of owner, admin, and member seem a skosh confining to you, then you're in luck. Say that you want to create a new role specifically for Roger, the head of marketing. Roger frequently hosts webinars for prospective customers. As a result, he needs to be able to do a few things that regular members can't. At the same time, though, you don't want to give him the keys to the kingdom.

Zoom lets admins and owners create new roles as needed. Just follow these steps:

1. **In the Zoom web portal, under the Admin header, click on User Management.**

2. **Click on Role Management to see the current roles in your organization.**

    By default, they are owner, admin, and member.

3. **On the right-hand side of the page, click on the Add Role button.**

4. **Enter a name for the role.**

5. **(Optional) Enter a description for that role.**

6. **Click on the blue Add button.**

    Zoom displays a boatload of options.

7. **Select the specific options that you want to grant to the new role.**

    At a high level, Zoom lets you determine what the people in the role will be able to do. Options include

    - View the setting or output

    - Edit the setting

    - Do both

    - Do neither (the default)

8. **When you finish, click on the blue Save Changes button at the bottom of the screen.**

    Zoom displays a temporary message in green at the top of the screen that confirms that your settings have been updated.

Your custom role is created, but it's not assigned to anyone in your organization.

WARNING

Tread lightly when creating new roles. Zoom grants users assigned to these new roles the power that you grant them. For example, in the preceding example, if you mistakenly allow Roger to delete users' accounts, then he will be able to do just that.

Changing an existing user's role

Employees and companies part ways. New hires come aboard. People transfer from one part of the company to another. Don't worry, though. Zoom recognizes that things change.

To assign someone in your organization a new Zoom role, follow these steps:

1. **In the Zoom web portal, under the Admin header, click on User Management.**

2. **Click on Users to see a list of users in your organization.**

3. **Click on the Edit button next to the name of the person whose role you want to change.**

   Zoom displays a new window that allows you to edit the user's information.

4. **Next to User Role, choose the user's new role from the drop-down menu.**

5. **Click on the blue Save button.**

   Zoom displays a temporary message in green at the top of the screen to confirm that you successfully changed the user's role.

TIP

Common courtesy dictates that you alert people when you've changed their roles.

For much more about Zoom roles, see `bit.ly/zmroles`.

IN THIS CHAPTER

» **Starting instant and scheduled Zoom meetings**

» **Sharing your screen**

» **Creating polls and in-meeting annotations**

» **Managing and interacting with meeting participants**

» **Recording your meetings for future use**

Chapter **4**

Connecting with Others via Zoom Meetings

have spent a great deal of time researching and writing about communication and technology. As such, I can make the following claim without fear of accurate contradiction: When it comes to those subjects, personal preferences vary.

Some people eschew actually talking to others at all costs. I'm talking about introverts, night owls, curmudgeons, misanthropes, and those who lack basic people skills. They'd rather go to the dentist than speak to another human being.

At the other end of the spectrum are loquacious individuals who need to talk about everything — even when sending a quick message would do the trick. These people generally fail to recognize that other viable communication methods exist.

Ideally, you don't fall into either category. You understand that when it comes to communication, one size doesn't fit all. Sometimes firing off a quick message is easiest. In other cases, hashing out a nuanced issue at work requires a real-time conversation — not a flurry of asynchronous emails. Aside from business scenarios, people want to hear the voices and see the faces of the most important people in their lives: friends, family members, and significant others. It's a basic human need.

This meaty chapter details Zoom's most popular service: meetings. As I discuss in Chapter 1, Zoom designed its flagship product from the ground up. The result is a modern, robust, convenient, consistent, reliable, intuitive, and user-friendly experience. As a result, Zoom makes holding single- and multi-person video and audio meetings a breeze. The phrase ridiculously simple comes to mind.

Bottom line: If you rue the very idea of a video meeting, Zoom's boatload of cool features may just change your mind.

Getting Started with Zoom Meetings

You may be anxious to jump right in and hold a Zoom meeting. I get it. Really. Zoom has created a powerful, user-friendly, flexible, and downright cool product.

I understand your excitement, and I cover the topic in the next section, "Hosting Zoom Meetings." Before I do, though, I need to cover some foundational material — and I urge you to read it. Developing a base understanding of Zoom's core functionality will help you use the service intelligently. What's more, it minimizes the chance of committing a *faux pas* or, even worse, exposing yourself and others to security or privacy issues.

Because I don't want to overwhelm you with a bevy of advanced options and features, I start with kid gloves.

TIP

Zoom appropriately names its flagship service Meetings & Chat because it performs both functions — and admirably to boot. This chapter focuses on the first half of Meetings & Chat. Chapter 5 goes deeper into the second half.

REMEMBER

Because of space considerations, this chapter simply cannot describe every meeting-related feature in Zoom. Zoom has packed quite a bit of functionality into its meetings. As a remedy and to let you find out more about the specific topics that interest you, I sprinkled plenty of contextual URLs throughout this chapter. I encourage you to visit them.

Reviewing Zoom's meeting-specific roles

Just like in real life, different people do different things in meetings. Zoom recognizes this reality by formalizing its meeting roles.

REMEMBER

The roles in the following section pertain only to the Meetings & Chat. That is, they differ from the proper user account roles discussed in Chapter 3. What's more, the following roles also overlap to an extent with their counterparts in Zoom Video Webinars — the subject of Chapter 8.

Host

Zoom by default assigns the person who starts or schedules the meeting the role of host. Say that Mary starts a meeting. Meetings & Chat assigns her the role of host. As such, she can perform the following tasks, among others:

» Start live streaming or, if you like, kick off the meeting in earnest

» End the meeting

» Share her screen with attendees

» Delegate another participant as co-host

» Start a breakout — a topic covered later in the chapter in the section "Using breakout rooms during meetings"

» Enable waiting rooms — a topic covered later in the chapter in the section "Enabling waiting rooms for all Zoom users in your organization"

Co-host

Depending on the size of your meeting, you may want to appoint a co-host. For the most part, these folks can perform the same tasks as hosts can with one main exception: They cannot start live streaming. They can, however, live stream once the host has started the meeting.

TIP

Zoom also lets meeting hosts designate surrogates. Visit `bit.ly/zfd-ahost` for more information on about what Zoom calls *alternative hosts*.

Participants

Say that you haven't scheduled the meeting; you just show up. In this case, Zoom refers to you as a meeting *participant*. Participants can perform tasks such as

» View the list of the other participants in the meeting

» Share their screens, with the host's permission

» Start and stop their own video

» Mute and unmute themselves

TIP

Visit `bit.ly/zfd-roles` to view a comprehensive list of the tasks that participants in each role can perform in a Zoom meeting.

Locating your personal Zoom information

Say that you're fortunate enough to sit in your own private office at work. If so, then your organization has effectively reserved space for you — whether you're at work or on vacation. For example, if you're traveling to Belize, you lock your office. No one else enters it without your consent. (Forget the janitorial staff for a moment.)

Zoom embraces the same general concept via what it calls a *Personal Meeting Room* (PMR). Think of the PMR as your very own, unique virtual meeting space. If Kramer wants to enter his PMR and host a meeting, then he'll need a key of sorts. Zoom refers to this key as a user's Personal Meeting ID (PMI).

You wouldn't give your house or office key to any Tom, Dick, or Harry. By the same token, you should treat your PMI with the same care. Once bad actors know your PMI, things can break bad. Specifically, if you are holding a meeting, others can join your PMR as uninvited guests, subject to the following two exceptions:

>> You lock the meeting — a topic that I cover in Chapter 9.

>> You enable Zoom's Waiting Room feature to individually admit participants. (For more on this subject, see the section "Enabling waiting rooms for all Zoom users in your organization," later in this chapter.)

To view both your PMR and PMI, follow these steps:

1. **In the Zoom web portal, under the Personal header, click on Profile.**

2. **On the right-hand side of the screen, you see the PMI.**

   By default, Zoom hides a few of its characters.

3. **Click on Show.**

   Zoom shows your PMI, as Figure 4-1 displays.

4. **(Optional) If you want to always use your PMI for instant meetings, click on Edit and then select the Use Personal Meeting ID for instant meetings checkbox.**

WARNING

   Checking this box introduces some risk that I cover in Chapter 9. I recommend leaving it unchecked.

FIGURE 4-1:
Zoom Personal
Meeting ID.

5. **(Optional) If you'd like to change your PMI, click on Edit and enter your new PMI.**

Zoom places some restrictions around PMIs. If Zoom doesn't like your new PMI, then it displays a red warning message.

6. **Click on the blue Save Changes button.**

WARNING

Giving out your PMR and/or PMI willy-nilly maximizes the chance of others crashing your meetings — or *Zoombombing*, as the kids say.

TIP

If you frequently host public meetings, then you should change your PMI every month or so.

TIP

You don't need to use your PMI when scheduling a meeting. I cover this topic in the section "Scheduling a Zoom meeting," later in this chapter.

Augmenting your Zoom meetings

Before hosting a single meeting, you may want to consider enabling three useful and underused Zoom options:

» Waiting rooms

» Breakout rooms

» Audio transcriptions (if your organization's Zoom plan allows)

Using these features lets you get more out of your meetings.

REMEMBER

Waiting and breakout rooms correspond to Meetings & Chat only. They have nothing to do with Zoom Rooms, discussed in Chapter 10. Bupkus.

Enabling waiting rooms for all Zoom users in your organization

Think about the last time that you visited your doctor. You didn't just barge in. You sat patiently or impatiently in the waiting room until the person at the front desk called your name.

Zoom lets meeting hosts follow the same protocol. If you are an account owner or admin, then you can enable waiting rooms for all users that fall under your organization's Zoom account. Follow these directions:

1. **In the Zoom web portal, under the Admin header, click on Account Management.**

2. **Click on Account Settings.**

3. **Scroll down to the Waiting room section and slide the toggle button to the right so that it turns blue.**

   Zoom asks you to confirm your decision.

4. **Click on the blue Turn On button.**

   Zoom confirms that it has updated your settings.

Of course, following these steps only means that members can choose to use waiting rooms. That is, admins cannot compel people to use them. I cover waiting rooms later in this chapter. (For more on this subject, see the section "Enabling waiting rooms for all Zoom users in your organization.")

TIP

Play around with Zoom's different waiting-room options. You can even customize your logo and the message that future meeting participants will see by visiting bit.ly/zfd-custwr.

Enabling breakout rooms during your meetings

John Keating teaches poetry at the Welton Academy in Middletown, Delaware. (Yes, I'm going all *Dead Poets Society* here.) He wants his class of 30 students to concurrently discuss Lord Byron's "She Walks In Beauty" in small groups. Unfortunately, he has to conduct his class via Meetings & Chat. Creating five or six distinct Zoom meetings isn't feasible.

What to do?

Enter breakout rooms, one of the most useful features of Meetings & Chat. Hosts can separate attendees into any number of smaller configurations during their meetings. The host can then drop in on each group and, in this case, bring the class back together — all without leaving the Zoom meeting or having to start a new one. If you think that feature would be beneficial in plenty of settings beyond classrooms, then trust your instincts. Even better, Zoom enables this feature on all plans, including the Basic one.

To enable breakout rooms for all members in an organization, an admin or owner needs to follow these steps:

1. **In the Zoom web portal, under the Admin header, click on Account Management.**

2. **Click on Account Settings.**

3. **Underneath the Breakout room section, slide the toggle button to the right so that it turns blue.**

   Zoom asks you to confirm your choice.

4. **Click on the blue Turn On button.**

   Zoom confirms that it has updated your settings.

Note that you need to enable breakout rooms only once. What's more, you can use them at your leisure. For more on how to enable breakout rooms for meeting participants, see "Using breakout rooms during meetings," later in this chapter.

TIP

At present, Zoom lets hosts create up to 50 separate breakout sessions per meeting.

Enabling meeting audio transcriptions

Zoom lets customers on its Business, Education, and Enterprise plans create audio transcriptions of their meetings. Even better, Zoom displays these transcriptions as different attendees speak. Think of it as watching a movie with subtitles.

To enable this setting for all members in an organization, a Zoom admin or owner needs to follow these steps:

1. **In the Zoom web portal, under the Admin header, click on Account Management.**

2. **Click on Account Settings.**

3. **Click on the Recording tab at the top of the page.**

4. **Underneath Advanced cloud recording settings, select the Audio transcript checkbox.**

5. **Click on the blue Save button.**

I cover this subject later in this chapter in the section "Viewing meeting transcriptions." Trust me. There is a method to my madness in this chapter.

TIP

Using breakout rooms is not a binary for all people under your organization's Zoom plan. For much more information on how you can configure them for different Zoom users and groups, see `bit.ly/zfd-bors`.

Hosting Zoom Meetings

Zoom calls its impromptu virtual get-togethers *Instant Meetings* or *Meet Now*. To start a meeting, launch the Zoom desktop client. Click on the Home icon and then on the New Meeting icon.

You are now hosting a live, one-person Zoom meeting, as Figure 4-2 displays.

FIGURE 4-2:
Zoom user interface during active meetings.

Astute observers may notice several things about Figure 4-2. First, I clearly haven't put my face on yet. Second, I love the band Rush and the 1995 crime movie *The Usual Suspects*. Third, in Zoom, background images appear inverted to hosts but normal to other participants. Trust me. I didn't buy backwards posters.

Fourth and most important for the purposes of this section, Zoom displays a series of icons from left to right when meetings begin, whether anyone has joined your meeting or not. Table 4-1 displays the menu icons that hosts see during their meetings.

TABLE 4-1   Zoom In-Meeting Menu Icons

Icon	Description
Mute	Control the audio output from your computer. The arrowhead lets you tweaks your computer's microphone and speaker settings for this meeting.
Stop Video	Let meeting participants see your visage. The arrowhead tweaks your computer's microphone and speaker settings for this meeting.
Security	Manage your meeting's security and privacy settings. Zoom added this new icon in April 2020 to make these features more prominent and easier to access. (Chapter 9 covers this subject in more detail.)
Participants	Determine who can do what during a meeting. For example, click here to quickly invite people to an existing meeting.
Share Screen	Minimize the main meeting window and share your screen with meeting participants. Stop sharing at any time by clicking on the red Stop Share button that appears. You can also momentarily stop sharing by — wait for it — clicking on the Pause Share button. The arrowhead lets you invoke additional screen-sharing options.
Record	Record your meeting. You can also stop or pause recording once you've started recording.
Reactions	Add simple emojis for all other meeting attendees to see.
End	Terminate the audio or video meeting for everyone.

Note: Table 4-1 intentionally omits two icons that you may see in the future, depending on how you configure Meetings & Chat.

>> **Polling:** I haven't created any polls for this meeting. I cover this subject in the section "Collecting participant input through polls," later in this chapter.

>> **Breakout Rooms:** I haven't enabled this valuable feature yet in my account. I address that topic in a later section called "Using during meetings."

REMEMBER

You can host only one meeting at a time per device.

Inviting others to your current meeting

Unless you've got split personalities or imaginary friends, you've probably never held a meeting with yourself. Rather, you need to talk with your boss or some colleagues about an issue. Maybe you want to catch up with your friends via a virtual happy hour. (Chapter 17 provides some neat ways to use Zoom socially.)

After starting your meeting, follow these directions to invite others:

1. **Click on the Participants icon at the bottom of the screen.**

2. **Click on the Invite button in the right-hand corner.**

3. **Click on the Email tab at the top of the screen.**

    In total, Zoom displays five options. The first three email-based invitation methods are:

    ● **Default Email:** Launches your computer's default email client. It may be Microsoft Outlook or Mail.

    ● **Gmail:** Launches a Gmail window or tab in your computer's default web browser, as Figure 4-3 displays.

    ● **Yahoo Mail:** Clicking here will launch a Yahoo Mail window or tab in your computer's default web browser.

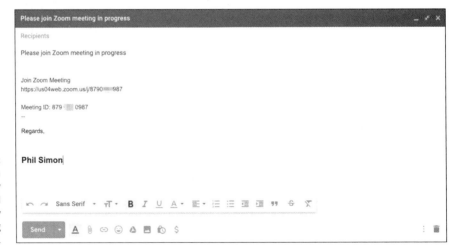

FIGURE 4-3: Zoom automatically generated Gmail message with key meeting information.

After sending your email, wait for others to join. Say, however, that you don't want to use Outlook or Gmail to invite others to your little shindig. No worries. Zoom provides two options unrelated to email:

- **Copy Invite Link:** Copies the meeting's URL to your computer's clipboard.

- **Copy Invitation:** Copies the words Join Zoom Meeting, the meeting URL, and the meeting identification number.

If you choose one of the last two options, then you can paste the copied text into a message in Slack, Microsoft Teams, WhatsApp, or just about any program or app that you could imagine. You could even write it down and fax it to someone if you like.

4. **Send the message and wait for others to join your Zoom meeting.**

   Once they do and assuming that all folks have enabled video on their end, Zoom displays something like Figure 4-4.

FIGURE 4-4:
Four-person
Zoom meeting
with Active
Speaker layout
enabled.

Note a few things about Figure 4-4. First, the folks in the lower left-hand corner have joined via Zoom Rooms. Chapter 10 explains that subject in more depth. Second, when three or more participants join a meeting, Zoom meetings default to what it calls its *Active Speaker* layout. (See the upper right-hand corner of Figure 4-4.) In this mode, Zoom automatically switches the large video window based upon who is speaking. Visit bit.ly/zfd-spkvw to discover more about this layout.

Say that your meeting consists of just two people, though. Your friend Roger and you are just catching up. In this case, from your perspective, Zoom displays your video in a small screen at the top, while Roger's video takes a more prominent position below yours. (From his perspective, the opposite is true.) For more on the other in-meeting layouts in Meetings & Chat, see `bit.ly/zfd-layouts`.

TIP

To watch a short video of a live Zoom meeting, see `bit.ly/zfd-mtg1`.

TIP

It's even easier to hold audio and video meetings people whom you've already added to your Zoom directory — a topic that I cover in Chapter 5.

Planning a future Zoom meeting

As former president Dwight D. Eisenhower once astutely observed, "Plans are worthless, but planning is everything." In the context of Zoom, convoking a spontaneous meeting makes sense in certain circumstances, especially when text-based communication just isn't working. Taken to the extreme, though, any given person's work life would be unmanageable and even downright chaotic if she couldn't at least try to plan her days.

To this end, Zoom makes it easy to schedule future meetings with others and to track attendee registration. What's more, by scheduling meetings, you unlock additional features that can make your meetings more valuable for all concerned.

Scheduling a Zoom meeting

To schedule a meeting with an individual or group of people in advance, follow these steps:

1. **Click on the Home icon at the top of the desktop client.**

2. **Click on the blue Schedule button.**

Zoom displays the Schedule Meeting window in Figure 4-5.

3. **Customize your meeting's settings.**

You can change its

- Topic and description

- Date

- Start and end time

- Meeting ID

- Audio and video options

FIGURE 4-5:
Scheduling a
future Zoom
meeting.

- Integration with third-party calendar tools, such as Microsoft Outlook and Google Calendar

- Advanced options, including whether you've assigned any alternative hosts

REMEMBER

Selecting Generate Automatically for the Meeting ID means that Zoom will produce and distribute a unique, disposable number. In other words, you won't be using your PMI for this meeting.

4. **When you finish, click on the blue Schedule button.**

You have now scheduled your meeting. Zoom displays a meeting-confirmation message with all the relevant information, such as the one in Figure 4-6.

From the meeting confirmation, you can perform the following actions by clicking on the related buttons:

» **Open:** Opens the calendar in your computer's default calendar program.

» **Close:** Closes the window.

» **Copy the invitation:** Sends the meeting's information to your clipboard. From here, you can paste it into an email or wherever you like.

Your meeting has been scheduled

MEETING INVITATION

Phil Simon is inviting you to a scheduled Zoom meeting.

Topic: Phil Simon's Zoom Meeting
Time: May 15, 2020 04:30 PM Arizona

Join Zoom Meeting
https://
pwd=S(

Meeting ID:
Password:
One tap mobile
                                    US (San Jose)
                                    US (Tacoma)

Dial by your location
    +1   US (San Jose)
    +1   US (Tacoma)
    +1   US (Houston)
    +1   US (New York)
    +1   US (Germantown)
    +1   US (Chicago)
Meeting ID:
Password:
Find your local number: https://us02web.zoom.us/u/

Open   Close   Copy Invitation

FIGURE 4-6:
Viewing a
scheduled Zoom
meeting.

TIP

View your scheduled meetings by clicking on the Meetings icon at the top of the Zoom desktop client.

Although you can host only one meeting at a time per device, you can schedule as many as you like in advance.

REMEMBER

Zoom also lets users schedule meetings via the web portal and through different browser extensions. Visit `bit.ly/zfd-sched` for instructions.

Editing your scheduled meeting

Say that you've successfully scheduled your meeting. After thinking about it, though, you decide that you'd like to make a few changes. Sure, you can junk your meeting and wreak havoc with others' calendars. A better way, though, involves editing your existing meeting — something that Zoom allows you to easily do by following these steps:

1. In the Zoom web portal, under the Personal header, click on Meetings.

2. Click on the name of the meeting that you'd like to edit.

Zoom presents basic information about your scheduled meeting.

3. **Click on the white Edit this Meeting button in the lower right-hand corner of the page.**

4. **Make whatever changes you like.**

   You can change the following:

   - Topic

   - Date and start and end time

   - Meeting ID

   - Audio and video options

   - Advanced options, including whether you have assigned any alternative hosts

5. **Click on the blue Save button.**

Collecting participant input through polls

Bruce has scheduled an upcoming meeting with members of his E Street Band. During the call, he wants to solicit everyone's feedback. Sure, attendees will be able to both chime in and enter text-based comments in the chat window. This type of unstructured data is often valuable, but collating it is typically messy and time-consuming, especially with larger groups. Structured data is far easier to collect and analyze. To this end, a better way in many cases is to conduct a poll — one that immediately displays results.

REMEMBER

Zoom reserves polls for customers on premium plans.

ENABLING POLLING AT THE ACCOUNT LEVEL

To enable polling for all members in an organization, an admin or owner needs to follow these steps:

1. **In the Zoom web portal, under the Admin header, click on Account Management.**

2. **Click on Account Settings.**

3. **Underneath the Polling section, click on the toggle button on the right-hand side of the page.**

   It turns blue. Zoom displays a new window asking you to confirm your choice.

4. **Click on the blue Turn On button.**

   Zoom confirms that it has updated your settings.

REMEMBER
You need to enable polls only once at the account level.

CREATING A POLL FOR YOUR SCHEDULED MEETING

After you activate polls, you can create one or more polls for an upcoming meeting:

1. In the Zoom web portal, under the Personal header, click on Meetings.

2. On the left-hand side of the page, under Upcoming Meetings, click on the meeting for which you want to schedule a poll.

3. Scroll to down the bottom of the page and click on the white Add button next to the words You have not created any poll yet.

4. In the window that appears, enter the title of your question.

5. (Optional) Select the Anonymous if you want to hide attendees' responses checkbox.

6. Type the name of your question.

7. Indicate whether the question is single or multiple choice by selected the related checkbox.

8. Enter the possible responses in the text boxes.

9. (Optional) To continue adding questions, click on + Add a Question and repeat Steps 4 through 8.

10. When you finish setting up your poll, click on the blue Save button.

You can now view the poll, as Figure 4-7 displays.

FIGURE 4-7: Saved poll for future Zoom meeting.

Note that Zoom ties polls to specific users' PMIs, a minor but important point. Say that Hank needs to set up a meeting with the other DEA agents in his office. He has read this book and, specifically, the earlier section on scheduling Zoom meetings. As such, he is weighing his two options:

>> **Using his PMI:** If he goes this route, then he can access all of the polls that he has created under his PMI.

>> **Allowing Zoom to automatically generate a disposable meeting ID number:** If Hank selects this option, then his poll applies only to that specific meeting. As a result, he would not be able to recycle them or transfer them to another meeting.

Either way, at some point during the meeting, hosts can launch their polls. I demonstrate how to do so later in the chapter in the section "Launching live polls."

REMEMBER

Do what you like, but I wouldn't let the transferability of polls drive your decision to use your PMI or not.

Handling meeting registration

While optional, requiring participants to register for future meetings confers a number of obvious benefits, including counting the number of heads in advance. Beyond that, a company or your manager may mandate attendance at certain meetings.

REQUIRING OTHERS TO REGISTER FOR YOUR MEETING

Brandt is holding an important department-wide meeting and wants to ensure that all employees attend. As such, he requires registration by following these steps:

1. **In the Zoom web portal, under the Personal header, click on Meetings.**

2. **Click on the name of the meeting whose registration information you'd like to view.**

3. **Click on the white Edit this Meeting button.**

4. **Scroll down to the word Registration and select the Required checkbox.**

5. **Click on the blue Save button.**

   Zoom returns you to the main meeting page.

6. **(Optional) To the right of Registration Link, copy the unique URL or click on Copy Invitation to view more detailed information about the meeting.**

7. **Distribute the link or meeting information to all meeting attendees however you choose.**

REGISTERING FOR A FUTURE MEETING

Brandt manages a staff of ten. He has required those folks to register for his monthly meeting. Further, he has distributed the link to attendees, maybe even via Zoom Meetings & Chat (discussed in Chapter 5). When others click on that URL, they will see a form similar to the one displayed in Figure 4-8.

FIGURE 4-8:
Zoom meeting
registration form.

VIEWING REGISTRANT DATA

After attendees fill out and submit a meeting registration form, Zoom stores their information. You can access it by following these steps:

1. **In the Zoom web portal, under the Personal header, click on Meetings.**

2. **Click on the name of the meeting whose registration information you'd like to view.**

3. **Scroll down to the Registration tab and to the right of Manage Attendees, click on View.**

    Zoom displays a window similar to Figure 4-9.

TIP

Click on the Edit button to customize your registration options even more.

FIGURE 4-9:
Viewing meeting
registrants.

Letting others in to your current meeting

Leo has scheduled a meeting with Johnny and Eddie in his corner office at 2 p.m. on Tuesday. They dutifully show up a few minutes early, but the door remains closed. Leo and Tom are arguing over what to do about Bernie, and the two have lost track of time. At 2:15 p.m., Leo finally opens the door and invites Johnny and Eddie in. The meeting can finally begin. (In case you're curious about the names, I'm paying tribute to the Coen Brothers' classic flick *Miller's Crossing*.)

The point of this little yarn is that, in the real world, a meeting's scheduled start time does not necessarily equal its actual start time. And the same principle applies to Zoom meetings.

Earlier in this chapter, I describe how hosts can enable waiting rooms for their meetings. (See the section "Enabling waiting rooms for all Zoom users in your organization.")

Say that you have enabled the waiting-room option. After folks have attempted to join your meeting, Zoom displays the message in Figure 4-10 until you let them in.

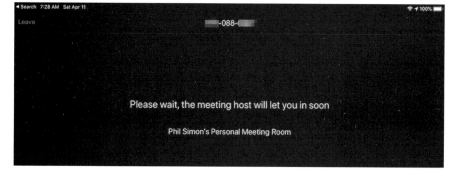

FIGURE 4-10:
Attendees' view
of the meeting
while they are in
the Zoom waiting
room.

As the meeting host, the Zoom desktop client notifies you with an orange blinking light on the Participants tab in Figure 4-11.

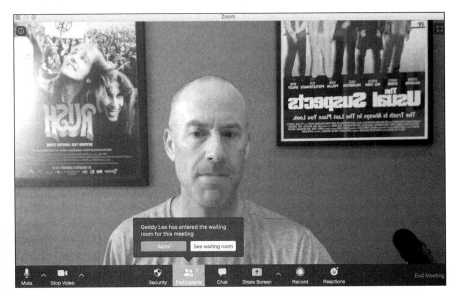

FIGURE 4-11:
Participant
notification in the
Zoom Meetings
desktop client.

Zoom provides meeting hosts with a number of options, as Table 4-2 describes.

TABLE 4-2   **Zoom's Waiting Room Options for Meeting Hosts**

Action	Directions and Results
Admit a participant	Click on the Participants icon and on the blue Admit button to let them into the meeting.
Send message	Click here to launch Zoom's in-meeting chat window. From here, you can send messages to everyone in the waiting room or single out a specific individual.
Do nothing	Self-explanatory: All attendees remain in purgatory.
Admit all participants	Click on the Participants icon and then click on the Admit all button in the top right-hand corner. All participants enter the meeting.

Joining others' Zoom meetings

Just like in real life, you won't always host a Zoom meeting. Sometimes you'll participate in meetings with people from external organizations. Zoom makes it remarkably simple to join an existing meeting, whether you know the host's PMI or the meeting's URL.

Joining a meeting using the host's PMI

Walter invites you to a meeting via email. His message includes his PMI as well as the meeting's password. You can join his meeting by following these instructions:

1. **Launch the Zoom desktop client.**

2. **On the Home screen, click on the Join icon.**

3. **From the prompt, enter the host's PMI.**

4. **(Optional) Enter the meeting password.**

    By default, Zoom began enabling passwords for all meetings starting on April 5, 2020. (You can uncheck this box to disable this option, but I recommend leaving it enabled for security purposes.)

5. **Enter your name or what you want others in the meeting to call you.**

6. **(Optional) Indicate whether you want to disable your audio by selecting the appropriate checkbox.**

    Zoom's default option connects you to the meeting with your computer's audio enabled.

7. **(Optional) Indicate whether you want to disable your video by selecting the radio box on the left.**

    Zoom's default option connects you to the meeting with your computer's video enabled.

8. **Click on the blue Join button.**

    (Optional) If you chose to join with your video enabled, then Zoom presents you with prompt that allows you to preview what other attendees will see, as see Figure 4-12 displays.

9. **If you like what you see, then click on the blue Join with Video button; if not, then click on the white Join without Video button.**

    Assuming that the host hasn't enabled meeting waiting rooms, you'll join the meeting momentarily.

    You'll also have to enter a password if the meeting host required it.

    You have now joined the Zoom meeting.

TIP

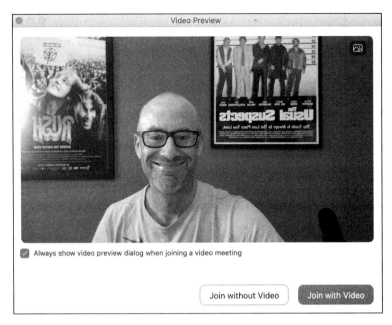

FIGURE 4-12:
Zoom video
premeeting entry
prompt.

Joining a meeting via a URL

Donnie invites you to a meeting by emailing you a URL. You can join him on Zoom by following these steps:

1. **Copy and paste the meeting URL into the address bar of your web browser and press the Enter key.**

   Assuming that you installed the Zoom desktop client, your browser prompts you to open it.

2. **Click on the Open or Allow button — or the equivalent button in your web browser.**

3. **Click on the blue Join button.**

4. **If you like the video preview, click on the blue Join with Video button; if not, then click on the white Join without Video button.**

Joining via a URL eliminates the need to enter the meeting's password because Zoom embeds the password in the link.

Waiting for hosts to begin their meetings

Say that you have arrived early for James's meeting, or he is running late. If James has turned on waiting rooms for his meeting, then you can expect to see a waiting room screen. (Refer to Figure 4-10 to see what it looks like.)

Putting your best foot forward

No one forces you to enable video during your Zoom meetings. You can always join via audio only. (Refer to the earlier section, "Joining a meeting using the host's PMI.") Still, from time to time you're going to want the world to see you.

Looking your best in Zoom

A seldom-used Zoom feature called Touch Up My Appearance purportedly helps smooth out the skin tone on your face. No, it won't transform me into Brad Pitt or Idris Elba, but think of it as the equivalent of putting on some digital makeup.

Follow these directions to enable this feature:

1. **Launch the Zoom desktop client.**
2. **Click on the Settings icon in the upper-right corner.**

   Zoom displays your settings.
3. **On the left-hand side, click on Video.**
4. **To the right of My Video, select the Touch up my appearance checkbox.**

TIP

Refrain from looking at other devices and screens during your meeting, especially if you've enabled video. Others will quickly pick up on your lack of concentration.

For some more sage advice on the best way to look your best during Zoom meetings, read the nearby sidebar "Presenting a professional appearance in Zoom."

To enable video during on Zoom's desktop client, you need to use your laptop's internal webcam or an external one.

Projecting a more professional visage isn't hard — in other words, to avoid the nostril-cam mentioned in the nearby sidebar "Presenting a professional appearance in Zoom." Just prop your laptop up on some books. If that doesn't work for you, then consider purchasing a proper laptop stand. For years I've happily used an inexpensive AmazonBasics ventilated one. (Find it at amzn.to/36p03vg.) As for external webcams, arguably the hottest one on the market now is the Logitech BRIO. (See amzn.to/3f04dyE for ordering information.)

Optimizing sound quality in Zoom

Of course, how you present yourself to others represents only part of the meeting experience. The other side is how you sound during your meetings — and, for that matter, how other participants sound to you. At a high level, a good deal hinges upon the quality of your computer's audio components. Contrary to what you may think, newer computers don't necessarily ship with better hardware in this regard than older ones did.

PRESENTING A PROFESSIONAL APPEARANCE IN ZOOM

People often ask me, "How can I make myself look as good as possible on my Zoom meetings?"

Here are a few simple tips on improving your shot. By following them, you will subtlety encourage meeting participants to engage with you.

- **Lighting:** If you sit in front of a bright window or lamp, then you'll be in silhouette. Likewise, don't sit directly under a bright lamp. Always place light directly in front of you.

- **Webcam:** Place it at or slightly above eye-level. No one needs to see your nostrils, half of your face, or your kitchen ceiling.

- **Framing:** TV stations deliberately shoot anchors from the mid-chest or mid-torso. By doing this, viewers can see the anchors' eyes and begin to establish trust with them. The same idea applies to your Zoom meetings. Also, remove the dead space around you. Place your head slightly below the top of the video box. Finally, sit front and center in front of your computer or tablet. Your body should fill up the video screen.

- **Personal appearance:** Avoid wearing red and white colors during your meetings. The first two notoriously cause lighting issues. Instead, consider a brighter hue that makes you pop against your background. Wear company-branded apparel if it fits into those parameters.

- **Background:** Viewers tend to find neutral backgrounds less off-putting than dark ones. What's more, they provide invaluable contrast. (Gangster move: If possible, hold your meeting in a room with light gray walls.)

If you take my advice, then you'll look your best during your Zoom meetings.

Kerry Barrett runs a full-service, media-prep, training, consulting, and camera-readiness firm based in New Jersey. She is a 20-year veteran of the broadcast news industry and an Emmy Award-winning TV news anchor, reporter, and producer.

Plenty of folks aren't satisfied with the sound emanating from their computer's native microphones and speakers. If you find yourself in this boat, you can tweak your computer's audio settings. Still disgruntled? Then consider purchasing an external microphone. I'm a fan of the Yeti Blue. (See `amzn.to/3cY5PbK`.)

As for headphones and speakers, I have found tremendous variation among Bluetooth devices. Some models work seamlessly, while others cut in and out throughout meetings.

Ask a trusted friend for honest feedback on A/V situations.

TIP

Finally, don't expect first-rate audio and video quality during Zoom meetings if your Internet connection is spotty. Zoom can only do so much. If you're having a tough time hearing others and vice versa, consider disabling your video. Ask others in the meeting to do the same.

Your overall audio and video quality during Zoom meetings stem from a number of factors. If you're experiencing problems, use the process of elimination. For example, try to connect to a friend's network when taking Zoom meetings. Does performance improve? Use a family member's computer instead of yours. Eventually, you'll figure out what's causing your issue.

TIP

Performing Mid-Meeting Actions

After you start your meeting and let everyone in, you don't just need to sit back. On the contrary, Zoom provides a boatload of valuable options for hosts to interact with meeting participants, sharing content with them, and much more.

Reviewing your recording options

In the days before videoconferences, recording calls required less-than-elegant solutions, such as tape recorders and then their digital equivalents. Fast forward a few years, and options vastly improved. For example, in my pre-Zoom days, I primarily relied upon Skype's free version. Back then, I happily used Ecamm, a neat third-party tool that recorded my calls.

Zoom requires no such workarounds. Meetings & Chat lets hosts easily record meetings. When they take advantage of this option, Zoom creates two separate files that hosts can access and distribute at a later point:

>> **Video:** Zoom's default video-file format is .mp4.

>> **Audio:** Zoom's default audio-file format is .m4a.

At the risk of stating the obvious, recording audio-only meetings in Zoom doesn't generate any video files.

Recording a Zoom meeting

To record a meeting, a host needs to follow the following directions:

1. **Launch the Zoom desktop client.**

2. **Start your meeting.**

3. **Mouse over the bottom of the screen so that Zoom displays the in-meeting menu.**

4. **Click on the Record icon.**

   Zoom displays a pop-up menu with two options:

   - Record on this Computer
   - Record to the Cloud

5. **Click on your desired option.**

   After you begin recording, Zoom replaces the Record icon with two adjacent icons:

   - Pause
   - Stop Recording

   If you click on Pause, then Zoom changes the icon again to Resume/Stop Recording.

6. **When you don't want to record anymore, click on the Stop Recording icon.**

TIP

Participants can ask to record meetings, but the host has to approve their requests.

Understanding your audio transcription options

Say that your organization pays for Zoom's Business, Education, or Enterprise plan. What's more, you have enabled this audio-transcription setting on your account, or your admin has done this for you. (See the section "Enabling meeting audio transcriptions," earlier in this chapter.)

It's imperative that you understand what Zoom can and can't do in this vein ahead of time. To this end, remember the following points.

» If you forgot to record your meeting to the cloud, then you're out of luck. Zoom cannot turn back time and record it for you.

» Second, if you have recorded your meeting locally, then you're partially out of luck. To transcribe your meeting, you would either have to do it yourself or send the file to someone else.

> » Zoom audio transcriptions are improving, but they are not perfect. (Chapters 11 and 13 have more to say about this subject.)

> » Zoom alerts you via email when it has processed the audio transcript of your meeting. Generally speaking, Zoom needs more time to process longer meetings than shorter ones.

Using virtual backgrounds

Musicians Jemaine and Bret need to take an early conference call in their studio apartment with their manager Murray to discuss band-related business. Unfortunately, the two of them haven't had time to tidy up. They prefer to let him see their faces, but they want to hide their unkempt environs during the meeting.

What to do?

TIP

They can take advantage of virtual backgrounds — hands down one of Zoom's coolest features and one that other vendors have copied. In other words, they can appear to join the meeting from the verdant fields in their home country of New Zealand, in space, or just about anywhere else they like. When they do, Murray won't know that their place is a mess.

Setting a virtual background

To use a virtual background for your meetings, follow these steps:

1. **Launch the Zoom desktop client.**

2. **Start a meeting and enable your video.**

3. **Click on the Settings icon in the upper right-hand corner.**

4. **On the left-hand side of the new window that appears, click on Virtual Background.**

5. **Click on the plus icon to the right of Choose Virtual Background in Figure 4-13.**

6. **Select an existing photo or video.**

    Zoom remembers this choice for your next video meeting.

7. **(Optional) If you're using a green screen, select the I have a green screen checkbox.**

    This selection helps Zoom optimize video quality during your meetings. Ignore this selection if you're not using one.

8. **(Optional) Uncheck the Mirror my video.**

   By default, Zoom displays the video as others see you, not as you see yourself.

9. **Close the screen and return to your meeting by clicking on the red circle in the top left-hand corner of the screen.**

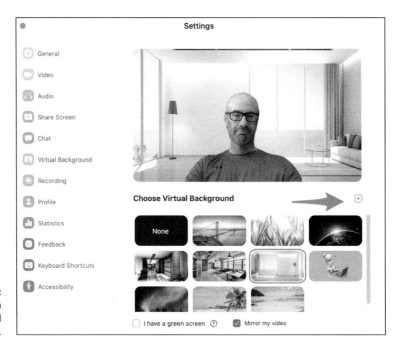

FIGURE 4-13:
Selecting a
custom virtual
background.

Colorful virtual backgrounds don't just allow employees to showcase their personalities and express themselves. Consider OpenText, a company that makes enterprise-information management software. OpenText's leadership has tried to preserve the company's culture while its people work from home, as have many organizations. CEO Mark Barrenechea told *The Wall Street Journal* that employees' use of company-branded videoconferencing backgrounds has helped in this regard. (Read the story at on.wsj.com/2ZIaY3V.)

Getting the most out of your virtual backgrounds

Virtual backgrounds don't work equally well on every type of computer. Its operating system needs to be current and its processor needs to be sufficiently powerful. (Good luck if you're still running Windows 98.) If Zoom determines that your computer isn't up to snuff in either case, then it displays a "Computer doesn't meet requirements" message.

Even if you're packing a powerful machine, Zoom's virtual backgrounds work best with green screens. I'm a fan of Corsair's collapsible and wrinkle-resistant Elgato Green Screen. Visit amzn.to/3dHnRP0 to learn more about it.

TIP

Say that you're using virtual backgrounds for your Zoom meetings without a green screen. For the best results, choose a room with neutral-colored walls.

TIP

My favorite virtual backgrounds involve videos of actual offices. Fans of the American version of popular show *The Office* will enjoy the one at bit.ly/zfd-office.

Managing and interacting with meeting participants

Just like in real life, during meetings, you'll interact with meeting participants and vice versa. To manage and interact with meeting participants, follow these steps:

1. **Click on the Participants tab.**

   Zoom shows a lists of Participants to the immediate right, as Figure 4-14 displays.

FIGURE 4-14: Meeting with the Participants panel displayed.

2. **Mouse over the name of the person with whom you want to interact and make your adjustments using the two blue buttons that appear.**

   Clicking on the Mute button temporarily disables the participant's ability to speak or generate sound. (In the case of the latter, perhaps ambient noise is making it difficult for others to hear.)

   If you click on the More button, Zoom provides you with the actions detailed in Table 4-3.

TABLE 4-3   **Meeting Participant Actions**

Actions	Description
Chat	Opens a new chat window that allows you to exchange private text messages with the participant. Participants can also use this feature to send private messages to each other during the meeting. For more information on how to configure and view chat logs, see bit.ly/zfd-chat.
Ask to Start Video	Sends a notification to the participant that you want him to start his video.
Make Host	Promote the participant to meeting host.
Make Co-Host	Promote the participant to meeting co-host.
Rename	Edit participant names. For example, three people named Emily have joined the meeting. Adding their last names may help clear up any confusion. If people pose as others, though, bad things can happen.
Put in Waiting Room	Click here to temporarily remove Hans from the meeting. From here, click on the white Remove button to kick him out of the meeting altogether. Click on the blue Admit button to let him back in.
Remove	Kick the participant out of the meeting. Note that Zoom displays a prompt asking you to confirm that you want to take this action. Click OK to proceed.
Report	Report a participant who is engaging in inappropriate behavior. See bit.ly/zfd-ruser for more on this subject.

TIP

Zoom displays all these options for meeting hosts only. Put differently, these features are role-dependent. For example, Hans is a regular meeting participant, not a host. As such, he cannot perform actions such as removing a colleague or promote himself to co-host.

Launching live polls

Earlier in this chapter, I discuss creating polls in the section "Collecting participant input through polls." After you create your poll, the final step is to launch it during your meeting:

1. **Launch the Zoom desktop client.**

2. **Start your meeting.**

3. **Mouse over the bottom of the screen to display the in-meeting menu.**

4. **Click on the Polling icon.**

    Zoom displays a screen with the poll that you previously created.

5. **At the bottom of this screen, click on the blue Launch Poll button.**

   Zoom displays your live poll. Figure 4-15 shows an example.

   As meeting participants vote, Zoom updates poll results in real time, as Figure 4-16 displays.

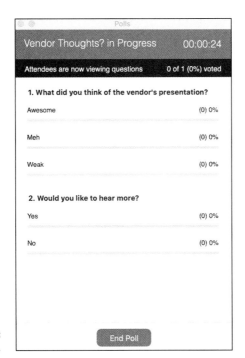

FIGURE 4-15:
Live Zoom poll.

6. **Stop the poll at any point by clicking on the red End Poll button.**

   Zoom displays the final results with two buttons at the bottom:

   - **Share Results:** Displays the results to all meeting participants. To cease showing this screen, click on the red Stop Sharing button.

   - **Re-launch Poll:** Resets the poll. Note that Zoom prompts you here. You'll have to click on the Continue button to proceed.

7. **Exit the poll altogether by clicking on the red circle in the upper left-hand corner of the poll window, not the Zoom desktop client.**

   You can now continue with the rest of your meeting.

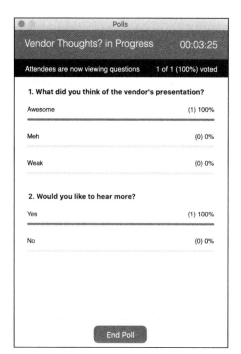

FIGURE 4-16:
Early results of a
simple Meetings
& Chat poll.

TIP

You can also access all your poll results via Zoom's reports, covered in Chapter 6.

Speaking of gathering feedback, Zoom allows participants to provide nonverbal reactions during meetings. Think of this feature as the equivalent of conducting *ad hoc* polls. They can click on buttons asking the host to speed up or slow down. They can also quickly indicate whether they agree or disagree with what the host has said.

TIP

See bit.ly/zfd-nvf for steps on how to enable and use this feature.

Using breakout rooms during meetings

I detail the benefits of Zoom's breakout rooms earlier in this chapter. (See the section "Enabling breakout rooms during your meetings.") To actually break meeting participants into different rooms, however, you need to follow these steps:

1. **Launch the Zoom desktop client.**

2. **Start a new Zoom meeting.**

3. **(Optional) If you have enabled the waiting room, then admit your participants.**

4. **Mouse over the menu and click on the Breakout Rooms icon.**

   Zoom displays a new window.

5. **Enter the number of breakout rooms into which you want to separate participants.**

6. **Manually or automatically break out meeting participants by selecting the checkbox that reflects your preference.**

   Zoom displays the window shown in Figure 4-17.

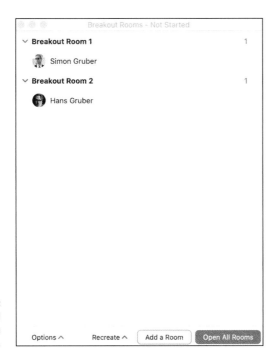

FIGURE 4-17:
Zoom initial breakout room host window.

7. **Click on the blue Open All Rooms button in the lower right-hand corner of the screen.**

   Zoom shows the meeting host a message indicating that you have now invited all participants into breakout rooms.

   Zoom prompts all meeting participants with an invitation to join the breakout room, as Figure 4-18 shows.

FIGURE 4-18:
Invitation for
meeting
participant to join
breakout room.

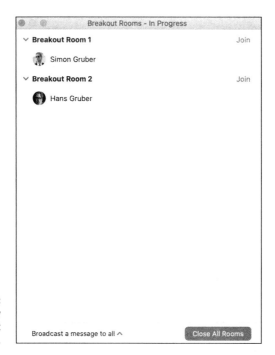

> **Breakout Rooms**
>
> The host is inviting you to join Breakout Room:
>
> **Breakout Room 1**
>
> Later   Join Breakout Room

8. **Wait for participants to join their breakout rooms.**

9. **Join participants in those individual rooms by clicking on Join next to your desired one.**

After you activate breakout rooms, Zoom displays Figure 4-19:

Breakout Rooms - In Progress

∨ **Breakout Room 1**   Join

   Simon Gruber

∨ **Breakout Room 2**   Join

   Hans Gruber

Broadcast a message to all ∧   Close All Rooms

FIGURE 4-19:
Zoom window
with breakout
rooms activated.

10. **To bring all meeting participants back together, click on the red Close All Rooms button in the lower right-hand corner.**

There's a great deal more that hosts can do with breakout rooms, including

» Renaming them.

» Creating new ones.

>> Deleting them.

>> Pre-assigning meeting participants to breakout rooms. (For more on this subject, go to bit.ly/zfd-boroom.)

>> Swapping meeting participants in and out of different rooms.

>> Setting expiration times for them.

REMEMBER

Say that you are hosting a meeting and are using breakout rooms. When you leave, breakout rooms end for everyone. To avoid this scenario, assign another participant the role of co-host before you bolt.

TIP

Visit bit.ly/zfd-br-rm4 to learn more about breakout rooms.

Sharing content with meeting participants

Screen-sharing and annotation tools have been around for decades. (Chapter 1 covers many of them.) In fact, if Zoom had failed to include these valuable features, many people would rightfully consider them glaring omissions, including yours truly.

Meetings & Chat is more than up to the task. You can share your screen with others and even allow them to control your computer's mouse and keyboard. What's more, you can allow others to mark up your screen — and vice versa.

Sharing your screen with others

As the meeting's host, you can easily share your screen with participants by following these steps:

1. **During your meeting, drag your mouse to the bottom of the screen.**

   Zoom displays the in-meeting menu.

2. **Click on the Screen Share icon.**

   Zoom displays all your computer's currently open programs, as you can see in Figure 4-20.

WARNING

   If you're using multiple monitors and programs, then expect a wide array of choices. I cover this point in the next section.

3. **Click on the specific screen, desktop, or application that you want to share with meeting participants.**

   You can also select Zoom's whiteboard or your tablet or smartphone if you've connected them to your computer via cables.

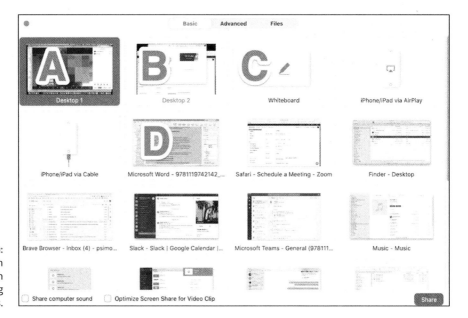

FIGURE 4-20:
Selecting a screen
to share with
meeting
participants.

4. **(Optional) If you want to share your computer's sound and/or optimize your screen-share session for playing videos, then select the corresponding checkboxes in the lower left-hand corner of the screen.**

5. **Click on the Advanced tab at the top of the screen to do the following:**

   • Share a portion of your screen

   • Share music or computer sound only

   • Share content from a second, external camera

6. **Click on the blue Share button in the lower right-hand corner.**

   Zoom adds both a green You are screen-sharing notification and a red Stop Share indicator to the bottom of the in-meeting menu, as Figure 4-21 displays.

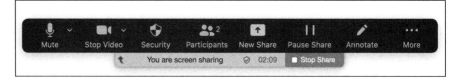

FIGURE 4-21:
Zoom menu
indicating active
screen-sharing.

   Zoom also places a green enclosure around the specific screen that you are sharing as a subtle reminder.

REMEMBER

Just because another meeting participant can control your screen doesn't mean that you are at his mercy. That is, you can still move your mouse, type your keyboard, and perform other normal computer functions.

Understanding exactly what you're sharing

Zoom's robust screen-sharing options can confound newbies and even experienced users. To eliminate this confusion, refer to Figure 4-20. Why did Zoom display all of those screens?

To answer this question, I need to supply some background information about how I work. My current computing setup includes a MacBook Pro and an ASUS external monitor. At the time that I shared my screen, I was running nine different programs on my computer. Taken together, you now understand why Zoom offered me so many different sharing options. (When it comes to screen-sharing, Meetings & Chat doesn't discriminate.) For the sake of simplicity, I'm highlighting only four of them:

>> **Desktop 1:** If I select this option (A), then I share any and all programs running on my MacBook Pro's screen. Say that I hit ⌘+Tab on my Mac to toggle to a different program. (PC users use Alt+Tab to do the same thing.) Because I previously chose Desktop 1, all participants would continue to see everything on my Mac's screen. Note that Zoom places a big white "1" on the left-hand side of my screen to remind me that I'd be sharing this desktop.

>> **Desktop 2:** If I select this option (B), then I share any and all programs that I have pinned to my external monitor. When I hit toggle to a different program, then participants continue to see everything that I'm showing that monitor. Note that Zoom places a big white 2 on the left-hand side of my external monitor to remind me that I'd be sharing this desktop.

>> **Zoom's whiteboard:** Selecting this option (C) means that I am sharing my Zoom whiteboard only with meeting participants.

>> **Microsoft Word:** Selecting this option means that I'm sharing Microsoft Word (D) only during my meeting. As a result, when I switch to a web browser or Spotify, then Zoom automatically pauses screen-sharing for all meeting participants because I have effectively moved Word to the background. That is, it is no longer the active program on my computer.

REMEMBER

There's nothing absolute about Zoom's screen-sharing options. Your specific choices will hinge upon your hardware and the applications that you're running. A simple example will illustrate my point.

Samir works at Initech and uses a Microsoft Surface and does not connect an external monitor to it. (I'm referencing *Office Space* here, by the way.) He's currently noodling with both a Microsoft Word document and an Excel spreadsheet. Figure 4-22 shows a crude mockup of Samir's screen.

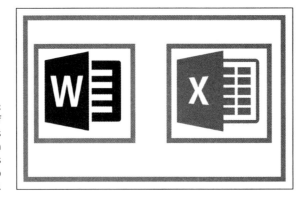

FIGURE 4-22:
Mockup of programs running on an employee's desktop computer.

It's time for Samir's weekly meeting with his boss Bill. Samir shares only Microsoft Word with him. In specific this case, the term *screen-sharing* is a bit of a misnomer. In other words, Samir isn't sharing his computer's entire screen. Rather, he is sharing only one specific program: Word.

If Samir wanted to share Excel with Bill, then he would have to end his new screen-sharing session and initiate a new one. Of course, if Samir shared his entire desktop, then he could have concurrently shared both programs with Bill from the start.

REMEMBER

Sharing a desktop with meeting participants can be very different than sharing a specific program.

When sharing your desktop, by default you cannot share the Zoom application itself. You can change this setting by following these steps:

1. **Launch the Zoom desktop client.**

2. **Click on the Settings icon in the upper-right corner.**

    Zoom displays your settings.

3. **Click on Share Screen on the left-hand side.**

4. **Select the Show Zoom windows during screen share checkbox.**

Performing different tasks while sharing your screen

Of course, you may want to do more than just share your screen. Zoom allows you to perform the following related functions during an existing screen-sharing session:

>> Pause your screen-sharing session

>> Stop sharing your screen altogether

>> Share a different one of your screens with users

To perform these options, follow whichever of the following directions you like:

>> If you want to temporarily stop sharing your screen, click on the Pause Share button. Zoom displays a message that reads, "Your screen sharing is paused."

>> If you want to share a different screen with meeting participants, click on the New Share button and follow the directions in the section "Sharing your screen with others," earlier in this chapter.

>> When you want to stop sharing your screen, click on the red Stop Share button underneath the in-meeting menu in the center.

TIP

Visit bit.ly/zfd-mscr for instructions on how to allow multiple meeting participants to simultaneously share their screens.

As the nearby sidebar "An unfortunately titled browser bookmark gets a professor fired" illustrates, those who don't exercise caution when sharing their screens run the risk of embarrassing themselves and even losing their jobs.

TIP

For a much more successful story of how a professor used Zoom's screen-sharing technology in the classroom, check out a blog post that I wrote at bit.ly/zfd-ps4.

Letting meeting participants control your screen

Peter works in IT, and he's helping Bob diagnose an issue on the latter's computers. For many reasons, Peter may want to control Bob's screen remotely:

>> It's just a more efficient way of working.

>> Peter doesn't want to keep barking orders at Bob. (This reason is my personal favorite for granting others the ability to control my screen.)

>> Bob doesn't care to know the exact steps required to solve it. He just wants Peter to take care of it for him.

AN UNFORTUNATELY TITLED BROWSER BOOKMARK GETS A PROFESSOR FIRED

In mid-March 2020, thousands of colleges and universities scrambled to put their classes online in the wake of COVID-19. Recording untold thousands of lectures in professional studios simply wasn't an option. I saw first-hand how ill-prepared institutions of higher education were for this sudden and massive change, but that's a conversation over drinks sometime.

Left with few alternatives, most professors held their classes via Zoom or similar tools from their homes. In most cases, those professors demonstrated concepts by sharing their screens with meeting attendees, often without incident.

The operative phrase in the last sentence is "in most cases."

In late April 2020, a business professor at the University of Miami gave a Zoom lecture that he won't soon forget. As it turned out, Professor X shared his screen via Zoom, and a few students noticed one of his lasciviously titled browser bookmarks. (I'll keep it PG here, but you can use your imagination.)

One student captured a short video of Professor X showing his screen to his class. The video included that bookmark. The student turned it into a meme and posted it on the social network TikTok. Needless to say, the video went viral, and the university soon fired Professor X.

Visit `bit.ly/zfd-prof` to read the story yourself.

Say that you want a meeting participant to control your computer. To let any current meeting participant *drive* (as the kids say), follow these steps:

1. **During your live meeting, drag your mouse or cursor to the bottom of Zoom.**

    Zoom displays the in-meeting menu.

2. **Click on the Share Screen icon and follow the directions in the "Sharing your screen with others" section, earlier in this chapter.**

3. **After you share your screen, click on the Remote Control icon.**

4. **(Optional) Select the Auto accept all requests option.**

TIP

To let a specific individual control your computer, follow the same steps but instead select Give Mouse/Keyboard Control to: and click on the name of the participant to whom you want to give control of your computer.

5. **Advise others in the meeting that they can control your screen if they request access.**

6. **Say that you don't want to automatically accept all requests. When you see a participant's request to assume control, click on the blue Approve button to grant her control of your screen.**

Requesting control of a host's screen

The following steps apply to meeting participants who would like to request control of the host's screen:

1. **Move your computer's cursor to the top of the Zoom desktop client window.** When you do, Zoom presents View Options menu.

2. **Click on the View Options menu and choose Request Remote Control from the menu that appears.**

   Zoom indicates that you are requesting control of the host's screen.

3. **Click on the blue Request button.**

   Zoom displays your request to assume control on the host's screen.

   At this point, the host needs to approve your request.

Regaining control of your computer

If you're the host and want to resume control of your computer, follow these steps:

1. **Return to the Zoom meeting.**

   In other words, control the mouse and tab over from whatever other program or screen you were sharing.

2. **Mouse over the in-meeting menu**

3. **Click on the red Stop Share button.**

TIP

Visit `bit.ly/zfd-mscrn` for directions on how to concurrently share multiple screens.

Annotating your screen

Zoom lets meeting participants do far more than just share their screens with each other. With a few clicks, you can annotate others' screens. In so doing, you can provide specific feedback, make insightful suggestions, or pinpoint a problem in a way that words alone often fail to do.

USING A DEDICATED WHITEBOARD

Odds are that you've seen a physical whiteboard at some point at work. Using markers, people in the room can sketch any number of diagrams on dry erase boards. They can document business processes, redesign org charts, mock up logos, write code, or just about anything else.

Why should Zoom be any different?

To share a whiteboard with meeting participants, follow the same steps in the earlier section "Sharing your screen with others" with one exception: Choose whiteboard when deciding which screen to share. (Refer to Figure 4-20.)

After you do, Zoom displays its whiteboard in Figure 4-23.

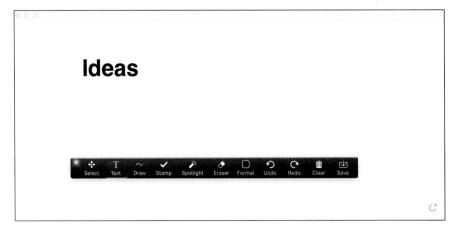

FIGURE 4-23:
Zoom whiteboard
with annotation
menu.

Table 4-4 displays the whiteboard's menu items and describes what they do.

TIP

Say that you lose track of Zoom's annotation tool menu. Just click on the Annotate button in the in-meeting menu. Zoom once again brings its annotation tools again to the front.

REMEMBER

Zoom's annotation tools are available only during screen-sharing sessions.

TABLE 4-4   Zoom Annotation Options

Name	Description
Select	Creates a box that engulfs your other annotations, allowing you to easily move them as a group.
Text	Enter text over any part of your screen.
Draw	Draw whatever you like with your mouse or touchpad. Zoom also lets you insert a number of basic shapes.
Stamp	Place different types of stamps. Examples include an arrow, checkmark, X, star, heart, and question mark.
Spot-light	Makes your computer's cursor more visible. You can turn it into a red circle or a rightward arrow.
Eraser	As its name states, clicking on this button allows you to erase prior annotations or parts of them.
Format	Clicking here lets you change the color, weight, and font of your annotation.
Undo	Reverse your previous annotation.
Redo	Repeat your previous annotation.
Clear	Invoke three options: clear all drawings, clear your drawings, and clear viewers' drawings.
Save	Saves the entire screen markup as a local file on your computer.

After you launch the communal whiteboard, others may want to add their own notes to it. If you're a participant and want to add notes to a communal whiteboard, follow these steps:

1. **From the desktop client, move your computer's cursor to the top of the Zoom desktop client window.**

2. **From the View Options menu that appears, choose Annotate.**

   You can now add whatever annotations to the whiteboard you desire.

Note that everyone in the meeting can annotate at the same time.

TIP

See `bit.ly/zfd-wboard` for more information on Zoom's whiteboard functionality.

ANNOTATING A SCREEN

Zoom doesn't force meeting hosts and participants to use a dedicated whiteboard to make annotations. Everyone in the meeting can mark up a regular screen and the program running on it. The possibilities here are limitless, but here's one common example.

Geno is developing a new version of a website for his client Jerry. Geno invites Jerry to a Zoom video meeting and follows these directions:

1. **Follow the steps in the section "Sharing your screen with others," earlier in this chapter.**

2. **Click on the Annotate button in the in-meeting menu.**

3. **From here, pinpoint design elements and changes in a far more specific way than mere words would allow.**

   Returning to the previous example, Jerry can now show Geno exactly where he wants to move a picture or the logo in the header.

TIP

Visit `bit.ly/zfd-annot` if you'd like to find out more about Zoom's screen annotation functionality.

Invoking other meeting options

Hosts can invoke a few other options to control their meetings.

Follow these steps to invoke these options:

1. **Launch the Zoom desktop client.**

2. **Start a meeting and enable your video.**

3. **Click on the Participants icon on the black in-meeting menu at the bottom of the screen.**

   Zoom displays a new screen on the right-hand side.

4. **In the lower right-hand corner, click on the More button.**

5. **Zoom presents the self-explanatory choices in Table 4-5.**

As you can see from this section, Zoom isn't exactly wanting for meeting options and features!

TABLE 4-5   **Additional Meeting Options for Hosts**

Action	Directions and Results
Mute Participants upon Entry	This feature does exactly what you expect. If you select this option, then Zoom prompts with you an additional window in which you can allow them to unmute themselves.
Allow Participants to Unmute Themselves	If you only want participants to listen during the meeting or part of it, then disenable this option at any point. Note that this feature is useful when an unknown participant is generating distracting background noise.
Play Enter/Exit Chime	This option lets you enable or disable the sound that Zoom plays when these events take place.
Allow Participants to Rename Themselves	This small but important feature means exactly what you think it does. Changing Lawrence to Larry is one thing. Think carefully about whether you want people to represent themselves as someone else entirely during the meeting, though.
Lock Meeting	This option prevents new participants from joining the meeting, even if they know the PMI, meeting ID number, and/or password. (Chapter 9 returns to this subject in the context of securing your communications.)
Clear All Feedback	If you have enabled nonverbal reactions, then Zoom allows the host to wipe them out in one fell swoop. Note that Zoom grays out this option if participants haven't provided any feedback. (For more information on this topic, see the section "Launching live polls," earlier in this chapter.)
Enable Waiting Room	Selecting this option means that participants cannot enter the meeting, even if they know the PMI, meeting ID number, and/or password.

Putting a Bow on Your Meeting

At some point, even marathon meetings come to an end. (Whether or not a two-hour one should only have taken 20 minutes is neither here nor there.)

When you want to exit stage left, Zoom provides two options:

» Ending the meeting for all

» Leaving the meeting

When you leave a meeting, Zoom presents you with some useful options. For more here, see `bit.ly/zfd-leavemtg`.

To wrap up your current meeting, click on the red End button on the far right-hand side of the menu. Then click on the red End Meeting for All button to end the meeting for all participants or click on the black Leave Meeting button to leave the meeting and let the others continue without you.

You have ended your meeting. Now what? If you want to do nothing, have at it. To quote the iconic Rush song "Freewill," "If you choose not to decide, you still have made a choice." Fortunately, inaction is not your only option. Zoom lets you perform a number of useful post–meeting actions. Your choices hinge upon the following factors:

>> Your organization's plan

>> Your formal Zoom role

>> Your role during the meeting

>> Your account settings

>> The actions that you took before and during the meeting

Viewing meeting transcriptions

Earlier in this chapter, I cover how to enable audio transcriptions of your meetings. (See the appropriately named section "Enabling meeting audio transcriptions.")

To access Zoom's meeting transcriptions, follow these steps:

1. **In the Zoom web portal, under the Personal header, click on Recordings.**

Note that your specific navigation may vary a bit based upon the options that your organization's Zoom owner or admin has disabled.

On the right-hand side, under the Cloud Recordings tab, Zoom defaults to display all the meetings that you recorded to the cloud.

2. **Click on the meeting whose transcription you want to access.**

WARNING

An owner or admin for your organization's Zoom may set all transcriptions to automatically delete after a certain number of days.

From here, Zoom presents the files that it has saved for your meeting.

3. **Select the file that you want.**

Your options include

- **Shared screen with speaker view:** Replay the video meeting with Zoom's transcription appearing on the right-hand side of the screen. Note that Zoom lets you replay video only if you held a video meeting.

- **Audio only:** Replay only the audio part of the meeting with the transcription appearing on the right-hand side of the screen.

- **Audio transcript:** Download the .vtt file of the recording. You can then open this file with most mainstream text editors and word-processing programs. (*Note:* You see this option only if your organization subscribes to a Zoom Business, Education, or Enterprise plan and you have enabled cloud recording.)

TECHNICAL STUFF

VTT files contain information about web videos. Specific elements typically include a video's subtitles, captions, descriptions, chapters, and related metadata. It does not contain any video data.

4. **From here, you can also perform the following tasks on each file:**

   - Sharing it

   - Deleting it

   - Copying a shareable link to it

TIP

Visit `bit.ly/zfd-vma` for information on Zoom's audio transcriptions.

Accessing your recorded meetings

In the section "Recording Zoom meetings" earlier in this chapter, I describe how Zoom lets you record meetings both locally and to the cloud. No matter which method you chose to record your meeting, you can access it as follows:

1. **Launch the Zoom desktop client.**

2. **Click on the Meetings icon at the top of the screen.**

3. **In the sidebar, click on the Recorded tab.**

   Zoom displays all your recorded meetings, irrespective of location. Figure 4-24 presents my recorded meetings.

4. **Click on a specific meeting in the sidebar.**

   For locally recorded video meetings, Zoom shows the following buttons:

   - Open

   - Play Video

   - Play Audio Only

   - Delete

TIP

   For meetings that you recorded to the cloud, Zoom displays only the Open button.

5. **Click on the Open button to open the link to the meeting in Zoom's web portal in your browser.**

FIGURE 4-24:
Viewing my
previously
recorded
meetings in
Meetings & Chat.

Performing other actions with meetings recorded to the cloud

Access the meetings that you recorded to the cloud by following these steps.

1. **In the Zoom web portal, under the Personal header, click on Recordings.**

On the right-hand side, under the Cloud Recordings tab, Zoom displays all the meetings that you recorded to the cloud.

2. **(Optional) Click on the white Share button.**

Zoom displays a window that allows you to invoke a number of additional options:

- Share this recording publicly or only with authenticated users. (See Chapter 9 for more information about this topic.)

- Add an expiration date to the link.

- Allow viewers to download the recording.

- Alter the password protection for the recording.

3. **(Optional) Click on the white More button to download the meeting files.**

Zoom displays a drop-down menu that lets you download the two files.

4. **Click on the blue Save button.**

Performing other actions with locally recorded meetings

You can also use the web portal to do a few neat things with locally recorded meetings. Just follow these directions:

1. **In the Zoom web portal, under the Personal header, click on Recordings.**

   On the right-hand side, under the Cloud Recordings tab, Zoom displays all the meetings that you have recorded to the cloud.

2. **(Optional) Click on the white Share button to customize your sharing settings.**

   Zoom displays a window that allows you to invoke the following options:

   - Share this recording publicly or only with authenticated users

   - Add an expiration date to the link

   - Allow viewers to download the recording

   - Alter the password protection for the recording

3. **(Optional) Click on the white More button to download the meeting files.**

   Zoom displays a drop-down menu that lets you download the two files.

4. **Click on the blue Save button.**

REMEMBER

You've got no shortage of options for tweaking your privacy and security for Zoom meetings. I go deeper into these critical subjects in Chapter 9.

Viewing your current data-storage level

Say that you always save your recording meetings on your main computer. If this is the case, the data-storage limits on your organization's Zoom plan don't apply. (See Chapter 2 for more on this subject.)

Many people, however, choose to save their recorded meetings in the cloud. As such, they can access them no matter where they are and no matter what device they're using. What's more, they keep all files forever. They've never heard of the word delete.

To quote Robert DeNiro in Michael Mann's epic crime saga *Heat,* though, there's a flipside to that coin. Specifically, by following that approach, you may bump up against the data-storage limits on your organization's Zoom plan.

To see how much data you're currently storing in Zoom, follow these steps:

1. **Launch the Zoom desktop client.**
2. **Click on the Settings icon in the upper-right corner.**

   Zoom displays your settings.

3. **Click on Recording.**

   To the right of Cloud Recording, Zoom displays how much data you're storing. Figure 4-25 shows the data that I'm currently using in my Zoom account:

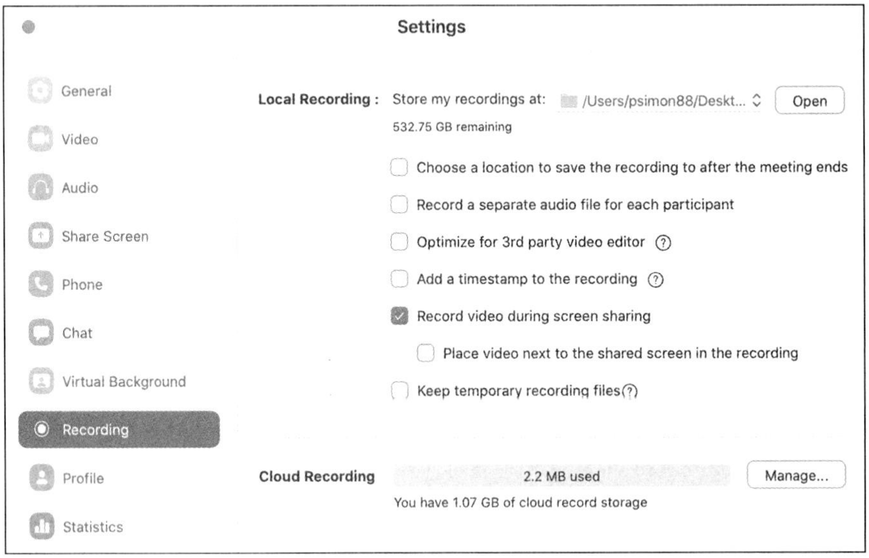

FIGURE 4-25:
A user's current data usage.

Note that your version of Figure 4-25 may appear a bit different based upon your organization's Zoom plan.

IN THIS CHAPTER

» Managing your Meetings & Chat
  directory and contacts

» Understanding your status and basic
  notifications

» Chatting with your Zoom contacts

» Finding what you need in Meetings &
  Chat

Chapter **5**

Getting to Know the Other Side of Zoom Meetings & Chat

Sociologists will invariably look back at the early months of 2020 as particularly instructive. Near the top of the list of lessons learned is that video meetings fill essential professional and social needs. At a minimum, they allow untold numbers of people to quickly, easily, and reliably talk to individuals and groups no matter where they are. Make no mistake: This type of synchronous communication is often invaluable, especially when you consider the alternative. Imagine trying to brainstorm an idea or interview a job applicant via email. What's more, in many cases, a quick conversation obviates sending a bevy of perplexing emails.

That's not to say, however, that all communications need to take place instantaneously. On the contrary, both while on and off the clock, there remains a legitimate need to send asynchronous messages to others. Odds are that you use email or text messages for this very purpose, but Meetings & Chat performs admirably here, too. In fact, Zoom's functionality here often makes it a superior alternative than the tried-and-true inbox.

This chapter explains how to perform many core functions in Meetings & Chat. I cover the Zoom directory, a simple way of managing the people with whom you frequently interact — whether they work for your organization or not. I also discuss setting your status, chatting with others, customizing notifications, and searching for valuable information.

Brass tacks: Don't be surprised if you and your colleagues begin using Meetings & Chat for far more than holding video meetings. Your inbox may just start getting a little jealous.

Managing Your Zoom Contacts

You may claim to have 812 friends on Facebook. Maybe you have convinced yourself that you actively follow 6,101 people on Twitter.

Not to pick a fight, but I'll bet my house that you have personally interacted with a small fraction of those people within the past year — and not just because of the global pandemic. I'd also wager that you regularly communicate with the same core group of individuals.

In proposing these bets, I'm hardly going out on a limb here.

In the early 1980s, the anthropologist Robin Dunbar theorized that human beings can maintain networks of a maximum of 148 people — subsequently rounded up to an even 150. To be sure, plenty of people have criticized his theory, and social networks didn't exist 40 years ago. Still, a good deal of solid research supports Dunbar's number. (For more on this subject, see `bit.ly/zxfd-dunb`.)

So, who are these people? (Insert *Seinfeld* inflection.) Perhaps they are colleagues, customers, friends, or family members.

Zoom lets people easily hold discrete video and audio calls with others, whether they are paying customers or not. (Chapter 4 goes deeper into this topic.) Zoom also lets users store their contacts in a dedicated directory.

Although not required, adding contacts to your Meetings & Chat directory offers a number of significant advantages:

>> You can quickly call them and send them text messages, photos, and just about any type of file you want.

>> In a matter of seconds, you can elevate the conversation from one mode (text) to another (audio or video).

>> You can view their statuses to see whether they're busy. (See the section "Understanding User Status in Zoom," later in this chapter, for more here.)

>> All things being equal, you will spend less time switching among different communications applications. Your brain will thank you.

What's more, let me allay your fears right here. Say that you have somehow defied Dunbar's number. A pox on my earlier cynicism! You are miraculously able to maintain close ties with each of your 812 Facebook friends. If so, then I stand corrected. You are Batman. Good news: You can keep tabs on all 812 of them in Zoom if and when they accept your invitations.

Adding contacts to your Zoom directory

At a high level, Zoom's Meetings & Chat directory separates contacts into two buckets:

>> **Internal:** These folks joined as members under your organization's parent Zoom account.

>> **External:** These people have created Zoom accounts independently or through other organizations. Regardless, you can still add them to your personal Meetings & Chat directory.

Adding internal contacts

By default and as long as your organization subscribes to a premium Zoom plan, your Meetings & Chat directory will contain all internal users tied to your account. (See Chapter 2 for more information on Zoom's different plans.) Zoom makes adding external contacts to your directory a piece of cake.

Manually adding a new external contact to your directory

Say that you frequently email Richard, the founder of Pied Piper, a hot new startup in Silicon Valley, California. You're starting to sour on email as a communications tool, though. Because of this, you'd like to move your conversations from email to Zoom.

To add Richard to your Zoom personal directory, just follow these steps:

1. **Launch the Zoom desktop client.**

2. **Click on the Contacts icon at the top of the screen.**

   By default, Zoom places you in your directory. Stay here.

3. **To the immediate right of the word Channels, click on the + icon.**

   Chapter 6 covers channels. Don't worry about them now.

4. **From the menu that appears, click on Add a Contact.**

5. **Enter the email address of the contact whom you'd like to invite.**

6. **Click on the blue Add button.**

7. **Click on the blue OK button.**

   Meetings & Chat notifies you if and when the person accepts your invitation. Until then, Zoom displays the word Pending to the right of their names under My Contacts.

TIP

Say that you want to add Verna as an external contact to your Meetings & Chat directory. Years ago, she created her Zoom account under verna@bernbaum.net — her main email address. Make sure that you invite her using that one. If you send Verna an invitation to one of her other email addresses (such as verna@coen.com), then she would have to register again under that one to accept your invitation.

TIP

Once an outside contact accepts your invitation, Meetings & Chat places the capitalized word External to the right of the person's name in the sidebar. You will see it on the left under the Contacts icon at the top of the page. This label is a not-so-subtle reminder that the person doesn't belong to your organization's Zoom account.

REMEMBER

Just because you invite external contacts to connect with you via Meetings & Chat doesn't mean that they will accept your invitation.

TIP

Zoom lets users on premium plans import their contacts from smartphones, tablets, or even spreadsheets into their directories. Regarding the latter option, users will need to create specific comma-separated value files, or CSVs. For more information on this process, visit bit.ly/zfd-csv.

IMPORTING OR SYNCING YOUR THIRD-PARTY CONTACTS

If the thought of manually adding your contacts to Zoom piecemeal makes you sick, then you're in luck. Meetings & Chat lets you easily import and even sync your contacts from popular email applications, including

- Google
- Office 365
- Microsoft Exchange

The precise instructions vary depending on the specific one that you use, so I excluded them from this book. For instructions on how to get the job done, go to bit.ly/zfd-contacts.

Removing an existing contact from your Meetings & Chat directory

Just like in real life, you may decide to break up with someone in Meetings & Chat. Say that I've had it with Jordan and want to remove him from my directory. To do so, I need to follow these steps:

1. **In the Zoom desktop client, click on Contacts icon at the top of the screen.**

   By default, Zoom places you in your directory. Stay here.

2. **Mouse over the name of the person whom you want to remove from your Zoom directory.**

   Zoom displays three new icons.

3. **Click on the ellipsis icon to the right of the person's name and then choose Delete Contact from the menu that appears.**

   Zoom warns you that deleting the contact will also clear your chat history with that user.

4. **Click on the Remove button.**

   Meetings & Chat dutifully banishes the user from your personal directory. If you want to reconnect, then you need to re-invite him and hope that he accepts your invitation. The process resembles reconnecting with people on Facebook, LinkedIn, and some other social networks.

REMEMBER

Say that you're a regular Zoom member and you remove someone from your personal directory. This action is not the same as revoking or deleting that person's Zoom account. As Chapter 3 covers, an admin or owner needs to do that. In other words, only users assigned to these administrative roles can effectively banish others from their organization's Zoom account.

Inviting an existing Zoom contact to a new meeting

While not imperative, adding Meetings & Chat contacts to your directory offers a number of advantages. For example, you can quickly invite them to meetings by following these steps:

1. **In the Zoom desktop client, click on Contacts.**

2. **Right-click on the name of the person whom you want to call.**

3. **From the menu that appears, choose Meet with Video or Meet without Video.**

   Zoom rattles off an email with a meeting invitation to that person.

Adding internal contacts to an existing meeting

Maude and Bunny are colleagues in the middle of an existing Zoom meeting. As the meeting host, Maude wants another one of her internal contacts to join the current meeting. To do so, she should follow these directions.

1. **Using the desktop client, click on the Participants icon at the bottom of the screen.**

   Zoom displays a new window on the right-hand side of the screen.

2. **Click on the Invite icon at the bottom of the screen.**

   Zoom displays a new screen.

3. **Select the name of the contact in your Zoom directory whom you'd like to invite to the meeting.**

TIP

   If you want to filter your contacts by name, simply type a few letters of the invitee's name. Zoom automatically restricts your results to people whose names contain those letters.

4. **Click on the name of the invitee.**

5. **Click on the blue Invite button in the lower right-hand corner.**

Zoom indicates that you have successfully invited that person to your meeting.

REMEMBER

Chapter 4 covers how to invite people who don't belong to your Meetings & Chat directory to your meetings.

Performing contact-specific actions

Over the course of sending messages to someone in Meetings & Chat, you may decide that it's time to move to a live meeting. Alternatively, you may want to bring others into the conversation or add the contact to your list of favorites.

Performing each of these actions — and many others — is easy. Just click on the downward arrowhead to the right of the contact's name in the sidebar. Meetings & Chat displays the useful options in Figure 5-1.

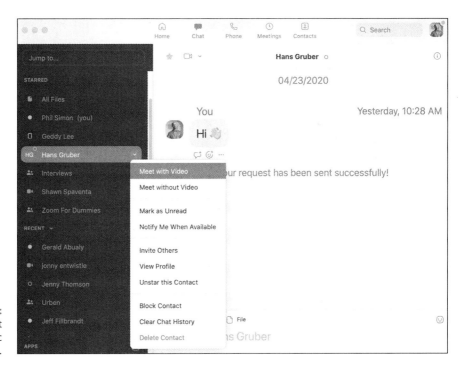

FIGURE 5-1:
Meetings & Chat contact-specific actions.

Table 5-1 describes each of these options in more detail:

TABLE 5-1   **Meetings & Chat Contact Actions**

Name	Description
Meet with Video	Launches a video meeting and concurrently invites the individual to it. (See Chapter 4 for more information on this subject.)
Meet without Video	Launches an audio meeting and concurrently invites the individual to it.
Mark as Unread	Marks the last message that you received from the contact as unread. Zoom also places a numeric badge to the right of the person's name in the sidebar. (I cover sending messages in more detail in the "Chatting in Zoom" section, later in this chapter.)
Notify Me When Available	Alerts you when a person's status changes to active. (If you've ever used Skype, then you will recognize this feature.) Note that Zoom grays out this option if the contact's status is already available. (I cover this topic more in the "Getting familiar with Zoom's status icons" section, later in this chapter.)
Invite Others	Displays a window in which you can invite others to a group chat with the contact.
View Profile	Displays the information that the contact has provided for others to see.
Star/Unstar this Contact	Moves the starred contact to the upper part of your Meetings & Chat directory. Unstarring the contact reverses that action.
Block Contact	Prevents the user from contacting you in Zoom in any way. If you change your mind, then you can unblock the user at a later point. Think of blocking as a trial separation, not a divorce.
Clear Chat History	Deletes your previous text-based conversations with the contact or group of contacts. Note that Zoom removes this information for you, but not for the other people participating in your chat.
Delete Contact	Permanently removes the contact from your personal Meetings & Chat directory.

Understanding User Status in Zoom

With a few mouse clicks, Meetings & Chat lets you hold calls and chat with the contacts in your directory. That's all well and good, but what if the person with whom you want to chat is offline or just plain busy?

Thankfully, Zoom lets users easily indicate their availability to everyone else — and vice versa. In this way, Meetings & Chat resembles many of today's popular collaboration tools. Notable examples include Slack and Microsoft Teams.

Getting familiar with Zoom's status icons

When you look at your new contacts, you will see different icons with different colors to the left of their names in the Meetings & Chat sidebar. In short, they connote members' statuses.

Table 5-2 presents the Meetings & Chat status icons as well as what they mean.

TABLE 5-2   Meetings & Chat Status Icons

Icon Color and Type	Status	Description
Empty white circle	Offline	Contact has not signed in to either the Zoom desktop client or a mobile app.
Green solid circle	Online (desktop)	Contact has signed in to the Zoom desktop client.
Green outlined rectangle	Online (mobile)	Contact has signed in only to the Zoom mobile app.
Gray circular clock	Away	Contact has signed in to the Zoom desktop client, but either her computer is inactive or she has manually set her status to away.
Red circle with white horizontal line in center	DND	Contact has manually set his status to DND. He won't receive notifications of new chat messages or phone calls. (For more information on this topic, see the section "Enabling do-not-disturb mode," later in this chapter.)
Red video camera	In a Zoom meeting	Contact has started a Zoom meeting or joined one.
Red video camera	Presenting	Contact is sharing her screen while in a Zoom meeting.
Red telephone	On a call	Contact is currently participating in a Zoom Phone call.
Red calendar	In a calendar event	Contact is currently participating in an event on his calendar, but is not in a proper Zoom meeting. (See Chapter 7 for information on integrating your existing calendar with Zoom. It's not hard.)
Red circle with white exclamation point	Chat error	Zoom failed to send the contact your chat message and/or file.

REMEMBER

Status icons are mere suggestions on availability; they're not absolutes. For example, just because Meetings & Chat shows that Steve is available doesn't mean that he necessarily is. He may have closed the Zoom desktop client because he is working on the new Marillion album. (Fingers crossed.)

Figure 5-2 displays the current status icons for all of my internal and external Zoom contacts.

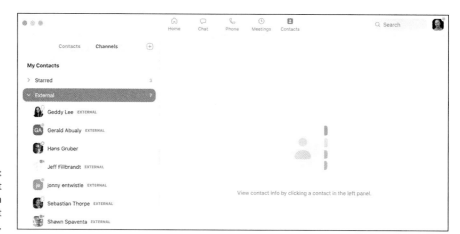

FIGURE 5-2:
Meetings & Chat
contacts with
their current
status icons.

As you can see, Johnny and Gerald are free at the moment. For their part, Jeff and Shawn are currently in Zoom meetings.

REMEMBER

Contacts who are currently in Zoom meetings are almost always unavailable.

Changing your status in Meetings & Chat

By default, when you're logged in to the Zoom desktop client, Meetings & Chat sets your status as online. Your colleagues will certainly know as much if they bother to look at your status. If they do, they will see a green solid circle appear in the upper right-hand corner of your profile image.

It's natural for others in your Zoom directory to assume that green means go. As a result, they may call you and/or chat with you. (I cover messages in the upcoming section "Chatting in Zoom.") These actions will interrupt your flow.

Yes, you can quit the Zoom desktop client, but that extreme action comes with downsides. Most obviously, you cannot use any of the features in Meetings & Chat. For example, you can bid *adieu* to accessing your prior conversations and finding valuable information. (See the section "Searching in Zoom," later in this chapter, for more on that subject.)

What to do?

Fortunately, Meetings & Chat provides a few options for people who want to keep the application open but, at the same time, don't want others pestering them.

Marking yourself as away

First, you can mark yourself as away. In theory, this status discourages others from pestering you in Zoom. In practice, though, your mileage here may vary.

To indicate that you are away, follow these steps:

1. **In the Zoom desktop client, click on your profile image.**

    It lies to the immediate right of the search bar.

2. **From the menu, click on Away.**

    When you're ready to indicate to others that you're available, simply click on your profile image and then click on Available.

Enabling do-not-disturb mode

Unfortunately, your away status may not deter your colleagues from calling you. They may still send you messages and expect an immediate response. When they do, Meetings & Chat promptly notifies you of these messages and calls.

To ignore them and focus, do you have to quit Zoom?

You do not.

To prevent others from bugging you, just enable Zoom's do-not-disturb or DND mode. When you do, Meetings & Chat knows not to interrupt you. In this way, Zoom works just like the comparable functionality on your smartphone.

Enable DND mode by following these instructions:

1. **In the Zoom desktop client, click on your profile image.**

2. **From the menu, click on Do Not Disturb.**

3. **(Optional) Indicate the length of time that you want to be left alone.**

    You're enabling DND mode here for a limited amount of time.

4. **(Optional) Select Set a Time Period to enable DND mode for daily intervals.**

    Zoom launches a new window in which you can change many of your account settings and defaults.

5. **Scroll down to the bottom of the screen.**

6. **Select the Do not disturb from: checkbox.**

7. **From the drop-down list, select the hours during which you want Zoom to leave you alone.**

WARNING

Meetings & Chat strictly obeys your preferences here. For example, say that you select 4:00 a.m. until 10 p.m. by mistake. Don't expect Zoom to send you any notifications during those 18 hours. Whether someone urgently tries to track you down by other means, however, is another matter.

8. **Close the Settings by clicking on the red circle in the upper left-hand corner of the screen.**

Regardless of how you've enabled DND mode, Meetings & Chat sends you notifications only when your period lapses.

DND MODE EXISTS FOR A REASON; USE IT LIBERALLY

I'm sure that you've heard the term *multitasking*. Many people take pride in their ability to ostensibly juggle four things at once. In fact, they may drop the word without giving it a second thought.

I've got some bad news for them: They are not multitasking at all. They are multichanging.

This difference isn't merely a matter of semantics. A boatload of research has demonstrated the pitfalls of switching back and forth among different activities and apps. Perhaps the most pernicious, though, is that you lose whatever momentum you've generated. Your work suffers when you're constantly interrupting what you're doing. Letting others interrupt you can be equally inimical.

For more on this subject, see the seminal Mihaly Csikszentmihalyi book *Flow: The Psychology of Optimal Experience* (Harper Perennial). *Deep Work: Rules for Focused Success in a Distracted World* (Grand Central Publishing) by Cal Newport is also worth a read.

You may not be able to go off of the grid for days at a time. At the risk of being preachy, though, don't be a slave to Zoom notifications — or notifications from other apps, for that matter.

Adding a personal note to your profile

You may find Zoom's current menu of statuses to be a bit limiting. I certainly do. (When it comes to user statuses, Meetings & Chat trails Slack, but that's neither here nor there.) At least Meetings & Chat lets you add a personal note to your profile. Follow these directions:

1. **In the Zoom desktop client, click on your profile image.**

2. **From the drop-down menu underneath your email address, click in the text box labeled "Add a Personal Note."**

   Meetings & Chat restricts you to 60 characters.

3. **Enter a few words and then press the Enter key on your keyboard.**

Now the contacts in your directory can see a bit more information about you when viewing your profile.

Staying current with Zoom notifications

Unless you've enabled DND mode, by default Meetings & Chat notifies you when your contacts send you messages and attempt to call you. Still, it's not hard to envision other scenarios that warrant your attention — that is, apart from people attempting to directly contact you.

Depending on how you use Meetings & Chat and the number of people in your directory, you may find its notifications a tad overwhelming. Here's one way that you can tweak them:

1. **In the Zoom desktop client, click on your profile image.**

2. **Choose Settings in the menu that appears.**

3. **On the left-hand side of the screen, click on the Chat icon at the top of the screen.**

4. **Under Push Notifications, select the circumstances under which you want to receive notifications.**

   If you select Only private messages or mentions, then Zoom won't notify you when new activity in your group chats takes place. (You can still view related badges in the sidebar at your leisure, though.)

   If you select Nothing, then you won't hear a peep from Zoom. The same disclaimer about badges applies, however.

5. **Close the Settings by clicking on the red circle in the upper left-hand corner of the screen.**

TIP

Chapter 6 has more to say about customizing the notifications that Meetings & Chat sends you.

TIP

Say that you selected the Notify me when available feature for a contact who is currently in a Zoom meeting. Meetings & Chat displays a little red bell to the right of the contact's name in the sidebar.

Chatting in Zoom

Every day, earthlings send billions of text-based messages. Of course, the tools of choice vary. Some people rely primarily on email. For others, WhatsApp, Snapchat, TikTok, old-fashioned Short Message Service (SMS) messages, Slack, and scores of other contemporary communications applications get the job done. Brass tacks: I'd be amazed if the idea of a sending text-based message is foreign to you.

In the rare case that it is, though, here's a quick example.

You run into your boss Kim in the hallway. You start talking about a few things, but she's in a rush to get to a meeting. She asks you to shoot her a quick reminder of what you briefly discussed so that she can review it later.

For far too many people today, the message in that simple example reflexively takes the form of a proper email. I can't stop you from sending your boss an email in these situations. Zoom, however, provides users with another — and I'd argue better — option: Send that note via Meetings & Chat. Its rich message functionality makes it a valid email alternative, especially for internal company communications.

Exchanging messages with your individual Zoom contacts

Geddy Lee is the lead singer and bassist extraordinaire of the legendary Canadian rock group Rush. I've met him twice in my life, most recently in the fall of 2019 in Tempe, Arizona. He was promoting his first book, appropriately named *Geddy Lee's Big Beautiful Book of Bass* (Harper Design). (Spoiler alert: It's awesome.)

Say that I connect with Geddy on Zoom. (Dare to dream.) I'd love to congratulate him and give him a quick call. Chapter 4 describes how easy that is to do. Because I don't want to seem pushy, though, I hesitate. Ringing him — much less initiating a Zoom video call with him — out of the blue seems a bit presumptuous. (As an aside, it's funny how proper phone etiquette today mandates that you text others before calling them.)

Returning to my earlier example, I want to send Geddy a quick Zoom message. To do so, I follow these steps:

1. **In the Zoom desktop client, click on Contacts.**

2. **Click on the name of the contact to whom you want to send a message.**

    In my example, it's Geddy.

3. **Click on the Chat button on the right side of the screen.**

    This button appears underneath the contact's profile picture, as Figure 5-3 displays.

    Zoom places my cursor in a text box at the bottom of the screen.

FIGURE 5-3: Chat button underneath a contact's profile picture.

4. **Type your message.**

5. **Press the Enter key on your keyboard.**

    Figure 5-4 displays the message that I sent Geddy congratulating him on his new book.

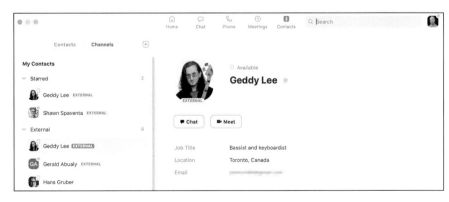

FIGURE 5-4: Simple Zoom message to an individual.

WHY I CAN'T SEND TOMMY MESSAGES IN ZOOM

Your ability to send others messages in Zoom is not absolute. Specifically, just because you have successfully added an external contact to your Zoom directory does not necessarily mean that you will be able to send that messages to that individual. An example from the classic flick *Tommy Boy* illustrates my point.

Tommy works as a salesman at Callahan Auto Parts in Sandusky, Ohio. (His Zoom role is member.) Richard is the company's Zoom admin. He does not want employees using Meetings & Chat to send messages to external contacts. As such, he has disabled this feature via IM Groups — a topic covered in Chapter 3. As a result, when I try to send Tommy a quick note, Meetings & Chat displays the following ominous error message: "Messages cannot be sent because Tommy has been restricted by their account admin."

Holy schnikes!

If I want to chat with Tommy in Zoom about his little coat or ordering chicken wings for lunch, then I need to contact him via email or another medium. In turn, Tommy would have to convince Richard to change this setting for Callahan's users.

TIP

Zoom often offers several ways to accomplish the same task. Don't be surprised if you stumble across one of them as you play around with Meetings & Chat.

Holding group chats

To be sure, the idea of a one-on-one chat is invaluable. Zoom would be pretty limited as a communication medium, however, if it could accommodate messages only between two individuals.

Fortunately, you don't have to worry. Meetings & Chat is more than up to the task.

Starting a new group chat

What if you want to concurrently exchange messages with David, Tim, and Gareth? Zoom's process for initiating a group chat is nearly identical to one covered in the section "Exchanging messages with your individual Zoom contacts," earlier in this chapter.

1. In the Zoom desktop client, click on the Chat icon at the top of the screen.

2. In the sidebar, click on the plus icon the right of Recent.

3. **Choose New Chat from the menu that Zoom displays.**

4. **At the top of the screen next to To:, type a few letters of the names of each of the people whom you want to invite to the group chat.**

    Their names should automatically appear. In this example, those folks are David, Tim, and Gareth.

5. **Click on the message pane at the bottom of the screen.**

6. **Enter your message and then press Enter on your keyboard.**

    Depending on whether they're active and how they've configured their notifications, Zoom alerts those folks that you're trying to start a group chat with them.

When you begin a new group chat, Zoom assigns you the role of chat administrator or admin. Don't get too excited, though. You won't receive any gifts in the mail. Also, don't confuse this designation with the admin role discussed in Chapter 3. Rather, Meetings & Chat has granted you a few special powers in this group chat. You — and only you — can do the following:

>> Delete the group chat altogether. (I cover this in the section "Editing and deleting your messages," later in this chapter.)

>> Designate another participant as the chat admin if you decide to leave the discussion. (I cover this in the section "Leaving a group chat," later in this chapter.)

Leaving a group chat

If you're like me, then you've become entangled in a few insufferable email threads over your career. After all, it takes inconsiderate or clueless people very little time to carbon copy or CC you on their messages. In highly political work environments, this problem is especially acute. I've wasted a great deal of time at work reading confusing emails that had ultimately nothing to do with me. Zilch.

Should the same thing happen to you in Meetings & Chat, fret not. Zoom makes extricating yourself from pointless or low-priority group chats easy. Just do the following:

1. **In the Zoom desktop client, click on the Chat icon at the top of the screen.**

2. **In the sidebar, click on the existing discussion that you want to leave.**

    Zoom highlights it in blue.

3. **Click on the arrow to display a drop-down list and then select Leave Chat.**

If you're the chat admin, then Zoom presents you with three options, as Figure 5-5 displays:

- **Delete Discussion:** You will be removing the discussion for all current participants. If you select this option, then Zoom prompts you with another window to ensure that you want to eradicate it. Click on the red Delete Discussion button to finish the kill.

- **Cancel:** Return to the previous screen. You can still participate in the group chat.

- **(Optional) Assign New Admin:** You are effectively delegating admin rights of this group chat to another current participant. If you go this route, then you'll need to select that person in an additional next step. Finally, complete the process by clicking on the blue Assign button.

REMEMBER

Zoom allows you to assign a new admin to the chat only if you started it or if someone else assigned you that role.

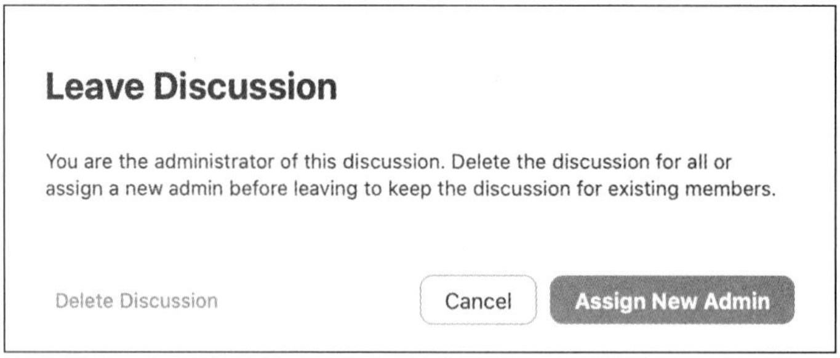

Leave Discussion

You are the administrator of this discussion. Delete the discussion for all or assign a new admin before leaving to keep the discussion for existing members.

Delete Discussion   Cancel   **Assign New Admin**

FIGURE 5-5:
Meetings & Chat prompt for leaving a group chat that you initiated.

4. **Select your desired option.**

REMEMBER

Say that you're a regular participant in this group chat. That is, you're not the admin. In this case, Meetings & Chat offers you a more limited menu of options when you want to bolt: Cancel and Leave Discussion. Because of your limited role, this restriction makes complete sense.

Once you leave, Meetings & Chat removes your name from the group chat in the sidebar.

TIP

When you're in a group of people in real life (or IRL, as the kids say), it's polite to say goodbye prior to leaving. The same principle applies here: Don't just bolt from a group chat. It's best to send the group a message explaining why you're leaving.

Inviting others to an existing group chat

Conversations are sometimes like improvisational jazz. That is, they occasionally take unexpected turns. For example, Taylor, Nate, and Pat are chatting about hiring Chris as the band's new guitarist. (Yes, I'm listening to Foo Fighters as I write these words.) Eventually, talks get serious, and it makes sense to bring Dave into the fold. Yeah, the three of them could forward Dave a bunch of separate chat messages, but that method is so 1998.

Fortunately, you need not create a new Zoom group chat and start from scratch. Meetings & Chat makes it insanely easy to add others to an existing discussion, allowing newbies to quickly catch up on all of the previous back-and-forth. (Foo Fighters' fans will get that last reference.)

Just follow these steps:

1. **In the Zoom desktop client, click on the Chat icon at the top of the screen.**
2. **In the sidebar, click on the existing discussion to which you want to add another person.**

   Zoom highlights it in blue.
3. **Click on the drop-down arrow to the right of the person's name.**
4. **Choose Invite Others from the menu that Zoom displays.**
5. **Select the people whom you want to invite to the group chat.**
6. **Click on the blue Invite button.**

   Zoom updates the names of the people in the active group chat in the sidebar.

   Figure 5-6 displays my initial message to the group about TPS reports.

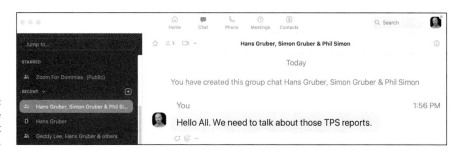

FIGURE 5-6:
Simple
group-chat
message.

Creating threads in Zoom

You and your colleague Ricky have exchanged a series of ten discrete messages, but you want to respond to a specific one. Say that he made a comment a week ago that you let slide. Upon further reflection, however, something about that message confused you. Now you would like to revisit it. Is there an easy way to refer to that prior message?

Like many modern communications tools, Meetings & Chat lets users create threads for specific messages. (If a Zoom thread sounds suspiciously like its email counterpart, trust your judgment.) This optional feature provides much-needed context to messages, especially if you and your colleague(s) have exchanged a bunch of them.

To create a thread on an existing message, follow these steps:

1. **In the Zoom desktop client, click on the Chat icon at the top of the screen.**

2. **Locate the specific message in the thread to which you want to respond.**

   As you hover over the message, Zoom displays a few new icons.

3. **Click on the chat-bubble icon.**

   It's the first one.

4. **Type your message and press the Enter key.**

   When you create a thread, Meetings & Chat indents your message and future ones in response to it. You and others can easily see that the thread stands apart from the other, unthreaded messages.

As Figure 5-7 shows, Shawn and I exchanged a bunch of messages in Zoom. I responded to one of them with "Thanks again." As such, I have provided valuable context to my message. Because I properly used the thread feature, he didn't respond with "For what?" If I had responded without a thread at the end of our messages, I probably would have confused him.

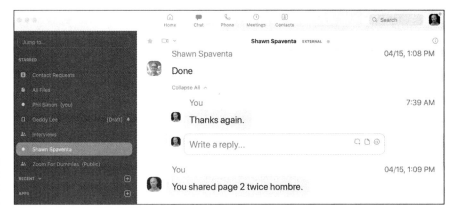

FIGURE 5-7: Example of a Meetings & Chat thread.

TIP

Threads are über-useful. Used properly, they minimize confusion and save everyone a good bit of time.

Saving message drafts

Have you ever spent 30 minutes drafting a critical email, only to get distracted? Alternatively, maybe you've composed your message and want to send it. A voice inside you, however, is telling you to think long and hard about hitting Send on a message that slams some of your colleagues. I'm talking not just about burning a bridge, but napalming it.

Just about every email program auto-saves drafts these days — and has for years. This feature allows users to return to email drafts when it's convenient for them. In a move that should surprise exactly no one, Zoom does the very same thing. Just follow these steps:

1. **In the Zoom desktop client, click on Contacts.**

2. **Click on the name of the contact to whom you want to send a message.**

   Zoom places your cursor in the message window.

3. **Type your message, but don't press the Enter key.**

4. **Click on another contact name or icon at the top of the screen.**

   Zoom auto-saves your draft and even places the text [Draft] in red to the right of the contact's name.

   You can return to your message draft at any point to finish and send it.

TIP

Unlike email, Meetings & Chat requires you to first select an entity before creating a draft. That entity may be another user, group, or channel. (Chapter 6 covers channels.)

TIP

You can also create drafts for yourself. Some users find prefer this method for jotting down in-call notes without leaving Meetings & Chat.

Editing and deleting your messages

Just about everyone has sent emails only later to have realized that they goofed. In my career, I have made every conceivable email-related mistake: Attached the wrong file, forgot to copy a key person, and emailed the wrong person altogether. You name it. I'm guessing that you have as well.

How does Meetings & Chat handle these issues?

Say that I sent Boris message by accident, and I want to take it back. No, Meetings & Chat won't erase Boris's memory if he has already read my message. You can't use it to summon hired goons to show up at his house. Still, I can delete it and minimize the chance that he views my errant note.

Delete a message that you previously sent by following these steps:

1. **In the Zoom desktop client, click on the Chat icon at the top of the screen.**

2. **Locate the specific message that you want to remove.**

As you hover over the message, Zoom displays a few new icons.

3. **Click on the ellipsis icon and then click on the Delete button.**

And like that, it's gone.

Perhaps your mistake is more benign. I'm talking about typos or misspellings here. Edit your sent message by following these instructions:

1. **In the Zoom desktop client, click on the Chat icon at the top of the screen.**

2. **Locate the specific message you want to change.**

As you hover over the message, Zoom displays a few new icons.

3. **Click on the ellipsis icon and choose Edit from the menu that appears.**

4. **Make whatever changes you like to your message.**

5. **Click on the Save button.**

Note that Meetings & Chat smartly displays the text (Edited) to the right of your original message next to its date and time. In this way, Zoom lets everyone in the chat see that you have altered your original message. Zoom is nothing if not transparent.

REMEMBER

For obvious reasons, Meetings & Chat prohibits users from editing and deleting others' messages. Talk about opening Pandora's box.

Referencing other Zoom members in a group discussion

Say that you are in a group chat with six other members, but you only want to ask Steven a question. It's best to specifically mention him using the @ symbol. This way, he'll likely receive a notification in Meetings & Chat. To reference a specific member of a group chat, follow these steps:

1. **In the Zoom desktop client, click on the Chat icon at the top.**

2. **In the sidebar, click on a specific discussion.**

   Zoom highlights it in blue.

3. **Type the @ symbol.**

   Zoom displays a list of the people involved in the current group chat.

4. **Select the name of the person whom you want to reference.**

   Zoom inserts that person's name in the message window in blue with the @ sign in front of it.

5. **Type the rest of your message and press the Enter key.**

TIP

Use @all to notify every chat participant.

You can use the same trick in channels, discussed in Chapter 6.

REMEMBER

Adding some flair to your messages

Sending a simple, format-free message often gets the job done. For example, when responding to a simple question of when today's meeting starts, you don't need to underline and bold your text. (A former colleague of mine used to regularly complicate his messages by applying superfluous styles. It drove me nuts. And don't get me started on people who use all caps with exclamation points to boot. Calm blue oceans.. . .)

Still, I'm not a complete formatting zealot. Sometimes a little message styling does wonders. For example, bullet points often make sense for meeting agendas.

Table 5-3 lists the current rich-text formatting options that Meetings & Chat offers.

TABLE 5-3   ### Rich-Text Message Formatting Options in Meetings & Chat

Icon	Description
B	Bolds text
I	Italicizes text
S̶	Applies strikethrough style
* —	Creates a bulleted list

Applying different formats to your text

To apply a style to specific text in your message, follow these directions:

1. **In the Zoom desktop client, create a new text message.**

2. **Type some text, but don't send the message just yet.**

3. **Highlight the text that you want to format.**

4. **In the formatting window that appears, click on the format that you'd like to apply to the selected text.**

   Zoom applies that format to that text — and only that text.

5. **Press the Enter key to send your rich-text message.**

Figure 5-8 displays a simple agenda with bullet points.

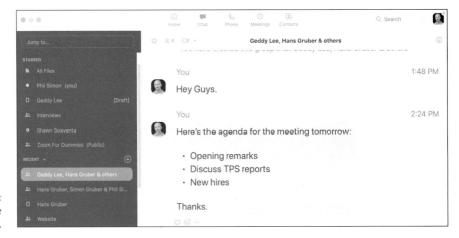

FIGURE 5-8:
Zoom message
with bullet points.

Hold down your Shift key and press your Enter key twice to create new paragraphs in your messages.

I'm not clairvoyant, but I expect Zoom to add some extra formatting options to Meetings & Chat in the near future. The ability to add hyperlinks, colored text, and headings, for example, would be especially useful.

Adding emojis and animated gifs

But what about emojis and animated gifs? Surely Meetings & Chat lets its users add these modern staples to our messages, right?

Nope, I was just teasing you.

I'm kidding.

To add either one of these accoutrements to your message, follow these directions:

1. **In the Zoom desktop client, create a text message.**

2. **Click on the smiley-face icon on the right-hand side of the screen.**

   Zoom displays the emoji and animated-gif picker in Figure 5-9.

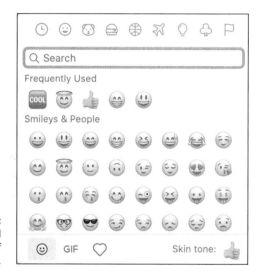

FIGURE 5-9:
Zoom emoji and
animated-gif
picker.

3. **Select the emoji or animated gif that you want to add to your message.**

4. **Press the Enter key on your keyboard.**

Speaking of emojis, Zoom doesn't make you send new messages to use them. In fact, you can add one as a response to someone else's message as follows:

1. **In the Zoom desktop client, click on the Chat icon at the top of the screen.**

2. **Locate the specific message to which you want to add an emoji.**

   As you hover over the message, Zoom displays a few new icons.

3. **Click on the smiley face.**

4. **Select your preferred emoji.**

Uploading and sharing files in Zoom

You run into your boss Kim in the hallway. She asks you to send her the latest version of your PowerPoint deck. She'd like to review it and give you notes.

Fulfilling her request does not necessitate scheduling a meeting and discussing it for ten minutes. (Of course, an actual conversation may make sense at a later point, but that's not important now.) In this scenario, you can certainly rattle her off an email and attach your file to it. You've probably performed that task hundreds or thousands of times. Again, though, a Zoom message also gets the job done.

Sharing files with other Zoom members

To send someone a file in Meetings & Chat, follow these steps:

1. **In the Zoom desktop client, click on Contacts.**

2. **Click on the name of the contact with whom you want share a file.**

3. **Click on the white Chat button on the right side of the screen.**

   Zoom places your cursor in text box at the bottom of the screen.

4. **Above your cursor, click on the File button to display a window.**

   Meetings & Chat provides a number of popular file-sharing options, including:

   - Microsoft OneDrive

   - Google Drive

   - Box

   - Your Computer

   In this example, I'm going to share my file via the last option.

5. **Double-click on the file that you want to share.**

   Zoom uploads the file to the chat.

   Figure 5-10 displays the file that I sent to Geddy — a copy of the cover of *Slack For Dummies*.

TIP

You also upload files to channels in this manner. Chapter 6 covers this subject.

FIGURE 5-10:
Example of file
shared with
Zoom user
via chat.

Quickly accessing your Zoom files

Imagine having to track down all your files in different Zoom chats. The word cumbersome comes to mind. Thankfully, Meetings & Chat lets you access all your shared files in one place by following these directions:

1. **In the Zoom desktop client, click on the Chat icon at the top of the screen.**

2. **At the top of the sidebar, click on All Files.**

   On the right, Zoom displays two tabs:

   - **My Files:** Access all the files you've uploaded to Meetings & Chat.

   - **All Files:** Access all the files that others have shared with you directly, via group chats, and via channels.

3. **Click on either tab to see related files.**

4. **(Optional) Double-click a file to open it.**

   Zoom launches the file's default program on your computer.

TIP

Meetings & Chat lets you do far more, however, than just open previously shared files. You can perform a number of other quick actions by mousing over them and clicking on one of the following three icons that appear:

» **Download:** Save this file to your computer.

» **Share:** Forward that file to a person, group chat, or channel.

» **More:** Options here include download and copy.

Sending screen captures

Have you and a colleague ever been in separate places as you viewed the same website, code, or spreadsheet? She has identified an error. For the life of you, though, you just don't see it. You just aren't connecting the dots. Sure, you can share your screen via Meetings & Chat, but that only works if both of you are available. What if she could capture a screenshot, mark it up, and send it to you?

Truth be told, the idea of sending a screen shot isn't exactly earth-shattering. For at least the last 25 years, anyone with basic computer skills could quickly generate them. Still, Meetings & Chat makes it easy to capture your screen, add simple markups, and send it to a colleague or a group chat. Just follow these instructions:

1. **In the Zoom desktop client, click on the Chat icon at the top of the screen.**

2. **In the sidebar, click on the person to whom you want to send a screenshot.**

    Zoom highlights the person's name in blue.

3. **Above the message prompt, click on the Screenshot icon.**

4. **Zoom lets you crop the part of your computer screen that you want to share.**

5. **(Optional) Mark up your image by using the icons that appear below the screen:**

    -   **Drawing:** Allows you to draw whatever you like on the screen.
    -   **Arrow:** Easily point to specific areas by inserting an arrow.
    -   **Box:** Lets you insert a box.
    -   **Circle:** Lets you insert a circle.
    -   **Text:** Enter whatever text you like.
    -   **Download:** Download the screen capture to your computer.
    -   **Undo:** Reverse your previous action.
    -   **Cancel:** Abandon ship and abort.

6. **Click on the Capture button, as Figure 5-11 displays.**

    Zoom includes the screen capture along with your message.

7. **Press the Enter key on your keyboard to send the message.**

    Zoom includes the screen capture along with your message.

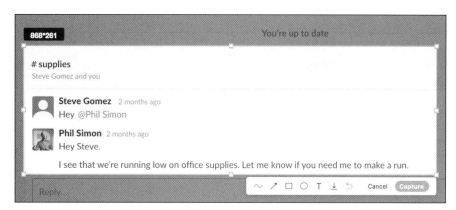

FIGURE 5-11:
Zoom screen
capture.

Performing message-specific actions

It turns out that you can do some other cool things with Zoom messages. Click on the ellipsis icon to the right of a message. In turn, Meetings & Chat displays the useful options in Table 5-4.

TABLE 5-4   **Zoom Message-Specific Actions**

Name	Description
Share Message. . .	Forward the message to another Zoom contact, group chat, or channel. This action resembles forwarding emails.
Copy	Copy the message's text to your computer's clipboard.
Follow Message	Ideal for messages in group threads and channels that don't specifically mention you with the @ symbol. Enabling it means that Meetings & Chat will send you a notification of new activity in the conversation.
Star Message	Places the message at the top of the Zoom desktop client in the Starred Messages container.
Mark as Unread	Much like email, restores the new message notification badge in Zoom in the sidebar next to the contact's name.

Figure 5-12 displays these actions in context:

TIP

For more information on Zoom's robust chat functionality, visit `bit.ly/zfd-chats`.

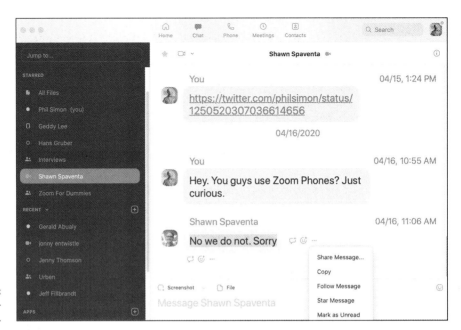

FIGURE 5-12:
Zoom message-
specific actions.

Searching in Zoom

Say that you intend to go all-in on Meetings & Chat. You're going to use it to send messages to colleagues or friends in lieu of email. In my humble opinion, it's a wise choice. I doubt that you will look back.

At first, Meetings & Chat is a tabula rasa or clean slate. As such, you may not need to conduct searches for one simple reason: You can easily find the relatively few messages and files. Make no mistake, though: Depending on how many messages you send and receive in Zoom, pretty soon hunting and pecking for messages and files will fail you. It's only a matter of time. At some point, you're going to need to employ a powerful and systematic way of locating key notes, tips, suggestions, and files.

Meetings & Chat answers the bell here by providing users with fairly robust search functionality. As a result, it's easy to conduct broad or even very specific queries and quickly find what you need.

Performing basic Zoom searches

Billions of people search both the web and their inboxes on a daily basis. At a high level, Meetings & Chat searches work in a similar manner: All three mechanisms attempt to locate the most meaningful mentions of your desired search terms or *keywords*.

Say that you're searching Meetings & Chat for the word "appreciate" in messages that you've exchanged with others. Follow these steps to conduct a basic keyword search.

1. **In the Zoom desktop client, click on the search bar in the upper right-hand corner of the screen.**

2. **Type your keyword.**

    In my example, I type the word "appreciate."

    Zoom displays a prompt underneath the search bar asking whether you want to restrict your search to messages or files.

    Ignore this prompt if you want to search everything in Zoom.

3. **Press the Enter key.**

    Zoom displays the results of your query, as Figure 5-13 shows.

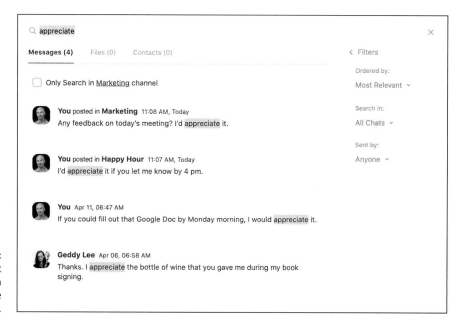

FIGURE 5-13: Meetings & Chat simple search results for the word *appreciate*.

A few things about Figure 5-13 stand out. First, Zoom displays three self-explanatory tabs at the top of the page:

>> **Messages:** Zoom displays chat messages — if any — that contain the keyword.

>> **Files:** Zoom displays the files — if any — that contain the keyword.

>> **Contacts:** Zoom displays the names of contacts — if any — that contain the keyword.

Second, note Zoom's default settings for search results in Figure 5-13:

>> **Ordered by: Most Relevant.** Click on the drop-down list to view Zoom's most recent results instead.

>> **Search in: All Chats.** Click on the drop-down list to restrict your search to conversations that you've held with specific individuals or in channels that contain the keyword. (Chapter 6 covers Zoom channels.)

>> **Sent by: Anyone.** Click on the drop-down list to restrict your search to messages sent by specific individual(s) containing your keyword(s).

REMEMBER

Meetings & Chat does not include message and file results from individuals' private messages. (Chapter 9 covers privacy and security in far more detail.)

It's also important to understand the dynamic and time-sensitive nature of your Meetings & Chat searches. That is, they reflect the message and file content in the app only at a particular time. For example, the Zoom search results in Figure 5-13 neglect to include any files for one simple reason: None existed at the time. A few minutes after performing that search, Simon Gruber posts a message and attaches a file.

A few days later, I perform the same search. Meetings & Chat displays new results (see Figure 5-14).

As a bonus, when you mouse over a specific search result, Meetings & Chat displays two additional, beneficial options:

>> **View Context:** Zoom expands the results and provides additional context.

>> **Jump:** Zoom takes you to the message in that channel or group chat.

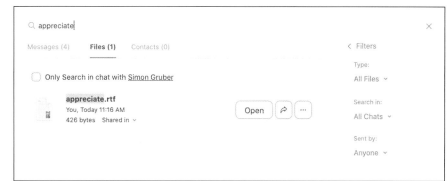

FIGURE 5-14: New Meetings & Chat search results for the word "appreciate."

Performing more advanced Zoom searches

Figure 5-14 presented four results underneath the Messages tab that contain the word "appreciate." But what if I wanted to restrict my search to the phrase "appreciate it"? That is, I want to see only the results that contain those two terms in that specific order.

Follow these directions to search for multiple keywords:

1. **In the Zoom desktop client, click on the search bar in the upper right-hand corner of the screen.**

2. **Type your phrase.**

    In my example, I type the words "appreciate it."

    Make sure to include the quotes.

REMEMBER

    Zoom displays a prompt underneath the search bar asking whether you want to search messages or files.

3. **Press the Enter key.**

    Zoom displays the results of your refined query, as Figure 5-15 shows.

Note how Zoom displays results that contain the full phrase "appreciate it." Meetings & Chat omits results that include only the word "appreciate" without "it."

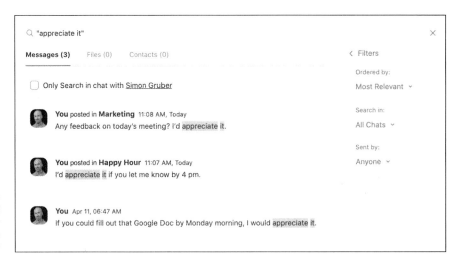

FIGURE 5-15:
Meetings & Chat
search results for
the phrase
"appreciate it."

To paraphrase the classic Rolling Stones song, you can't always get what you want. In the context of Meetings & Chat searches, you may not find what you need for a few reasons.

>> **Your search query is too specific.** For example, you're searching for the term "party" from Hans. Other Meetings & Chat users have used that term in conversations with you, but Hans never has.

>> **You're searching for a term that exists, but its privacy and security settings prohibit you from viewing it.** Again, you're searching for a term "party." It exists, but only in a private group chat. Unfortunately, you're not a member of it.

>> **You're searching for something that simply doesn't exist in Zoom.** For example, as Figure 5-16 displays, I search for the phrase "don't appreciate" and Zoom returns nothing. No shocker here. No results exist anywhere in Meetings & Chat that meet my search specific criteria.

REMEMBER

Meetings & Chat search is quite literal and not all that smart yet. For example, I type "apreciate" and Zoom returns nothing. Yes, I misspelled the word, but Zoom doesn't recognize users' search intent yet. At some point in the future, I suspect that Zoom will overhaul its search capabilities. (Chapter 13 covers my predictions on the other ways in which Zoom will improve in the future.)

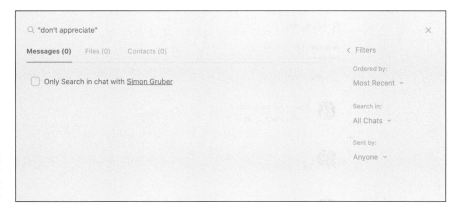

FIGURE 5-16:
Meetings & Chat
search results for
the phrase "don't
appreciate."

Performing searches with wildcards

Say that you'd like to search on all permutations of the word "in." That is, you want Meetings & Chat to return all results that contain those two letters in succession. For example, you'd like to see things such as:

>> I'll send you that *in*formation shortly.

>> I get here early. Call me, and I'll let you *in*.

>> Any Word documents, PDFs, or other files in Meetings & Chat that contain the word *in*.

You may think that you'll have to conduct separate searches.

You certainly can, but Meetings & Chat provides a better way to perform these types of imprecise queries. By using powerful wildcards, you view the parts of a specific keyword or phrase.

Wildcards can save you an enormous amount of time, especially when dealing with thousands of files and messages. To be fair, Slack, Microsoft Teams, and collaboration tools have supported wildcards for years. Put differently, Meetings & Chat isn't unique in supporting them.

To search with wildcards, follow these instructions:

1. **In the Zoom desktop client, click on the search bar in the upper right-hand corner of the screen.**

2. **Type your phrase.**

   In my example, I type in "*in*."

TIP

Hold down your Shift key and hit the number 8 on your keyboard to generate the asterisk.

Meetings & Chat displays a prompt underneath the search bar asking whether you want to search messages or files.

Limit your search if you like — or don't.

3. **Press the Enter key.**

Figure 5-17 displays the results of the wildcard search in Meetings & Chat.

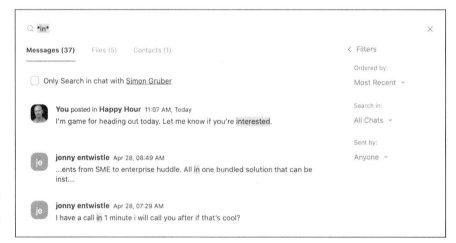

FIGURE 5-17:
Meetings & Chat search results with wildcards.

REMEMBER

You need not use wildcards at both the beginning and the end of your keyword in your searches. You can opt for either. Just remember, though, that Meetings & Chat may well return different results. What you get out of your search hinges upon what you put into it.

3

Becoming a Zoom Power User

Learn how to customize Zoom to your liking.

Easily connect Zoom to your favorite productivity and communications apps.

Hold powerful and interactive webinars in Zoom.

Chapter **6**

Getting Even More Out of Meetings & Chat

Whoa! I didn't know that you could do that.

Has someone ever uttered that sentence to you after you performed a task on your phone, in a software application, or with a programming language? If not, then have you ever said the same thing to someone under those circumstances?

Plenty of people are downright oblivious of many technologies' useful and time-saving features — sometimes for years. Don't take my word for it, though.

Presenting his research at a tech conference in 2002, Jim Johnson — the founder and chairman of The Standish Group — confirmed what many industry types have long suspected: In a typical software program or system, the majority of users ignore nearly two-thirds of its available features. Put differently, most folks usually know just enough to get by. When we spoke in May 2020, Johnson relayed that his firm's subsequent studies have confirmed that not much has changed since then.

Generally speaking, power users understand that using the basics of any application gets them only so far — and that same adage certainly applies to Meetings & Chat. If you use it only to make video calls, then you're missing out on oodles of its useful and timesaving features.

Are you willing to open your mind? If so, then you'll find that you can do so much more, especially if your organization subscribes to a premium Zoom plan. Along these lines, this chapter describes some of the valuable but lesser used features in Meetings & Chat: IM groups, channels, snippets, reporting, and more.

Managing Users via IM Groups

As I cover in Chapter 3, account owners and admins can enable or disable certain settings — ones that affect all users in an organization's Zoom account. That is, they can make global decisions that regular Zoom members cannot override. People in administrative roles can also perform tasks that their non-administrative brethren cannot.

In that chapter, I cover creating user accounts, roles, user groups, and more. To be sure, customers on Meetings & Chat premium accounts get quite a bit of mileage out of these features. Far too often, however, they fail to take advantage of one particularly useful piece of Zoom functionality.

Understanding the need for IM groups

Lucy manages Marillion, a five-member progressive rock band based in England. She uses Meetings & Chat to coordinate events, conduct band meetings, and generally stay in touch with all of its members. In this simple scenario, it's unlikely that her directory will become unwieldly.

Now, assume that you work for a global conglomerate that consists of 6,000 employees distributed across the globe. Employees can use Meetings & Chat to manage their internal communications, but it's not hard to imagine logistical difficulties associated with such a large workforce.

To this end, IM groups fulfill a key need. (IM here stands for *Instant Message*.) This *administrative* tool allows owners and admins to corral users into specific buckets. (That is, a regular Zoom member cannot create IM groups for herself.)

Think of IM groups as different subdirectories. They allow individual members to easily find and connect with specific peers in their organization and discuss relevant topics. Even better, you can place the same member in your Zoom account into multiple IM groups. For example, a company hires Grace as its new head of northeastern sales. Its Zoom admin places her into two IM groups: one for new hires and one for sales.

REMEMBER

Like user groups, Zoom restricts IM groups to customers on premium plans.

If you create IM groups, then you should encourage employees to use them.

TIP

Examples of IM groups run the gamut. A large retailer decides to create IM groups for its sales, accounting, and HR departments. A restaurant chain uses separate IM groups for its store and district managers. School districts create them for different types of teachers across districts — as well as a massive IM group for all teachers in all districts.

Zoom gives account owners and admins the ability to create three types of IM groups:

>> **Shared:** All Zoom members can search for the group and view it.

>> **Private:** Only existing IM group members can view the IM group. Members who don't belong to this group can search for users who are in the group. (In its online help text, Zoom sometimes refers to private groups as *normal groups*.)

>> **Restricted:** Only group members can view the group and find the members in it.

Depending on the type of IM group(s) that you create, Zoom users in your organization may or may not be able to view all of them.

REMEMBER

Note that IM groups are different than user groups, discussed in Chapter 3.

Adding a new IM group

To add a new IM group, just follow these steps:

1. **In the Zoom web portal, under the Admin header, click on Account Management.**

2. **Click on IM Management.**

3. **Click on the blue + Add IM Group button on the right-hand side of the screen.**

4. **Under Group Name, enter a name for the new IM group.**

   In this case, I am calling it Internal.

5. **Select whether it's a shared, private, or restricted group.**

6. **Click on the blue Save button.**

Adding users to IM groups

Of course, adding an IM group makes little sense unless you populate it with Zoom members. To place existing Zoom users into an existing IM group, follow these steps:

1. **In the Zoom web portal, under the Admin header, click on Account Management.**

2. **Click on IM Management.**

3. **Under Group Name, select the name of the existing IM group to which you want to add members.**

   For this example, I selected Internal.

4. **Click on the blue + Add Members button on the right-hand side of the screen.**

5. **Enter at least three letters of an individual's email address.**

   Note that a person's email address may not contain any of the same letters as his name.

6. **After Zoom recognizes your text string, select that person's name from the drop-down list.**

   Repeat this step as often as you like for new members.

7. **Click on the blue Add button.**

Figure 6-1 displays my new IM group Internal, along with its two members.

REMEMBER

IM groups appear in the Contacts section of users' Zoom desktop clients.

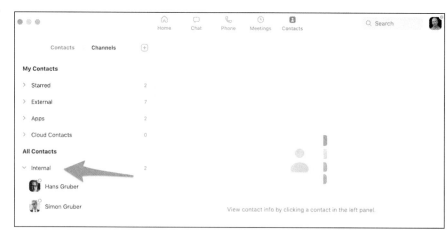

FIGURE 6-1: New Zoom IM group with members.

Exploring Additional Options and Features in Meetings & Chat

You may not like how owners and admins have locked down certain Zoom features or required others. Feel free to disagree with them or, if you're feeling particularly bold, politely discuss your bone of contention.

Make no mistake, though: Regular Zoom members can still do plenty to customize their experience.

Understanding Zoom Channels

Say that your local high school employs 200 teachers. Some teach math, while others cover history, English, science, and physical education. The math teachers would like to discuss math-related issues with their colleagues. They frequently share numbers-oriented techniques and exercises with each other — plus the occasional horror story about helicopter parents and students who can't do simple addition. In this scenario, the district's nonmath teachers don't care too much about algebra and trigonometry.

All teachers do, however, need to know about district-wide announcements, faculty meetings, and safety issues. Sure, the school superintendent could blast out all-employee emails, but that one-size-fits-all solution isn't terribly elegant. What's more, hitting the Reply All button is bound to cause chaos. At a minimum, users will receive plenty of irrelevant emails and subsequent responses.

What if there were a way to create specialized containers of conversations? And what if teachers could join only the ones that interest them? While I'm at it, what if newly hired teachers could search for — and view —prior conversations and digest them at their own pace?

If you followed my logic, then you now understand the general idea behind channels. They allow users connected in Zoom to discuss specific subjects with one another — whether they are in the same organization or not. Channels let people engage in targeted group discussions and send files and images. Channel-mates can also start instant group meetings with or without video.

In short, channels are incredibly useful. If you're not using them, then you are missing out.

Zoom offers users the ability to create their own channels, functionality that tools such as Slack and Microsoft Teams have also embraced.

As of this writing, Zoom users can start two types of channels:

>> **Public:** Anyone in the organization can join these channels.

>> **Private:** To join this type of channel, an existing member needs to invite you.

Private channels for customers on premium plans can consist of a maximum of 5,000 members. On its Basic plan, Zoom restricts private channels to 500 members. Zoom public channels can accommodate up to a downright bawdy 10,000 members.

On their surface, channels resemble IM groups, discussed in the section "Managing Users via IM Groups" earlier in this chapter. There's a subtle but important difference between the two features, though: Regular Zoom members can create channels on their own. That is, they don't need to solicit prior owner or admin approval. As such, channels tend to be smaller and more topic-specific than broad IM groups.

Why channels tend to beat group chats

Astute readers may be furrowing their brows at this point. Don't Zoom channels overlap to some extent with group chats? (Chapter 5 discusses the latter topic.) The answer is yes. For several reasons, though, channels generally represent a better way of holding group discussions.

First, Meetings & Chat users can freely discover public channels on their own. Put differently, public channels are more open and democratic than private group chats. By default, Zoom lets members discover and join public channels for themselves. That is, they don't need to receive formal invitations. (For obvious reasons, private channels are a different story.)

Second and just as important, channels are more permanent than group chats. For example, say that Arthur, Michael, and Barry are all attorneys at the New York law firm Kenner, Back and Ledeen. (Yes, these characters are from the excellent flick *Michael Clayton*.) The three lawyers discuss a complicated legal matter in a Zoom group chat. Six months later, all leave the firm. Their discussions technically still exist, but Zoom's privacy settings will prevent others from accessing them. (Chapter 9 goes much deeper into this subject.) Had they created and used a public channel, then others could easily join it and view their previous conversations.

REMEMBER

Channels also overlap to some extent with IM groups, discussed in the "Managing Users via IM Groups" section earlier in this chapter. There's one key difference, though: IM groups are administrative or top-down tools. For their part, Zoom users drive channels. As such, they are bottom-up tools.

Creating a new channel

To create a Zoom channel, abide by these steps:

1. Launch the Zoom desktop client.

2. At the top of the screen, click on Contacts.

3. In the sidebar, click on Channels.

4. Click on the plus icon to the immediate right of the word Channels.

5. From the menu that appears, choose Create a Channel.

   Zoom displays the Create a Channel window.

6. Enter the name of your new channel in the Channel Name text box.

7. (Optional) Invite members to your new channel by entering parts of their names.

8. (Optional) Restrict the channel to just members on your organization's Zoom plan.

9. Select whether you want to create a private or public channel by clicking on the checkbox to the left of each option.

10. Click on the blue Create Channel button.

    Your channel is created.

After you create a public channel, Zoom places the word Public in parentheses to its immediate right in the sidebar. Meetings & Chat makes no such annotation for private channels.

REMEMBER

Zoom places a people icon to the left of the channel in the sidebar.

Browsing and joining existing public channels

If you're new to an organization, you're going to want to stay informed. To this end, it's best to explore public channels and join those that interest you.

To join an existing public channel, follow these steps:

1. Launch the Zoom desktop client.

2. At the top of the screen, click on the Contacts icon.

3. In the sidebar, click on Channels.

4. Click on the plus icon to the immediate right of the word Channels.

5. **From the menu that appears, click on Join a Channel.**

Zoom displays the Join a Channel window, allowing you to view all public channels.

6. **(Optional) In the search bar, type a few letters of the name of the public channel that you want to join and press the Enter key.**

7. **Underneath the search bar, identify the name of the public channel that you want to join and click on it.**

8. **Click on the blue Join button to the right of the name of the public channel.**

Zoom takes you back to the desktop app's Chat window.

Viewing information about specific channels

For each channel, Zoom makes it easy to get a lay of the land. That is, with a few clicks, you can view important information about each channel, what members have already shared in it, and more.

Just follow these directions:

1. **Launch the Zoom desktop client.**

2. **At the top of the screen, click on Chat.**

3. **In the sidebar, click on a channel to which you already belong.**

Zoom highlights it in blue.

4. **Underneath your profile picture in the upper right-hand corner, click on the circled _i_ icon.**

Zoom displays Figure 6-2 — a new pane with a number of items, each of which displays a right-arrow to its right.

FIGURE 6-2:
Zoom
information on
#Announcements
channel.

5. **Click on the menu items to perform the action you'd like:**

- **Channel Info:** Add a description to the channel.

- **Members:** View the channel's current members.

- **Images:** View the images (if any) that members of the channel have shared.

- **Files:** View the files (if any) that members of the channel have shared.

- **Starred Messages:** View the messages in the channel (if any) that members of the channel have starred.

- **Notifications:** Customize your channel notifications. (See the section "Setting keyword-specific notifications," later in this chapter, for more information on this topic.)

- **More Options:** Perform additional channel actions, all of which I cover in this chapter.

Starring a channel

Say that you spend a great deal of time in the #TechTips channel and want it to appear at the top of your channel list in the sidebar. To indicate that a particular channel is a favorite, follow these steps:

1. **Launch the Zoom desktop client.**

2. **At the top of the screen, click on Chat.**

3. **In the sidebar, click on the channel.**

   Zoom highlights it in blue and displays a drop-down arrow.

4. **Click on the drop-down arrow to the right of the HR channel and choose Star this Channel from the pop-up menu that appears.**

   Zoom moves the channel up to the top of your sidebar within the starred section.

Deleting channels

Say that you create a public channel and give it a chic name, such as #ZoomBeasts. Six months later, no one uses it. Alternatively, no one has used it for months because users have flocked to a different channel.

As long as you are the channel admin, you can delete a channel as follows:

1. **Launch the Zoom desktop client.**

2. **At the top of the screen, click on Chat.**

3. **In the sidebar, click on the channel that you want to delete.**

Zoom highlights it in blue.

4. **Click on the drop-down arrow next to the channel and choose Delete Channel from the menu that appears.**

Zoom prompts you to confirm that you want to delete the channel.

5. **Click on the red Delete Channel button.**

Say that you're only a channel member, not an admin. In this case, Zoom forbids you from deleting that channel. You won't even see it as an option.

Channel deletions are permanent. Say *adios* to all of the correspondence that previously took place and the files that people shared in it.

REMEMBER

Leaving channels

If you join a channel by mistake or lose interest, you don't have to remain in it. You can leave it whenever you like by following these steps:

1. **Launch the Zoom desktop client.**

2. **At the top of the screen, click on Chat.**

3. **In the sidebar, click on the channel that you want to leave.**

Zoom highlights it in blue.

4. **Click on the drop-down arrow next to the channel and choose Leave Channel from the menu that appears.**

Zoom prompts you to confirm that you want to leave the channel.

5. **Click on the blue Leave Channel button.**

If you leave a public channel, then you can always rejoin it. For private channels, though, a current member will need to re-invite you.

Converting channel types

Beanie runs Speaker City, a 50-employee outfit in the Midwest. He uses Zoom to create an #HR channel. He figures that it represents the best way to make general announcements about employee pay and benefits policies. Unfortunately, the types of conversations that take place in the channel are more sensitive in nature. For example, employees ask about specific disciplinary issues and volunteer information about their private lives that just aren't appropriate for public consumption.

What should Beanie do?

He certainly can delete the channel. That move, however, poses a problem: All of the information in #HR goes poof. A better alternative is to convert the public channel to a private one:

1. **Launch the Zoom desktop client.**

2. **At the top of the screen, click on Chat.**

3. **In the sidebar, click on the HR channel.**

   Zoom highlights it in blue.

4. **Click on the drop-down arrow next to the channel and choose Edit Channel from the menu that appears.**

   Zoom prompts you to edit the channel.

5. **Under Group Type, select the Private (Invited members only) checkbox.**

6. **Click on the blue Save Changes button.**

   Zoom removes the text (Public) to the right of the channel name in the sidebar.

Zoom lets you easily reverse this process as well. If you want to make a private channel public, follow the preceding steps and select Public in Step 5. Just because you can, though, doesn't mean that you should. Employees may have posted certain messages and files in a private channel with the understanding that others would not be able to view them. Making that channel public violates that compact.

WARNING

Tread lightly when converting private channels to public ones. Carelessly making this decision is bound to cause strife with its members.

Inviting other members to an existing private channel

You are discussing a potential acquisition with your four colleagues. It's very much under the radar. To this end, the five of you are using a private channel. A few of them recommend bringing your company's VP of Finance into the discussion.

Follow these steps to invite a new user into your existing private channel:

1. **Launch the Zoom desktop client.**

2. **At the top of the screen, click on Contacts.**

3. **In the sidebar, click on Channels.**

4. **Click on the name of the private channel to which you want to add members.**

5. **Click on the ellipsis icon and click on Invite Others from the menu that appears.**

6. **From the new window, select the people whom you want to invite.**

   Either type a few letters of their names in the search bar or select their names from the list.

7. **Click on the blue Invite button.**

Referencing channels in messages

While not a requirement, it's wise to reference public channels in your messages when appropriate. Referencing extraneous channels for the sake of doing so is bound to confuse people.

This practice offers a number of benefits. First, when others click on the channel in your message, Zoom takes them directly to that channel. Beyond that, it encourages others to join those public channels — something that they may have missed when they joined your organization.

Follow these steps to reference a public channel in an individual or group message:

1. **Launch the Zoom desktop client.**

2. **Create a new message for an individual, a group, or another channel.**

3. **Before you enter the name of the public channel, enter the # symbol.**

4. **Press the Enter key.**

For example, I reference the marketing message in my message to Hans Gruber, as Figure 6-3 displays.

FIGURE 6-3:
Zoom message referencing the public #Marketing channel.

Zoom does not let members reference private channels in this manner.

Starting quick channel meetings

Say that you're bandying ideas back and forth with some channel members via chat. At some point, Walter suggests actually discussing the matter and moving away from text-based chatting. In no time, Zoom lets you change the medium from text to a real-time audio or video call.

Follow these steps to start a quick video meeting with all channel members:

1. **Launch the Zoom desktop client.**

2. **At the top of the screen, click on Chat.**

3. **Click on the name of the channel with which you want to hold an audio or video meeting.**

4. **Click on the video camera icon in the main screen, as Figure 6-4 shows.**

    Zoom prompts you with a new window asking whether you want to invite all members to join.

FIGURE 6-4:
Video camera icon to hold a quick channel meeting.

5. **Click on the white Yes button.**

    Zoom attempts to notify all channel members of the impending call.

    Members who accept the invitation will join the channel video chat.

I'm hard-pressed to imagine a simpler way to elevate the discussion to a better medium.

Don't be afraid to move from text to a real-time meeting. If you haven't put your face on, just opt not to enable the video on Zoom calls.

Turning group chats into proper channels

By default, Zoom isn't terribly creative when it names a group chat. It just lumps the participants' names together.

Of course, assigning a more descriptive topic to a group chat is prudent. While you're at it, why not turn the informal group chat into a more formal channel? To do so, follow these steps:

1. **Launch the Zoom desktop client.**

2. **At the top of the screen, click on the Chat icon.**

3. **In the sidebar, click on the existing group chat.**

   Zoom highlights it in blue.

4. **Click on the drop-down arrow next to the group chat and choose Edit Chat from the menu that appears.**

   Zoom prompts you to enter a new topic.

5. **(Optional) Select the checkbox if you want new members to be able to see the group's message history.**

6. **Click on the blue Save Changes button.**

Posting messages in channels

The process for posting messages in channels is the same as sending messages to individuals and groups. The only difference is the audience for your messages. For more on this subject, see Chapter 5.

Searching specific channels

Say that I'm looking for the word feedback, but I'd like to search only a specific channel for that keyword. Follow these directions:

1. **Launch the Zoom desktop client.**

2. **Click on the search bar in the upper right-hand corner of the screen.**

3. **Type your keyword.**

   In this case, I type the word feedback.

   Zoom then displays a prompt underneath the search bar asking whether you want to restrict your search to messages or files.

TIP

   If you have previously highlighted a channel, the search defaults to that channel.

4. **If you want to search everything in Zoom, then ignore the prompt that appears and press the Enter key.**

   Zoom displays the results of your query.

5. **(Optional) If you want to restrict your results to a specific channel, select its name from the Search in: drop-down menu, as Figure 6-5 displays.**

FIGURE 6-5:
Zoom channel-
specific search
for the word
feedback.

GETTING STARTED WITH CHANNELS

In the course of writing and researching this book, I connected with plenty of Zoom employees — or Zoomies, as they call themselves. They couldn't have been more informative and helpful. *Zoom For Dummies* is richer for their contributions, such as this one.

I connected with them in Zoom, and we used channels to communicate. I asked one of them to provide some simple examples of channels that Zoom's clients typically create and use. Esther Yoon is Zoom's Product Marketing Lead for Room Solutions. She provided the following sage recommendations:

- **Topical-update channels:** These types of ongoing channels include public relations (PR) updates or company announcements.

- **Project-based channels:** Channels here involve discrete projects, such as a website relaunch, an enterprise-system upgrade, a marketing campaign, or the launch of a new internal tool — maybe even Zoom itself.

- **Team-based or functional channels:** Teams here include enterprise sales, PR, or product-marketing.

- **Open Q&A channels:** Useful channels in this vein often include #AskIT, #AskHR, #AskEngineering, and #AskSales.

Of course, these channels are just suggestions. You can create as many channels — and types of channels — as you like.

Comparing channels to similar Zoom features

Table 6-1 compares and contrasts some of the related Zoom features in this book.

TABLE 6-1   **Feature Comparison**

Feature	Type	Type of Plan	Description and General Uses
User groups	Administrative	Premium	Provide the ability to manage users and their settings en masse. Admins can save time by concurrently changing or locking the settings for multiple users.
IM groups	Administrative	Premium	Assign users under the organization's Zoom account to groups that automatically display within their directories.
Channels	Non-administrative	All	Start more formal and permanent conversations about particular topics.
Group chats	Non-administrative	All	Start informal, temporary, and possibly disposable conversations about particular topics.

TIP

If you are new to Meetings & Chat, then bookmark or highlight Table 6-1.

Refining your Zoom notifications

Basic Zoom notifications are indeed useful. (For more on this subject, see the section "Staying current with Zoom notifications" in Chapter 5.) In a way, though, they are a bit limited because of their global nature. That is, when users set them, Zoom applies their choices to all messages and/or mentions.

Many Zoom users don't realize that Meetings & Chat provides two additional ways to customize their alerts. These options allow you to stay informed without feeling overwhelmed.

Setting specific notifications for channels and group chats

As you use channels and group chats, you'll invariably find that some of them are busier, noisier, and more relevant than others. In this respect, they are just like people. For example, some channels may thrive with interesting activity and relevant content to your job or industry. You'll want to pay close attention to them. Others, though, may annoy you, although you don't want to leave them altogether.

Luckily, Meetings & Chat allows users to customize their notifications for individual channels and group chats. Doing so lets them strike a balance between staying informed and losing their sanity. Zoom accommodates that legitimate need. For example, what if you'd like to receive certain #Announcements notifications but different ones for #HappyHour?

Follow these steps to customize your notifications for a particular channel or group chat:

1. **Launch the Zoom desktop client.**

2. **At the top of the screen, click on Chat.**

3. **In the sidebar, click on the channel or group chat whose notifications you want to modify.**

   Zoom highlights it in blue.

4. **Click on the drop-down arrow next to the channel and choose Notifications from the menu that appears.**

5. **From the menu that appears, choose the notification options you want to enable.**

   Figure 6-6 displays your options.

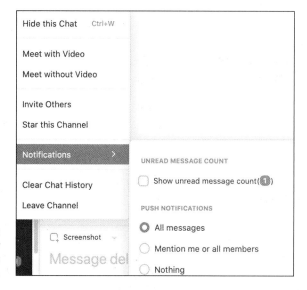

FIGURE 6-6:
Customizing your notifications for a specific channel.

- Enabling the **Show unread message count** option under the Unread Message Count header means that Zoom displays in red the number of new messages in the channel or group chat.

- The Push Notifications header contains three options:

  - **All messages:** Zoom alerts you to all messages posted in the channel or group chat.

  - **Mention me or all members:** Zoom notifies you when someone tags you with the @ symbol or uses @all. (See Chapter 5 for more on this subject.)

  - **Nothing:** Clicking here means that you're muting the channel or group chat.

Quickly setting your notifications for all channels and group chats

If you belong to — and participate in — multiple channels, then individually tweaking their notification settings can become a bit time-consuming. Fortunately, Meetings & Chat provides users with a single place to change all channel and group-chat settings. Follow these directions:

1. **Launch the Zoom desktop client.**

2. **At the top of the screen, click on your profile image and choose Settings from the menu that appears.**

3. **On the left-hand side of the screen, click on Chat.**

4. **(Optional) Under Push Notifications, select the With exception for checkbox and click on the Channels button.**

   Meetings & Chat displays a new window allowing you to customize your alerts from your essential channels and group chats. See Figure 6-7.

   Note that Zoom intelligently places starred channels and group chats at the top of the screen. The rest appear in alphabetical order.

5. **Customize each channel's and group chat's notifications by selecting the appropriate checkboxes.**

   You have three options:

   - **All messages:** Zoom notifies you of all new messages, whether they mention you directly or not. (This option is the most inclusive.)

   - **Only private messages or mentions:** Think of this option as a middle ground. If someone references you in a message, then Zoom notifies you.

   - **Nothing:** This option represents the equivalent of muting the channel or group chat.

6. **Click on the blue Save button.**

7. **Close the Settings by clicking on the red circle in the upper left-hand corner of the screen.**

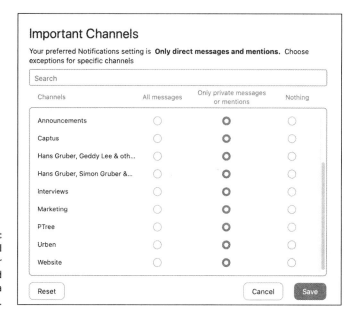

FIGURE 6-7:
Customizing all
notifications for
all channels and
group chats in a
single screen.

TIP

Say that you want to restore your notification settings to their default values. Just click on the white Reset in the bottom left-hand corner of Figure 6-7.

Setting keyword-specific notifications

Setting channel-specific notifications can keep you informed of key activity that takes place within them. Still, as the following example illustrates, plenty of scenarios exist in which they may not be optimal or even practical.

Benicio is the head of marketing at Kobayashi Porcelain. As such, he belongs to several public channels. Kobayashi has released some new mugs, but rumor has it that they are not terribly durable. Benicio is particularly concerned about a blow-back on social media sites, such as Facebook and Twitter. He doesn't want to constantly check all of his public channels for the word "fail." In other words, he'd like Zoom to notify him when a colleague mentions that word in any of the public channels to which he belongs. Meetings & Chat lets him do just that.

To enable keyword-specific notifications, follow these steps.

1. **Launch the Zoom desktop client.**

2. **At the top of the screen, click on your profile image and choose Settings from the menu that appears.**

3. **On the left-hand side of the screen, click on Chat.**

4. **(Optional) Under Receive notifications for, click on the Keywords button.**

5. **Enter the keyword(s) for which you want Zoom to send you alerts.**

   Select more than one keyword by separating them with commas.

6. **Click on the Done button.**

   Now, when someone uses one of your keywords in a public channel, Zoom displays a numeric red badge to its immediate right.

REMEMBER

Keyword-specific alerts work only for public channels and private channels to which you already belong. That is, say that members in your organization use a private channel of which you are not a part. When they use your predefined keywords, Meetings & Chat doesn't notify you.

TIP

Mess around with channel- and chat-specific notifications until you find a system that works for you. Meetings & Chat is very flexible in this regard.

Sharing code snippets

Software engineers are fond of *snippets,* a term that connotes a relatively small region of reusable code. As such, it should be not a surprise that Zoom allows you to create and share them with others individually, in group chats, and even in channels.

You don't need be a proper programmer, though, to benefit from snippets. Web designers, business analysts, and other folks who occasionally dabble in code also tend to find them useful. An example will help illustrate my point.

Amy is the head of marketing at Hudsucker Industries. She sometimes wants to make small changes to her company's website. In the past, she has followed this process:

>> She generates some simple Hypertext Markup Language (HTML).

>> She copies and pastes it into a Word document.

>> She emails it as an attachment to her web developer, Norville.

>> He receives the email, downloads the attachment, copies the new code, and then inserts the updated code into the website.

Amy and Norville can certainly continue to follow this process. A more efficient way, however, involves using snippets.

Enabling snippets

Before you can create a snippet, you have to enable it in the Meetings & Chat user interface or UI. Follow these instructions to perform this one-time task:

1. **Launch the Zoom desktop client and click on the Home icon at the top of the screen.**

2. **Click on the Settings icon underneath your profile picture.**

   Zoom launches its Settings screen.

3. **On the left-hand side of the screen, click on Chat.**

4. **Under Chat Settings, select the Show Code Snippet button checkbox.**

5. **Close the screen and return to your meeting by clicking on the red circle in the top left-hand corner of the screen.**

   Zoom displays a new ‹/› Code icon in the message pane, as Figure 6-8 displays.

FIGURE 6-8:
Zoom new snippet icon.

REMEMBER

You need to follow this process only once. After completing it, you can add snippets as often as you like, whenever and wherever you like.

Creating a snippet

I'm a fan of the programming language Python, although I'm hardly an expert at it. Sometimes I write code for fun and to keep my axe sharp. (If you haven't figured it out by now, I'm a bit of a geek.) If I find myself stuck on a Python script, I can create a snippet and share it with my Zoom contacts who know the programming language better than I do. To create a snippet, follow these steps:

1. **Launch the Zoom desktop client.**

2. **At the top of the screen, click on Chat.**

3. **Click on the name of the contact with whom you want to share a snippet.**

4. **In the message pane, click on the </> Code icon above the area in which you'd normally enter text for a message.**

Zoom launches the Create Code Snippet window.

5. **(Optional) In the Title box just underneath Create Code Snippet, give your snippet a descriptive name.**

6. **(Optional) To the right of the Title box, choose the specific programming language from the drop-down list.**

You can also just leave the default language of Text, if you like.

7. **Type or paste your software code into the main box, as Figure 6-9 displays.**

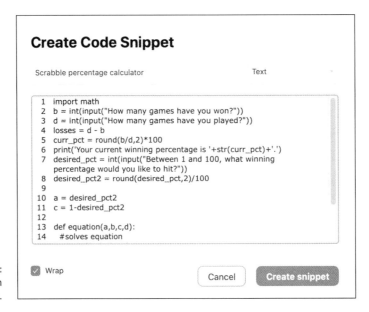

Create Code Snippet

Scrabble percentage calculator   Text

```
 1  import math
 2  b = int(input("How many games have you won?"))
 3  d = int(input("How many games have you played?"))
 4  losses = d - b
 5  curr_pct = round(b/d,2)*100
 6  print('Your current winning percentage is '+str(curr_pct)+'.')
 7  desired_pct = int(input("Between 1 and 100, what winning
    percentage would you like to hit?"))
 8  desired_pct2 = round(desired_pct,2)/100
 9
10  a = desired_pct2
11  c = 1-desired_pct2
12
13  def equation(a,b,c,d):
14      #solves equation
```

☑ Wrap   Cancel   **Create snippet**

FIGURE 6-9: Creating a Zoom snippet.

8. **(Optional) Select the Wrap checkbox if you'd like to — wait for it — wrap your text.**

9. **Click on the blue Create snippet button.**

Zoom posts the snippet where you decided, as Figure 6-10 shows.

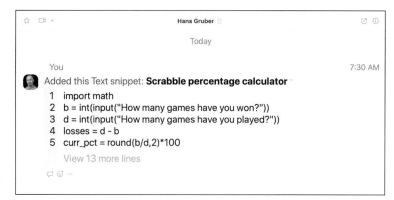

FIGURE 6-10:
Completed Zoom
snippet sent to
contact.

Running Reports in Zoom

Say that you are an inquisitive, data-driven person. As such, you may be scratching your head at this point. After all, Meetings & Chat can store a tremendous amount of valuable data. You may want to ask insightful and analytical questions. Specific queries may include

>> Which employees at our company are using Meetings & Chat the most?

>> What about Zoom Phone and Video Webinars?

>> How does Meetings & Chat usage vary by department?

>> What are the most popular days and times of the week for meetings?

>> On which devices do employees most frequently use Meetings & Chat?

>> Which employees aren't using Zoom much or even at all?

As it turns out, customers on premium plans can answer these questions in spades — and many more. Zoom provides a robust set of reports, graphs, and easily exportable data for additional analysis. Trust me: I could expand this chapter into a separate 200-page book.

Suffice it to say that Zoom offers users a bevy of different reports. That's not to say, however, that you'll be able to view absolutely everything that takes place in Zoom from all users in perpetuity. At a general level, users' reporting capabilities hinge upon the following restrictions:

>> The individual's formal Zoom role. (See Chapter 3 for more on this subject.)

>> The Zoom plan and add-ons to which the organization subscribes.

>> The number of users in her organization's Zoom account.

>> The specific reports and features that her account owners and administrators have locked down.

>> Her organization's data-retention policies.

Reviewing Zoom's role-based reporting

At a high level, Zoom grants account owners and admins greater reporting access than it does to regular members. No shocker here.

Account owners

Zoom account owners tend to look at things through an organization-wide perspective. That is, they're not just concerned about what Zoom-related actions they, as individuals, are performing. Along these lines, by default account owners and admins can access two different report buckets:

>> **Usage reports:** These reports display data on the Zoom services that account members have used.

>> **User-activity reports:** These logs typically provide audit trails in the event that the organization needs to investigate a security event.

To view these buckets, account owners should do as follows:

1. **In the Zoom web portal, under the Admin header, click on Account Management.**

2. **Click on Reports.**

   Zoom takes account owners and admins to the main reporting page. Figure 6-11 displays a partial view of this screen.

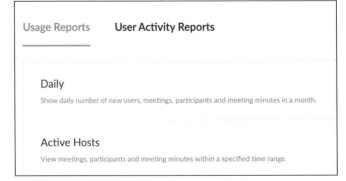

Usage Reports   **User Activity Reports**

Daily
Show daily number of new users, meetings, participants and meeting minutes in a month.

Active Hosts
View meetings, participants and meeting minutes within a specified time range.

FIGURE 6-11:
Partial view of
Zoom admin and
account report
main screen.

Table 6-2 explains the first bucket of reports.

TABLE 6-2 ## Bucket 1: Usage Reports

Sub-category	Description
Daily	Displays daily number of new users, meetings, participants, and total meeting minutes per month.
Active Hosts	Displays meetings, participants, and meeting minutes within a user-defined time range.
Inactive Hosts	Displays inactive users during a specific period.
Upcoming Events	Displays information on upcoming meetings and webinars.
Meeting	Displays registration and poll reports for meetings.
Cloud Recording	Displays detailed information about calls that users have recorded to the cloud.
Phone System	Displays users' activity on Zoom Phone for specific time periods. Note that you can view this option only if your organization subscribes to Zoom Phone, covered in Chapter 11.
Remote Support	Displays users' in-meeting support sessions during certain time periods.

Note that Table 6-2 excludes the option for running webinar reports. Expect to see it, though, if your organization subscribes to Zoom Video Webinars.

Table 6-3 shows the types of user activity reports that account owners can run.

TABLE 6-3 ## Bucket 2: User-Activity Reports

Sub-category	Description
Operation Logs	View account activity, including adding and deleting different types of groups, adding new users, changing passwords, and much more.
Sign In/Sign Out	Determine when different users logged in and out of Zoom, along with their Internet Protocol (IP) addresses.
Phone System Operation Logs	View data about the phone-related actions that admins have taken. (Chapter 11 goes much deeper into Zoom Phone.)

Zoom owners can access these report buckets by following these steps:

1. **In the Zoom web portal, under the Admin header, click on Account Management.**

2. **Click on Reports.**

   Zoom displays two tabs: Usage Reports and User-Activity Reports.

Refer to Tables 6-1 and 6-2 for more information on your specific report choices here.

3. **To view the specific reports available to you, click on one of the selections.**

For example, I selected the Active Hosts report under the Usage Reports heading. By default, Zoom displays activity only during the past two days, as Figure 6-12 shows.

FIGURE 6-12:
Zoom daily usage report.

For how to run a report, see the section "Running a simple report," later in this chapter.

TIP

Admins for Zoom customers on Business and Education plans can access a separate reporting dashboard. Visit `bit.ly/zfd-dash` to learn more about this topic.

Note that certain Zoom reports contain graphs and/or charts to go along with the raw data. For example, as Figure 6-13 shows, the Daily Usage Report provides these simple bar charts at the bottom.

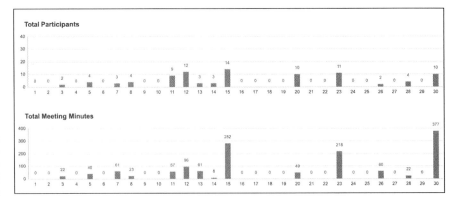

FIGURE 6-13:
Zoom participants-usage reports for April 2020.

Members

Zoom restricts the types of reports that members can run. Still, they can access limited information on their activity, as Table 6-4 shows.

TABLE 6-4   ### Types of Member Reports

Name	Description
Usage	Members can view a list of meetings, participants, and meeting minutes for meetings that they have hosted.
Meeting	Members can create meeting-specific registration reports and poll reports.
Webinar	Members can run reports based upon webinar registration, attendees, performance, Q&A, and polls. (Chapter 8 covers Zoom Video Webinars in depth.)

Account admins

To be sure, Zoom grants account admins greater reporting access than regular members. At the same time, though, admins' reporting powers fall short of those of full account owners. While understandable, this restriction can be problematic.

Say that your job requires you to analyze data on how members in your organization communicate. Unfortunately, your current admin role makes this impossible. You find yourself constantly asking Mark — the Zoom account owner — to run reports for you and send you the results. Importantly, Mark doesn't want to promote you to the role of owner.

What to do?

Fortunately, Zoom allows account owners to create new roles and assign them. In this case, a Reporting Analyst role would enhance your default your reporting capability to include ones that you currently cannot access. For more information on this subject, see Chapter 3.

TIP

To watch a quick video of how I did this very thing, visit bit.ly/zfd-newrole.

Running a simple report

To run a simple report, follow these steps:

1. **In the Zoom web portal, under the Admin header, click on Account Management.**

2. **Click on Reports.**

3. **Click on the type of report that you want to run.**

Again, Zoom's default categories are Usage and Meetings.

4. **Click on either one.**

Note that only account owners can view User Activity Reports.

Depending on the report that you select in the previous step, Zoom may display a blue Search button that allows you to restrict your results to a specified date range, specific users, and more.

I return to this subject in the section "Selecting a date range," later in this chapter.

Figure 6-14 displays the results of this simple usage report.

FIGURE 6-14: Zoom simple member-usage report.

Much like Zoom search (covered in Chapter 5), your report may fail to show data for any number of reasons. Examples here run the gamut. Perhaps your criteria are too restrictive or have no data for Zoom to display. Alternatively, your Upcoming Events report comes up blank because no one has scheduled any meetings or webinars. (Chapter 8 covers webinars.)

REMEMBER

Users cannot access reports in the Zoom desktop client. They have to use the Zoom web portal.

Customizing your reports

Regardless of your role, Zoom provides a few useful ways to customize your reports.

Selecting a date range

In the abstract, reports are certainly useful. Those that provide too little or too much information, however, often cause more problems than they solve. It's usually helpful to restrict reports to a certain period of time. Doing so allows you to answer questions such as

>> What were users doing last January?

>> After our company's TV commercial ran, how many calls did our call-center reps receive?

>> And how long was the average call?

To tweak your report's date range, follow these steps:

1. **Log in to the Zoom web portal and run a Zoom report.**

   If you're unsure how to run a report, see the section "Running a simple report," earlier in this chapter.

TIP

   Note that Zoom's different reports provide different options. That is, there's no one-size-fits all approach to running reports. Visit bit.ly/zfd-rpts to watch a quick video of me running a few reports.

2. **(Optional) At the top of the report, select your desired date range.**

   Depending on the specific report that you're trying to run, you may be able to filter dates by

   - A specific month

   - A specific date range

3. **(Optional) Click on the blue Search button.**

   Zoom displays the results — if any — that meet your new date criteria.

TIP

Some Zoom reports default to the current month's activity. To state the obvious, if you want to go back in time, just select a new month from the drop-down menu.

WARNING

Zoom currently restricts date ranges for some reports to 30 days. In these cases, say that you want 60 days' worth of data. You will have to run the report twice — once for each 30-day period. You'll then have to stitch them together. (For more on this subject, see the section "Exporting raw report data," later in this chapter.)

Toggling columns

By default, many Zoom reports include a host of different fields, some of which might not matter to you. For example, employees in your organization may not include their department in their profile, so why display it in the report? Alternatively, you may not use Zoom Rooms, the subject of Chapter 10.

To hide fields from your report, follow these directions:

1. **Log in to the Zoom web portal and run a Zoom report.**

   If you're unsure how to run a report, see the section "Running a simple report," earlier in this chapter.

2. **To the right of the report, click on the Toggle columns link.**

3. **In the menu that appears, uncheck the box to the left of the field that you want to hide.**

   Zoom immediately removes those fields from your report.

Exporting raw report data

Some folks may find Zoom's standard reports a bit wanting. Sure, they present information in a simple way, but what if you want to do more with that data? Like me, you may prefer to analyze your data in Tableau (my personal favorite), Microsoft PowerBI, Microsoft Excel or Access, Google Sheets, or another data-analysis tool. Those applications let users slice and dice their data and, even better, create interactive visualizations.

To export report data to a comma-separated value or CSV file, follow these steps:

1. **Log in to the Zoom web portal and run a report.**

   For a refresher on how to run a report, see the section "Running a simple report," earlier in this chapter.

2. **Click on Export as CSV File link.**

   Zoom alerts you that the download will start automatically when ready. Depending on the size of your dataset, Zoom may need a few minutes to generate the report and the download file.

3. **From the prompt, decide where on your computer you want to save the file and click on the Save button.**

4. **(Optional) Open the file in another program and go nuts.**

TIP

All mainstream reporting and analysis programs allow you to easily import data from CSVs for additional analysis.

Chapter 8 covers this topic in the context of webinars.

Chapter **7**

Enhancing Zoom with Third-Party Apps

Z oom's suite of tools isn't exactly wanting for features. In other words, its out-of-the-box functionality by itself helps hundreds of millions of people communicate and collaborate better. Through videoconferences, audio and video calls, webinars, text messages, and more, Zoom consistently rises to the challenge.

Despite the power and utility of Zoom's features, a little reality check is in order: Zoom won't eliminate your need to use other critical applications. For example, even if you go all-in on the Zoom suite, don't expect to abandon your current email and calendar programs anytime soon. You will still work with G Suite, Microsoft Office, and productivity tchotchkes. Ditto for collaboration suites as Slack and Microsoft Teams and file-sharing services, such as Google Drive, Box, and more.

Then why bother with Zoom? What if the very thought of adding another productivity application to the fray makes you dizzy? After all, you're probably not keen on complicating your work life and multitasking even more. Fair enough.

Fortunately, there's a simple way to integrate Zoom's services with your email, calendar, and other essential programs. Brass tacks: By supercharging Zoom, you can have your cake and eat it, too.

This chapter introduces third-party apps. At a high level, they can save users time and make their work lives easier and less chaotic. Apps tightly integrate with a growing number of mainstream programs, web services, and even some enterprise systems. Put differently, say that Zoom's native features already impress you. You ain't seen nothin' yet.

Understanding the Rationale behind Third-Party Apps

I'm willing to wager that you own a smartphone — and have for years. I'll also bet that you regularly use several apps on that iOS or Android device. Perhaps you enjoy playing games, sharing photos via Instagram, sending messages via Snapchat, listening to music on Spotify, or watching videos on YouTube and Netflix. In some cases, you can perform the same task on your phone without one of these apps, but the app improves the experience and saves you time.

The same rationale applies to Zoom's third-party apps. Like your smartphone, you can certainly get a great deal of mileage out of Zoom's services by themselves. That is, installing apps isn't mandatory. If you neglect to use them, Zoom won't send a bunch of hired goons to your home or workplace.

Benefits of using third-party apps

Make no mistake, though: Apps are useful in a number of important ways. First, they extend the power of Zoom's services. Second, they can save you and your colleagues a great deal of time. The following example illustrates my point.

Say that you work at Wernham Hogg Paper Merchants in Slough, a large town in Berkshire, England. (Yes, I'm a big fan of the English version of *The Office*.) You and your colleagues record all Zoom client meetings. Someone then manually uploads those recordings and their transcripts to Google Drive, Wernham Hogg's file-storage tool of choice. You then manually delete these recordings from your Zoom account to keep within your plan's storage limit. The process is a bit manual for your liking, and you wish that you could automate it.

Fortunately, you can.

The slpain.io Google Drive for Zoom app automates this entire process. That is, it automatically transfers your Zoom video recordings and their transcriptions to

Google Drive. It then deletes Wernham Hogg's Zoom recordings. (For more information on that particular app, see `bit.ly/slpain-Zoom`.)

To paraphrase Larry David on *Curb Your Enthusiasm,* pretty, pretty, pretty good.

Why Zoom relies upon external developers

You may wonder why Zoom —a $60-billion company as of this writing— relies upon third-party software developers to build timesaving apps.

It's a fair question.

Although Zoom employs plenty of smart cookies, it can't possibly address every one of its customers' needs. Zoom clients are anything but monolithic. For example, the specific communication needs of a large government agency don't overlap all that much with those of an eight-employee Pilates studio. Ditto for a university with 50,000 students and an independent consultant.

What to do?

In a nutshell, look outside for help.

Lest you think that Zoom management is lazy for outsourcing its app development, I'll disabuse you of that notion right now.

Like most successful software vendors these days, Zoom's top brass understands the importance of building a vibrant ecosystem of external software developers. Microsoft, Amazon, Slack, Twitter, Facebook, Salesforce, Apple, and scores of other companies harness the engineering talents of coders all over the world. These companies all encourage third-party developers to create their own apps.

In Zoom's case, the company wants developers to build bridges that link Zoom to other services, such as the ones that I mention in this chapter. How? The nearby sidebar details the three main types of tools that developers use.

REMEMBER

Don't confuse Zoom's third-party apps with the Zoom's tablet and smartphone apps. You cannot install, much less use, Zoom's proper Outlook and Gmail apps on your computer without having first downloaded and installed the Zoom desktop client. (See Chapter 3 for more on that subject.)

REMEMBER

At the risk of confusing you, many web browsers offer Zoom *extensions.* Think of these items as diluted apps. That is, they let users perform a limited number of related tasks directly within Chrome, Firefox, Safari, or another browser.

THOMAS CARLYLE AND ZOOM

British philosopher and writer Thomas Carlyle once famously said, "Man is a tool using animal. Without tools he is nothing, with tools he is all."

Trust me: He wasn't talking about Zoom. Carlyle died in 1881, but his words are no less relevant today than they were over a century ago.

Zoom provides external developers with the following software-development tools:

- **Application programming interfaces (APIs):** An API acts as a sort of a software intermediary that allows two applications to talk to each other. Zoom's API serves as a primary access point for interactions with third-party apps.

- **Webhooks:** Webhooks are automated messages sent from apps when events take place. At a high level, Zoom embraces them to do a number of really cool things under the hood.

- **Software development kits (SDKs):** At their core, SDKs allow developers to easily create powerful new applications. In the case of Zoom, its SDK lets coders embed Zoom directly into iOS, Android, MacOS, iPadOS, and Windows apps.

With these tools, and developers can go nuts. That is, they build interesting and innovative bridges between Zoom and other applications and web services.

Introducing the Zoom App Marketplace

With all of these developers building cool apps Zoom, where does one go to find them? Look no further than the Zoom App Marketplace. To access it, follow these directions:

1. **In the Zoom web portal, hover over Solutions in the top left-hand corner of the page.**

2. **From the menu that appears, choose App Marketplace.**

Zoom takes you to `marketplace.zoom.us`, displayed in Figure 7-1.

As of this writing, Zoom sports more than 200 different third–party apps. This number will only increase in the future as Zoom becomes more popular and attracts ambitious developers.

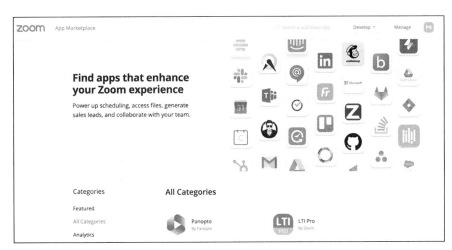

FIGURE 7-1:
Zoom App
Marketplace.

This variety is a bit of a double-edged sword. On one hand and at the risk of getting all existential, personal choice is objectively a good thing. Say that you can easily install a Zoom app for Microsoft Outlook. Great, but you're a longtime Gmail user. Would you change your email service to accommodate Zoom? I doubt it.

On the other hand, though, human beings struggle when faced with too many choices — and oodles of research supports this claim. (For more on this topic, see Barry Schwartz's 2004 book *The Paradox of Choice: Why More Is Less* [Ecco].)

Zoom squares this circle by offering two different, familiar ways to locate useful apps: searching and browsing.

Searching for a specific Zoom app

Say that you know exactly which Zoom app you want. Follow these directions to locate it:

1. **Go to the Zoom App Marketplace.**

2. **Click on the search bar at the top of the page.**

3. **Type the name of the app that you want to install.**

4. **Press the Enter key.**

   Zoom displays the results.

I cover how to install your desired app in the upcoming section "Installing a Zoom app."

Browsing for Zoom apps

In Zoom as well as in life, sometimes people don't know what they want. For example, say that you go to a bookstore and start gandering at the new nonfiction titles. You wander around and ultimately buy a classic tale of fiction. Bookstores encourage browsing, and the Zoom App Marketplace does, too.

To poke around for interesting apps, follow these steps:

1. **Go to the Zoom App Marketplace.**

2. **Scroll down to the different categories on the bottom of the page and click on the name of the category that you want to explore.**

    Examples here run the gamut: education, finance, healthcare, productivity, and many more.

    TIP

    It's not uncommon to find a specific app in more than one category. After all, an app can fall into more than one bucket. Case in point: An app can qualify as both healthcare- and productivity-related.

    Zoom displays the apps that fall into your selected category.

3. **(Optional) Under the Works with header, filter apps by the type of Zoom offering.**

    REMEMBER

    Zoom's different offerings do different things. What's more, your organization may subscribe to only some of them. For example, your organization may subscribe to both Meetings & Chat and Zoom Phones. As a result, you may want to exclude apps for Zoom Rooms from your browsing.

    By default, Zoom displays apps that work with all of its offerings. To filter, select one or more of the checkboxes:

    -   Zoom Meetings

    -   Zoom Webinars

    -   Zoom Rooms

    -   Zoom Phone

    -   Zoom Chat

4. **(Optional) Filter apps by permission granted.**

    As covered in Chapter 3, Zoom allows customers on premium plans to take advantage of user roles. To this end, a Zoom admin may have already locked down your app-installation permissions. Your choices here include

    -   **Pre-approved only:** An admin has explicitly allowed or whitelisted all members to install these apps.

- **Admin Installable:** Only admins can install these apps.

- **Member Installable:** Only members can install these apps.

TIP

The more checkboxes you select in Steps 3 and 4, the more Zoom restricts your search results. Depending on the specificity of your browsing needs, these restrictions may help or hinder your efforts.

5. **Click on the name of the app that you'd like to install.**

REMEMBER

There's no one right way to find an app.

Managing Your Zoom Apps

Browse the App Marketplace until your heart's content. Eventually, though, you'll want to install one. To this end, it's important to note a few things from the get-go.

First, Zoom offers premium customers tremendous flexibility around apps and roles. (For more on the latter topic, see Chapter 3.) To keep this book at a reasonable length and cost, I simply cannot cover all of Zoom's different options regarding user roles, security, and app configuration. Instead, I focus on the most important ones.

Second, there's no one single, universal app-installation process. At a high level, apps do different things and often require different authentications. For example, say that you want to install the Zoom Microsoft Outlook app — as millions of people have no doubt done. (See `bit.ly/zfd-out`.) In this case, you have to explicitly grant Zoom and Microsoft access to share some of your account data. Figure 7-2 displays the message that you see when you attempt to install this particular app.

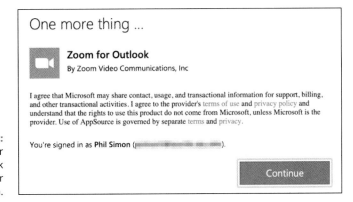

FIGURE 7-2:
Zoom for Microsoft Outlook request for user permission.

Third, depending on your Zoom role, you may not be able to install a specific app — or any apps, for that matter. It's entirely possible that an account owner or admin has prohibited Zoom users in her organization from installing apps.

Installing a Zoom app

Follow these general steps to install a third-party app:

1. **Locate the app that you want to install in the Zoom App Marketplace.**

In this example, I'm going to install the Zoom Gmail app.

2. **Click on the app icon to go to its main page.**

The exact web page and URL hinges upon the app that you want to install, but it should look something like Figure 7-3.

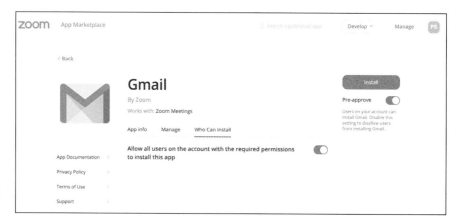

FIGURE 7-3:
Zoom home page
for the Gmail app.

3. **(Optional) Underneath the Install button, click on the Pre-approve toggle button.**

By doing this step, you're effectively permitting others in your organization to install this app. Depending on the rules that admins in your organization have established around your role, you may not be able to perform this step.

4. **Click on the blue Install button in the upper right-hand corner of the page.**

Note that some apps may require you to have previously set up an existing account using the same email address as the one that you used to set up your Zoom account. This restriction may complicate your attempt to install an app.

WARNING

Say that you're unable to click on this button. It's possible that someone in your organization has explicitly forbade members from installing it. Check with your IT department or the Zoom admin.

5. **(Optional) If necessary, click on the blue Authorize button.**

    Depending on the app that you're trying to install, Zoom may display a message requiring you to verify that you are granting the app permission to access your Zoom account. (For more on this topic, see Figure 7-2.)

    Zoom sends you an email confirming that you have successfully installed the app similar to the one in Figure 7-4.

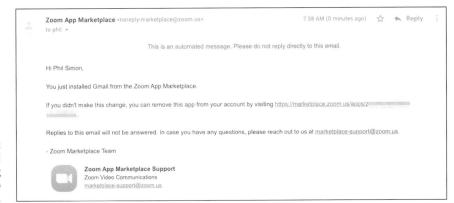

FIGURE 7-4:
Zoom email
confirming
successful app
installation.

A third-party app may occasionally notify you via the Zoom desktop client. For example, I am a fan of the project-management app Trello. After installing it, Trello's bot sent me a message letting me know that I could interact with it if I liked. Figure 7-5 displays its welcome message.

For more information on managing text messages, see Chapter 5.

Uninstalling a Zoom app

You may find that an app sounded better in theory than in practice. As such, you decide that you no longer need it. Once again, there's no one single, universal app-removal process.

To remove an app from Meetings & Chat, follow these general directions:

1. **Locate the app that you want to remove in the Zoom App Marketplace.**

2. **Click on the app to go to its main page.**

3. **Click on the Manage tab.**

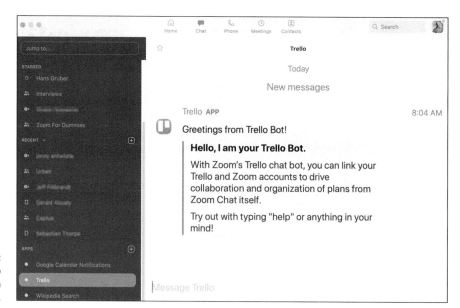

FIGURE 7-5:
Zoom in-app
message from
the Trello app.

4. **Click on the white Uninstall button underneath the Manage tab.**

5. **(Optional) If Zoom requests your feedback about why you're breaking up with the app, click on whatever reason you want.**

   You may also be able to provide app developers with feedback.

6. **Click on the white Uninstall button.**

   Zoom displays a new window to confirm that you want to uninstall the app.

7. **Click on the blue Uninstall button.**

8. Zoom sends you an email confirming the breakup (see Figure 7-6).

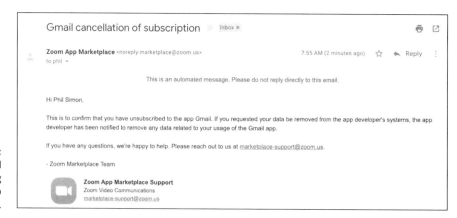

FIGURE 7-6:
Zoom email
confirming
successful app
removal.

Viewing your organization's installed apps

Account admins and owners can view all the apps available to employees in their organization by following these directions:

1. **Go to the Zoom App Marketplace and sign in.**

2. **Click on the Manage button in the top right-hand corner.**

   Zoom takes you to a new web page.

3. **Under My Dashboard, click on Installed Apps.**

   Zoom presents a list of the apps that users in the organization have installed, including valuable app metadata. It looks like Figure 7-7.

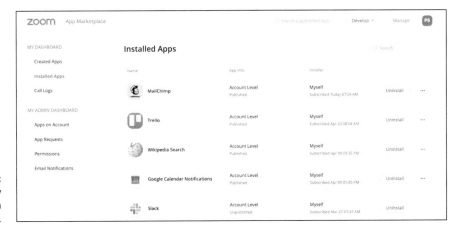

FIGURE 7-7:
Currently installed Zoom apps.

Restricting apps in Meetings & Chat

By default, Zoom allows all members in your account to access installed apps during text-based chats, the subject of Chapter 5. If you like, you can restrict users from using specific apps in Meetings & Chat by instant message (IM) group — a topic covered in Chapter 3.

For example, say that your company uses Vimeo to post corporate marketing videos. It wants only certain employees to see notifications on these videos and comment on them in Meetings & Chat.

To do restrict the app to a IM group in Meetings & Chat, follow these instructions:

1. **Go to the Zoom App Marketplace and sign in.**
2. **Click on the Manage button in the top right-hand corner.**
3. **Under My Dashboard, click on Installed Apps.**

    You are now at https://marketplace.zoom.us/user/installed.

4. **Click on the ellipsis icon to the right of the app that you want to restrict.**
5. **From the drop-down menu, choose Set Chat Visibility.**
6. **Slide the toggle button to the left.**
7. **Type the name of the IM group to which you want to restrict the app in Meetings & Chat.**
8. **Click on the blue Add button.**
9. **Click on the blue Save button.**

    Zoom confirms that it has saved your settings.

REMEMBER

By going this route, a member will need to belong to the IM group for which you have approved the app. For example, say that I had restricted the Wikipedia app to only the Management IM group. Unless company president Donna is a member of that IM group, she won't be able to install it.

Limiting apps that members can install

Zoom's account owners and admins, by virtue of their default roles, are able to install and uninstall apps at their discretion. Organizations on premium Zoom plans, however, can enable user roles and limit what regular members can do in a number of important ways.

Pre-approving specific apps

Say that you want to explicitly allow employees at your firm to install a particular app. That is, you want to create an app whitelist. For example, you run the Bluth Company. Its employees are avid Slack fans. As such, you want to let them start Zoom meetings with a single mouse click in Slack. As long as you are a Zoom admin or owner, you can perform this task by following these directions:

1. **Sign in to the Zoom App Marketplace.**
2. **Locate the app that you want to let other members install and click on its icon.**

3. **(Optional) In the top right-hand corner of the page, slide the Pre-approve toggle button to the right so that it turns blue.**

   After a few seconds, Zoom displays a new toggle button that reads as follows: Allow all users on the account with the required permissions to install this app. Selecting this option means that all users under your firm's Zoom account are able to install this app.

4. **(Optional) If you want to restrict the app to a subset of Zoom account users, click on the Who Can Install tab on the app's web page.**

5. **To the right of Allow all users on the account with the required permissions to install this app, slide the toggle button so that it turns gray.**

   Zoom allows you to limit the app to

   - **Individual users:** Enter the email address(es) of the person(s) who will be able to install the app.

   - **User groups:** Enter the user group(s) whose members will be able to install the app. (See Chapter 3 for more on user groups.)

   If you change your mind, then you can simply click on the trash can icon next to one of these new restrictions.

6. **Click on the blue Add button.**

Others in your organization can now download and install a specific Zoom app.

REMEMBER

With many apps, a little reciprocity lets you get the most out of them. For example, to make my life as easy as possible, I install the Slack app for Zoom as well as Zoom app for Slack.

Viewing which members have already installed a specific app

Perhaps you're curious about which members in your organization have installed a specific Zoom app. You can send a mass email or conduct a poll, but Zoom makes this process a cinch:

1. **Sign in to the Zoom App Marketplace.**

2. **Locate the app that you want to investigate and click on its icon.**

   Zoom takes you to that app's home page in its App Marketplace.

3. **Click on the Manage tab.**

   Zoom displays the users — if any — who have installed the app.

Requesting approval to install a specific app

Say your employer subscribes to a premium Zoom plan. Unfortunately, however, you're not an account owner or admin. Normally, this state of affairs doesn't bother you. One day, though, you find an app that you'd like to install, such as the email marketing tool MailChimp. There's just one problem: An owner or admin hasn't placed MailChimp on the organization's whitelist.

What to do?

Regular members can certainly send their managers emails or quick messages in Meetings & Chat. They can kick and scream as well, but Zoom has made it remarkably simple for members to request permission to install a currently unapproved app by following these instructions:

1. **Sign in to the Zoom App Marketplace.**

2. **Locate the app that you to install and click on its icon.**

   Zoom takes you to that app's home page in its App Marketplace.

3. **In the upper right-hand corner, click on the blue Request pre-approve button.**

   Zoom lets you know it has sent your installation request to your account admin. It then rattles off an email to the account owner advising him or her of the employee's request.

At this point, the account owner can add the app to the organization's whitelist by following the directions in the "Pre-approving specific apps" section earlier in this chapter.

TIP

For much more information on how admins and owners can customize and lock down Zoom apps for your organization's members, go to bit.ly/zfd-app.

Recommending a Few Useful Zoom Apps

In addition to the valuable Zoom apps I mention throughout this chapter, Table 7-1 displays some more, with a specific focus on Meetings & Chat. That is, I have intentionally omitted apps for Zoom's other three core offerings. Don't let Table 7-1 stop you, though. If you want to find dedicated apps for Zoom Video Webinars, Zoom Rooms, and/or Zoom Phone in the very same Zoom App Marketplace, knock yourself out.

TABLE 7-1   Popular Zoom Apps

Name	Useful App Features
Epic	COVID-19 brought the idea behind telehealth to the front lines. Epic lets providers and patients launch Zoom meetings from their Epic online health appointments.
Github	Developers are particularly fond of this robust code repository. The Zoom Github app sends them different types of notifications via Zoom Meetings & Chat.
Google Calendar	This app makes scheduling, joining, and managing Zoom meetings a breeze.
Microsoft Teams	This app lets users start, schedule, and participate in Zoom meetings right from a Team space.
Otter.ai	Otter.ai integrates with Zoom and provides both interactive, real-time, and post-meeting transcripts. Participants can view, highlight, comment, and add photos. They can also share meeting notes.
Salesforce	The world's largest vendor of customer-relationship management (CRM) software tightly integrates with Zoom. Salesforce lets its own customers easily hold Zoom calls and even webinars with only a few clicks.
Slack	The Slack app lets you make Zoom calls directly from the world's most powerful and user-friendly collaboration tool.
Zapier	Zapier's Zoom app lets you connect a number of different apps and automate manual actions in more ways that I can possibly describe here. Scheduling tool YouCanBook.me is one of go-to apps.
Zendesk	The gold standard for customer-service software also plays nicely with Zoom Meetings & Chat. After installing it, reps can receive and view notifications related to their support tickets.
Zoom for Doodle	Doodle is a simple tool that makes scheduling meetings for users on different calendar systems a piece of cake. I've used it for years — long before I started Zooming.
Zylo	As I describe in Chapter 6, Zoom's native reports are pretty straightforward. Zylo provides a far greater level of sophistication. The app allows its users to answer more penetrating questions on how a specific company and its employees use Zoom.

To be sure, vast differences exist among and between apps — even those that fall within the same category. Some are far more robust than others. Some are free while others require payment — to the app maker, not to Zoom directly. Typically, apps in the latter group offer some type of trial period or other free offering.

REMEMBER

Don't gloss over an app's pricing terms. You don't want to get stuck with a large bill at the end of the month because you forgot to read its terms of service.

Treading Lightly with Apps

At a high level, apps connect one company's core offering with those of a third-party. This statement holds up whether you're using the wares of Apple, Google, Slack, Facebook, Microsoft, or dozens of other technology companies. Because of their tight integration with their host apps, third-party ones often do amazing things. In the case of Zoom, its apps can

>> Extend its native functionality.

>> Alert users to important events.

>> Consolidate communications in one place.

>> Automate manual actions.

>> Save employees time.

Sounds great, right?

Economists have said for years that there's no such thing as a free lunch. The same principle applies to apps.

Consider two organizations:

>> **ABC:** Employees install third-party apps at will. Zoom admins have given them *carte blanche.*

>> **XYZ:** Zoom admins have approved only a small number of apps. IT carefully monitors those apps that employees install and use.

All things being equal, which one is more secure?

If you picked XYZ, trust your judgment.

WARNING

I do not mean to imply that any particular Zoom app is fundamentally unsafe, let alone all of them. Still, precisely because they connect to other companies' applications and databases, apps by definition create additional risk for organizations and their employees. The nearby sidebar presents a fictitious example of an all-too-real problem.

If you're skeptical that such an event can ever take place, then riddle me this: When you sign up for new online accounts, services, and apps, do you ever read those lengthy documents?

A HYPOTHETICAL EXAMPLE OF THE PERILS OF THIRD-PARTY APPS

Say that Zoom's four core services are completely secure. No black hat can penetrate them. Period. The file compression startup Pied Piper releases a third-party app that compresses the sizes of files that people send to each other via Meetings & Chat. (I'm referencing the HBO series *Silicon Valley* here.) Zoom reviews Pied Piper's app and approves it for download in its App Marketplace.

Unfortunately, Pied Piper engineer Dinesh forgot to lock down a critical setting. Expert hacker Mia ultimately discovers the flaw and exploits it to download thousands of Zoom recordings.

In this case, the security issue didn't stem from Zoom directly, but from an app that accessed Zoom. Ultimately, that semantic distinction won't give you any comfort.

I'm betting that you just scroll to the bottom of the page and click on the Accept button.

I'm not judging you. Really. I almost always do the same thing.

Companies call these opaque, dense, and legalese documents *end-user license agreements* or EULAs. (Read one if you ever suffer from insomnia.) To be sure, EULAs vary on many levels; some are far more verbose and restrictive than others. A few contain patently ridiculous clauses. (Check out `bit.ly/zm-eula` for some real doozies.)

For the most part, though, a EULA attempts to absolve an organization from blame in the event of a security breach or some other type of malfeasance — by its current and former employees, partners, and/or vendors. Oh, and they typically run far longer than the one displayed in Figure 7-2.

TIP

For more information on this timely subject, watch the fascinating 2013 documentary *Terms and Conditions May Apply*.

TIP

With apps, strike a balance among utility, convenience, and security.

Chapter **8**

Connecting with the Masses through Webinars

A nyone with a lick of business sense knows the following: It's wise to stay in touch with your constituents on a regular basis. I'm talking about your colleagues, employees, vendors, and partners.

In the inimitable words of *The Simpsons*' C. Montgomery Burns, "Duh!"

Circumstances permitting and absent global pandemics, odds are that most *recurring* meetings at your organization have historically taken place in person. Some people stick to the meeting agenda, while others routinely ignore it. Is the conversation equally distributed? Maybe not. A few folks may routinely tend to dominate these meetings and drive you crazy in the process. Still, you expect a decent amount of back and forth during these many-to-many conversations.

But what about information sessions and product demonstrations? In these one-to-many presentations, hosts generally don't want others interrupting them. If people have any questions, then they should wait until the end of the meeting. What's more, participants don't expect to regularly attend these types of presentations. They're essentially one-offs. Normal Zoom meetings just don't make sense here.

Welcome to Zoom Video Webinars, a special type of Zoom meeting that lets organizations disseminate knowledge, acquire leads, answer group questions in an organized forum, and more. For their part, webinar attendees can learn new things and receive timely information.

This chapter provides a boatload of information about Zoom webinars: how to set one up, collect registrant data, administer them, answer attendees' questions, record them, run reports on them, and share them for others to view in the future.

Taking Your First Steps

Before going too far down the rabbit hole, a few disclaimers are in order.

First, video webinars are old hat. People of a certain age remember when they rose to prominence in the mid-1990s. In this vein and in the interest of transparency, Zoom hasn't exactly reinvented the wheel. In keeping with this analogy, however, Zoom has created a better, smoother ride, and its customers rarely have to deal with flat tires.

Second, Zoom webinars largely rely upon the same technology required to its run video meetings — a topic I cover in Chapter 4. Yes, there are a few differences between the two, particularly with regard to roles. Still, if you understand the basic idea behind Zoom meetings, then you'll pick up webinars in no time.

Next, webinars represent an add-on to Zoom's core Meetings & Chat plan. (See Chapter 2 for more information here.) That is, Zoom doesn't include webinars in its Free or even Pro plans. If your organization wants to host webinars, then it will have to pony up. Trust me, though: The juice is well worth the squeeze.

Finally, this chapter does not cover every feature or option in Zoom Video Webinars. I could have easily written a separate 180-page book on this meaty subject. For lots more information on this subject, visit bit.ly/zfd-webz.

REMEMBER

To host your own webinar, Zoom requires more than just subscribing to a premium Meetings & Chat plan. Participating in other hosts' and organizations' webinars, however, costs attendees nothing.

Creating your first Zoom webinar

As long as your organization's current Zoom plan includes webinars, scheduling them is remarkably easy:

1. **In the Zoom web portal, under the Personal header, click on Webinars.**

2. **Click on the blue Schedule a Webinar button.**

   Zoom displays the Schedule a Webinar window, shown in Figure 8-1.

My Webinars   ›   Schedule a Webinar

Schedule a Webinar

Topic   My Webinar

Description (Optional)   Enter your webinar description

When   05/07/2020   7:00 ⌄   PM ⌄

Duration   1 ⌄ hr   0 ⌄ min

Time Zone   (GMT-7:00) Arizona   ⌄

                               ☐ Recurring webinar

Registration   ☐ Required

FIGURE 8-1: Scheduling a new Zoom webinar.

3. **In the Topic text box, enter the name of your webinar.**

   You can always change it later.

4. **(Optional) Enter a description.**

   Don't skip this step. You'll want to provide prospective attendees with more information about what they can expect to learn if they attend.

5. **Enter a date and time.**

6. **Enter a duration.**

   Zoom defaults to one hour. This duration is for scheduling purposes only. That is, Zoom doesn't cut you off once the host reaches the end time.

7. Override the time zone, if you like.

Zoom defaults to the time zone associated with your account, but you can override it.

8. (Optional) Enter whether the webinar is recurring.

9. Indicate whether your webinar requires users to enter a password to join; if so, then enter the password.

TIP

Only provide this password to webinar registrants unless you want it to be useless.

10. Under the Video header, select whether the hosts and/or panelists can show their faces.

11. Indicate your audio preference.

Zoom defaults to Telephone and Computer Audio, but you can override that option.

12. Under webinar options, indicate whether you want to allow the following options by selecting the appropriate checkboxes:

- Q&A
- Enable Practice Session
- Only authenticated users can join (See Chapter 9 for details.)
- Make the webinar on-demand
- Record the webinar automatically

13. (Optional) Enter the email addresses of any alterative hosts.

I cover this option in the section "Reviewing Zoom's webinar-specific roles," later in this chapter.

TIP

Say that you've enabled a practice session for your webinar. When you start the webinar, Zoom displays the following orange text at the top of the window: Practice Mode Only: Attendees cannot join until you broadcast.

TIP

None of these webinar options is set in stone. That is, you can edit all of them later — up until the point that you begin your webinar.

Setting your registration options

By default, Zoom doesn't require people to register for webinars. As such, as long as they know the URL, they can just show up without providing any of their contact information. This option is certainly viable. For many reasons, though, you may want to require registration and collect their basic data in advance.

To tweak your webinar–registration options, follow these steps:

1. **In the Zoom web portal, under the Personal header, click on Webinars.**

2. **Click on the title of one of your upcoming webinars.**

They appear under the Topic tab in the middle of the page.

3. **In the Invitations tab, click on the blue Edit link to the far right of the word Approval.**

Zoom displays the window in Figure 8-2 with three tabs:

- **Registration:** Make decisions about webinar registration and approval. For example, when you require registration via a unique URL, Zoom sends one to each registrant. Also, you can disable attendees' ability to join from multiple devices so that they can't share their unique URLs with other people and circumvent the registration process.

- **Questions:** Select the checkboxes here if you want to require attendees to include additional information to register for the webinar. Examples include their phone number, employer, industry, job title, and more.

- **Custom Questions:** Create your own multiple-choice or short-answer questions.

By asking a few targeted registration questions, you may be able to determine which topic(s) attendees would value most ahead of time.

TIP

4. **Make whatever changes you want and click on the blue Save button.**

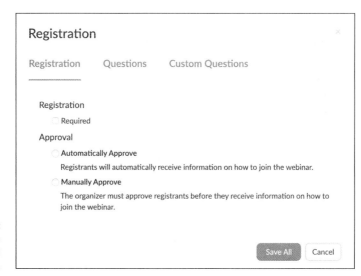

FIGURE 8-2:
Zoom registration
options and
questions.

Registration

Registration   Questions   Custom Questions

Registration
☐ Required
Approval
○ Automatically Approve
Registrants will automatically receive information on how to join the webinar.
○ Manually Approve
The organizer must approve registrants before they receive information on how to join the webinar.

Save All   Cancel

Tread lightly with webinar registration. You don't want to required too many questions. Try to strike a balance. If you come across as too nosy, then you run the risk of minimizing the number of webinar registrants and attendees. On the other hand, your goal should not necessarily be to maximize these numbers.

Consider two scenarios:

>> **Option A:** Twenty people attend your webinar, each of whom is legitimately interested in your company's product or service. Attendees ask penetrating and insightful questions.

>> **Option B:** Fifty, mostly aloof, people attend your webinar. Attendees constantly fidget with their devices as you present. They ignore your polls and other chances to interact. When it's time for questions at the end of the webinar, you hear crickets.

Option A beats B any day of the week and twice on Sunday.

TIP

Visit `bit.ly/zfd-webreg` for ways on how you can customize your webinar-registration options.

Preparing for your webinar

As the famous philosophical query goes, "If a tree falls in a forest, and no one is around to hear it, does it make a sound?"

By the same token, if you hold a webinar without any attendees, does anyone gain any knowledge from it? For now, forget whether they view a recording of it a few weeks or months later. (I cover that subject later in this chapter in the section "Accessing your recorded webinar and sharing it with the world.")

I never advocate spamming people. Still, if you're hosting a public webinar, then you should promote it and encourage people to register for it. Doing so allows you to get a sense of your audience in advance — specifically, their interests, job titles, locations, and more. As a result, you can customize your webinar's content to provide the most valuable experience for as many attendees as possible.

Inviting others to your webinar

To share your webinar link with others, follow these directions:

1. **In the Zoom web portal, under the Personal header, click on Webinars.**

2. **Click on the title of one of your upcoming webinars.**

3. **In the Invitations tab, to the right of the Webinar attended limit, click on Copy the invitation.**

Zoom displays the full invitation, including detailed directions on how to join and links, as Figure 8-3 shows.

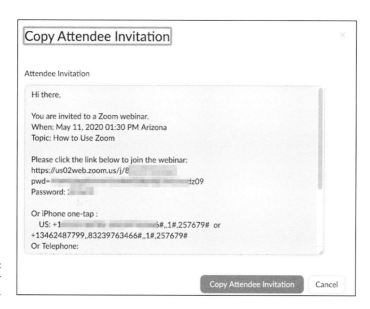

FIGURE 8-3: Zoom webinar invitation.

4. **Click on the blue Copy Attendee Invitation.**

TIP

You can email an invitation to yourself by selecting Email me the invitation. After clicking on a blue button, Zoom emails you the details.

Zoom lets you know that it has copied the text to the clipboard.

5. **Paste your text into an email or as a post on one of your social networks.**

TIP

Play around with Zoom's different options for creating tracking links. This feature allows you to see which marketing channels yield the most registrations. The data will inform you how to promote your webinars in the future.

Sharing a link to your webinar with others

Blasting emails is certainly one way to encourage others to sign up for your webinar. For example, you can send the invitation to members of your organization's mailing list.

But what if you don't want to limit your potential audience to people with whom you've already connected? After all, the whole point of many webinars is to connect with new people — individuals whose email addresses you just don't know yet.

To this end, you may want to share your webinar link on Facebook, Twitter, LinkedIn, and other high-traffic sites. What's more, it's wise to create a simple page that links to the webinar on your company's website. (I do the same thing myself when I host webinars for my clients.)

To find the registration link for your webinar, follow these steps:

1. **In the Zoom web portal, under the Personal header, click on Webinars.**

2. **Click on the title of one of your upcoming webinars.**

3. **In the Invitations tab, to the right of Invitee Attendees underneath Registration Link, copy the full link.**

4. **Share that link however you want.**

   When other people click on it, they'll see something like Figure 8-4.

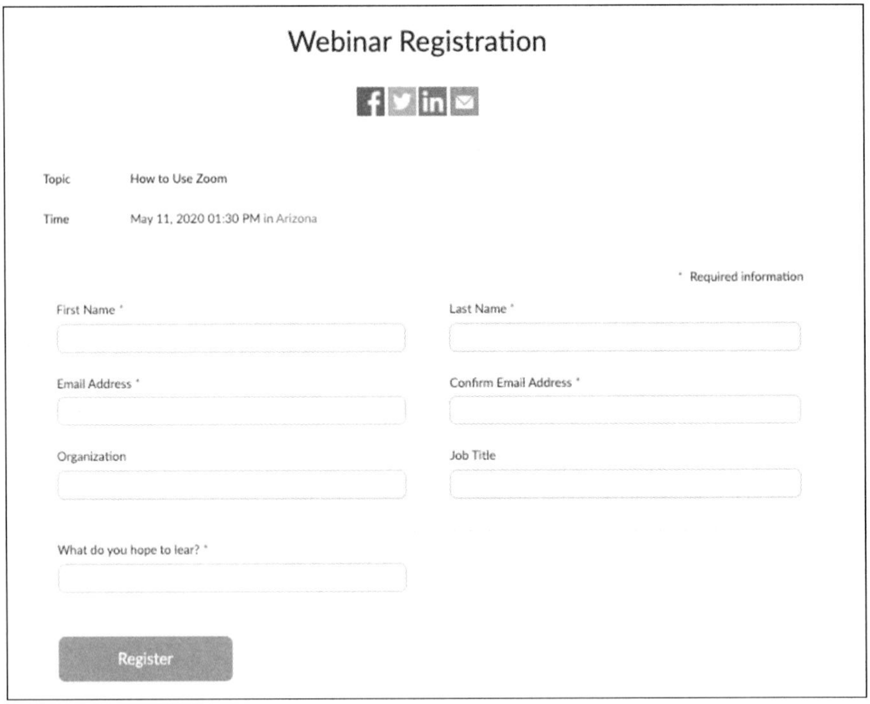

FIGURE 8-4:
Unbranded
Zoom webinar
registration page.

Webinar Registration

Topic   How to Use Zoom

Time   May 11, 2020 01:30 PM in Arizona

* Required information

First Name *

Last Name *

Email Address *

Confirm Email Address *

Organization

Job Title

What do you hope to lear? *

Register

By filling out the form, attendees can register for your webinar. Once they do, Zoom displays a confirmation, such as the one in Figure 8-5.

Webinar Registration Approved

Topic   How to Use Zoom

Time   May 11, 2020 01:30 PM in Arizona

📅 Add to calendar ▾

Webinar ID   832-3976-3466

To Join the Webinar

Join from a PC, Mac, iPad, iPhone or Android device:

Please click this URL to join. https://us02web.zoom.us/w/83

To Cancel This Registration

You can cancel your registration at any time.

FIGURE 8-5:
Zoom attendee webinar registration confirmation.

TIP

If you want to add a banner or logo to your webinar URL, click on the Branding tab on the same page and go nuts.

Viewing and removing webinar registrants

Ideally, loads of people will sign up for your webinar. Great news, right? Perhaps, but maybe a few of them participated in previous webinars and acted like knuckleheads. To view which people have already registered and block a few knuckleheads from participating, follow these steps:

1. **In the Zoom web portal, under the Personal header, click on Webinars.**

2. **Click on the title of one of your upcoming webinars.**

3. **Click on the Invitations tab.**

4. **To the far right of Manage Attendees, click on the blue View link.**

   Zoom displays a screen similar to Figure 8-6.

5. **(Optional) To remove a registered attendee from your list, select the checkbox to the immediate left of that person's name.**

6. **(Optional) Click on the white Cancel Registration button.**

   Zoom adds the user to the Denied/Blocked list.

FIGURE 8-6:
Viewing list of
registered
attendees for
webinar.

Disabling attendee questions

Zoom enables attendee Q&A by default. (See the section "Creating your first Zoom webinar," earlier in this chapter.) If you want to change this option at any point prior to starting the webinar, then follow these steps.

1. **In the Zoom web portal, under the Personal header, click on Webinars.**

2. **Click on the title of one of your upcoming webinars.**

3. **Click on the white Edit this Webinar button.**

4. **Uncheck the checkbox to the left of Q&A.**

REMEMBER

You can also enable anonymous attendee questions if privacy is a concern.

Setting up polls

Real-life and virtual meetings tend to involve multiple people talking to each other. By contrast, webinars tend to consist of one or two people doing the vast majority of the talking.

That's not to say, however, that you can't add a little interactivity to your webinars beyond enabling Q&A. Polls let you do just that. What's more, they allow the webinar host to collect valuable data on any number of subjects.

Before the webinar begins, follow these steps to create a poll that you can invoke after you kick it off:

1. **In the Zoom web portal, under the Personal header, click on Webinars.**

2. **Click on the title of one of your upcoming webinars.**

3. **Click on the Polls tab and click on Polls.**

4. **To the immediate right, click on the white Add button.**

   Zoom displays a new window.

5. **Enter the title of your question.**

6. **(Optional) Select the Anonymous if you want to hide attendees' responses checkbox.**

7. **Type the name of your question.**

8. **Indicate whether the question is single or multiple choice by clicking in the related radio box.**

9. **Enter the possible responses in the text boxes.**

10. **(Optional) Click on + Add a Question to repeat this process and proceed with Steps 5 through 9 again.**

11. **When you finish, click on the blue Save button.**

    Zoom takes you back to the main webinar page and displays a brief message that lets you know that you were successful.

Repeat these steps as necessary. You can invoke up to 25 polls per webinar.

I prefer to set up polls ahead of time because it leaves fewer things to chance. Still, as the next section describes, creating polls on the fly is simple as long as your permissions are sufficient. This ad hoc approach allows you to respond to new issues and questions that attendees have raised during the webinar.

Reviewing Zoom's webinar-specific roles

Like just about all popular webinar tools, Zoom understands that one size does not fit all. Zoom users can perform different actions during a webinar.

TIP

Note that the roles in the following section pertain only to Zoom webinars. That is, they differ from the proper user roles discussed in Chapter 3. Also, they overlap a bit with the roles in Zoom Meetings & Chat (see Chapter 4).

Host

Think of the webinar host as an omnipotent king or queen — one whose permissions include the following actions:

» Stop and start the webinar

» Promote panelists to co-hosts

>> Mute panelists and stop their ability to project video

>> Create and edit polls

>> Remove disruptive attendees

Say that Geddy creates a new webinar. Zoom defaults his role to host. Of course, it's wise for him to share his hosting duties with someone — and Zoom makes that task easy to accomplish.

Alternative host

Say that 1,000 people have registered for your upcoming webinar. Much like a wedding, it's foolish to expect all registrants to actually attend. Make no mistake, though: The larger the number of webinar registrants, the more attendees you can expect.

You may get only one bite at the apple with webinar attendees. What's more, emergencies happen. You don't want all of them waiting for a tardy host to arrive or get her Internet connection working.

To this end, Zoom lets hosts assign as many alternative hosts to their webinars as they like. (For how to do so, see the "Creating your first Zoom webinar" section, earlier in this chapter.) Alternative hosts can do almost everything that hosts can. Most important here is that they can start the webinar in the event that the primary host is MIA. (For more on roles, see `bit.ly/zfd-alth`.)

TIP

Alternative webinar hosts can't ride for free. That is, an individual must be a licensed user under your organization's Zoom Meetings & Chat plan to serve as an alternative webinar host.

Panelist

Panelists are full webinar participants, but their powers lie somewhere between hosts and attendees. They can perform the following actions:

>> Participate in webinar practice sessions

>> Raise their hands

>> Locally record the webinar

>> View the list of attendees

To assign panelists to an existing webinar, following these steps:

1. **In the Zoom web portal, under the Personal header, click on Webinars.**

2. **Click on the name of the upcoming webinar to which you want to add panelists.**

3. **Click on the white Edit this Webinar button.**

4. **To the right of Panelists, select the Panelists radio button.**

5. **Click on the blue Save button.**

6. **Under Invitations, click on Edit next to Invite Panelists.**

7. **From the prompt, enter the panelists' names and email addresses.**

8. **When you finish, click on the blue Save button.**

   Zoom rattles off emails to those people that include links that let them enter that webinar as panelists by default. That is, no one will have to promote them.

REMEMBER

Panelists cannot anoint themselves; primary and alternative webinar hosts must designate them — either ahead of time or after they join as regular attendees.

Co-host

At a high level, co-hosts can perform most of the same actions that hosts can. In this way, think of the co-host as the host's right-hand man or woman during the webinar. (If you're a fan of the seminal HBO series *The Larry Sanders Show*, then the co-host conjures up images of "Hey Now" Hank Kingsley.)

More specifically, co-hosts can perform the following actions during webinars:

» Manage attendees

» Start and stop the recording

» Remove disruptive attendees

» Open polls

REMEMBER

Co-hosts cannot start webinars independently — a key difference compared to Zoom's alternative host role.

The co-host is an essential role. As such, it's wise to assign at least one to each webinar that your organization hosts. In my earlier example, say that Hank is feeling ill and cannot serve as the webinar co-host. Larry should designate a different webinar co-host as soon as possible.

If you're still on the fence about using a co-host, here's the final nail in the no-co-host coffin:

» **Scenario A:** You fly solo on the webinar and opt not to appoint a co-host.

» **Scenario B:** You appoint a co-host.

During the webinar, your Internet connection suddenly dies. Under Scenario A, Zoom terminates the webinar for everyone. Under Scenario B, Zoom automatically transfers hosting responsibilities to the co-host and keeps the webinar running.

TIP

Zoom doesn't require hosts to assign co-hosts to webinars, but it's certainly a best practice — particularly for large webinars.

To enable webinar co-hosts at the account level, account owners and admins should follow these directions:

1. **In the Zoom web portal, under the Personal header, click on Settings.**

2. **Slide the Co-host toggle button to the right.**

   Zoom turns the toggle blue and confirms your new settings.

Note that Zoom remembers this selection for all webinars held under your organization's account. That is, you need not perform this step for every webinar that you and others under your account host.

Oddly, at present, Zoom does not grant webinar hosts the power to pre-assign co-hosts. To receive their promotions to co-hosts, panelists have to wait until a host starts the webinar. At that point, the host can promote panelists to co-host status by following these directions:

1. **Launch the webinar.**

2. **From the icons at the bottom of the screen, click on Manage Participants.**

3. **Click on the Participants tab.**

4. **Identify the person whom you want to make your co-host.**

5. **Mouse over that person and choose Make Co-Host from the menu that appears, as Figure 8-7 displays.**

6. **Select Make Co-host.**

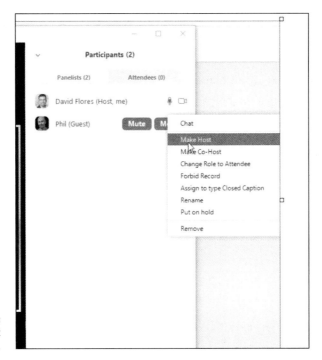

FIGURE 8-7:
Zoom panelist
options.

HOW AN EXPERIENCED CO-HOST ENABLES A SUCCESSFUL WEBINAR

In April 2020, I held a Zoom webinar on remote work for my alma mater Carnegie Mellon University. (Go Tartans.) Over the course of the first 30 minutes, I presented to more than 200 people on the differences among today's three most popular collaboration tools: Slack, Zoom, and Microsoft Teams. I then took questions from inquisitive webinar attendees. (To watch a replay, visit bit.ly/zfd–web.) Long story short: It went smoothly for a few reasons.

First, after I agreed to host the webinar, I connected with emcee and CMU employee Melissa Turk. Over the course of a few weeks, the two of us exchanged basic information via Slack and Google Docs. She shares my aversion to interminable email threads. Needless to say, we got along spectacularly.

(continued)

(continued)

Second, a few days before showtime, we held a 30-minute trial webinar. (Turk's knowledge of Zoom webinars is extensive. She even shares some of her wisdom in the "Advice on handling attendee Q&A from an experienced webinar professional" sidebar, later in this chapter.) We worked out the audio, video, and screen-sharing kinks beforehand, not in front of hundreds of impatient attendees. The two of us left no logistical issues to chance.

Third, Melissa served as the webinar co-host. She handled all attendees' questions and comments and ran the polls. As such, I had to worry only about presenting my content in a professional manner.

As the sidebar illustrates, an experienced webinar co-host is worth her weight in gold.

TIP

Ask a colleague whether he would be interested in being a webinar panelist or co-host. Don't spring these responsibilities on folks at the last minute.

TIP

Zoom provides a host of other options here for adding and managing co-hosts. (Pretty good pun, eh?) Visit `bit.ly/zfd-web-h` to learn more about this topic.

If you're the host, then you cannot remove a co-host from the webinar in one fell swoop. You have to demote him first and then kick him out of the webinar.

REMEMBER

Attendee

Compared to the other roles, attendees can't do all that much. They certainly can view the webinar and participate in it, but they remain fairly passive observers — and that's very much the point. Specifically and if hosts enable these features, attendees can perform the following actions during webinars:

>> **Participate in polls:** When a host or co-host launches a poll, they can choose to respond.

>> **Raise their hands:** Attendees can indicate that they need something from webinar panelists.

>> **Ask the webinar host questions:** Attendees can indirectly submit questions to the host, subject to panelist or co-host moderation.

>> **Chat with others:** By clicking on this icon, they can send messages to the group or to individuals privately. They can also ask questions.

To be sure, attendees can certainly troll webinars via chat. Panelists and co-hosts can remove these disruptive individuals.

TIP

To ensure a successful webinar, think carefully about who should be able to do what. Granting people too much or too little power is bound to cause problems.

TIP

Visit `bit.ly/zm-web-role` to view a comprehensive list of the actions that people in each role can perform during Zoom webinars.

Taking Zoom webinars up a notch with third-party apps and integrations

Chapter 7 covers third-party apps that extend the native power of Zoom Meetings & Chat. If you would like to do the same thing with Zoom Video Webinars, you're in luck.

Generally speaking, Zoom's webinar-specific apps and integrations fall into the following three buckets:

>> **CRM and Marketing Automation:** Many organizations use customer-relationship management (CRM) and marketing automation tools. Popular choices include Salesforce, Marketo, Pardot, and HubSpot. By installing these apps for Zoom Video Webinars, users can automatically capture registrants as leads in these systems. Say goodbye to dual-data entry.

>> **Content Distribution:** Zoom's Kaltura and Panopto integrations allow users to easily share their videos with large audiences.

>> **Monetization:** While many or most companies provide their webinars for free, some charge a nominal fee. With a few clicks of your mouse, you can directly connect Video Webinars with PayPal. Say that you use Eventbrite, CVent, or another event management site and want to charge for your webinar. If so, then you can use the popular and multifaceted automation tool Zapier to stitch those tools together.

TECHNICAL STUFF

Laypeople don't need to worry about the technical differences between Zoom *apps* and *integrations*. At a high level, they effectively do the same types of things — namely, automate manual tasks and make your life easier.

TIP

For more on how to use these apps and integrations, check out Zoom's informative 12-page ebook *Running Engaging Online Events* at `bit.ly/zfd-onlineev`.

Canceling your webinar

John is an accomplished guitarist who works at a Guitar Center in Long Island, New York. He decides to hold a webinar called "How to Play a 12-String" and show his considerable chops. For whatever reason, though, attendance is sparse. Despite his best efforts to promote it, only two people have registered. After mulling it over, he pulls the plug on the webinar.

To cancel your webinar before it starts, follow these directions:

1. **In the Zoom web portal, under the Personal header, click on Webinars.**

2. **To the right of the webinar that you want to cancel, click on the white Delete button.**

   Zoom displays a window allowing you to easily notify registrants that you are canceling the webinar, as Figure 8-8 shows.

FIGURE 8-8:
Zoom screen allowing host to notify registrants of webinar cancelation.

3. **(Optional) Uncheck the Topic checkbox and click on the red Delete button if you want to cancel the webinar without alerting registrants.**

WARNING

If you cancel the webinar, leave the checkbox selected here to alert registrants. It's bad form to cancel a webinar without notifying them.

4. **Customize your cancelation email as desired.**

5. **Click on the red Delete button.**

Zoom sends all registrants the email that you specified.

Whether you alert registrants or not, Zoom sends the webinar host a separate email confirming the cancelation.

Running Your Webinar

Say that you have already scheduled your webinar, promoted it, reviewed the registrant list, assigned webinar roles, created a few polls, and did a walkthrough. To quote Saul Goodman on AMC's *Better Call Saul*, "It's showtime." That is, it's time to launch your webinar and demonstrate to the world how much you know about your topic.

Launching your webinar

Follow these directions to kick off your webinar:

1. **In the Zoom web portal, under the Personal header, click on Webinars.**

2. **Click on the title of one of your upcoming webinars.**

3. **Click on the white Start button.**

Zoom launches the desktop client, and displays a screen similar to Figure 8-9.

TIP

You can and should begin your webinar at least 20 minutes early. Doing so allows you to assign webinar co-hosts, test your computer's audio and microphone again, and generally relax before it's time to rock and roll. Starting your webinar early does not mean that registrants will be able to participate ahead of time.

FIGURE 8-9:
Zoom webinar
launch screen.

Table 8-1 displays the controls that Zoom offers hosts once they kick off their webinars. They largely overlap with the controls for Zoom meetings, discussed in Chapter 4.

TABLE 8-1   ## Zoom In-Webinar Controls for Webinar Hosts

Name	Description
Mute	Mutes and unmutes your microphone. Click on the down-pointing arrow to the right of this button to invoke a number of other sound-related options, including testing your speaker and microphone.
Stop Video	Enables and disables your video. Click on the down-pointing arrow to the right of this button to invoke a number of other video-related options, including choosing a virtual background.
Participants	Displays a new panel on the right-hand side of the screen showing the panelists and attendees for your webinar. From here, you can allow them to talk, rename them, lower their raised hands, promote them to panelists, or boot them from the webinar altogether.
Chat	Displays a window in which you can send messages to other panelists and attendees.

Name	Description
Share Screen	Prompts you to share a screen with webinar attendees. After sharing your screen, Zoom provides a separate menu with powerful annotation options. (Table 8-3 covers these options.)
Polling	Launches one of the polls you created specifically for this webinar. (See the section "Setting up polls," earlier in this chapter.)
Record	Records your webinar either locally or to the cloud.
Q&A	Displays the questions that attendees have asked. Zoom displays three tabs: Open, Answered, and Dismissed. When an attendee raises his hand, Zoom displays a red badge to indicate that he requires attention.
End	Discontinues the webinar for good.

TIP

Always record your webinar — even if you're not sure that you'll need it for future use. To paraphrase the German writer Franz Kafka, it's better to have and not need than to need and not have.

Of course, Table 8-1 displays the options available to webinar hosts. To state the obvious, Zoom does not grant everyone on the webinar the same power. In fact, Zoom limits the tasks that attendees can perform to the ones listed in Table 8-2.

TABLE 8-2   ## Zoom Options for Webinar Attendees

Name	Description
Audio Settings	Invokes the audio settings for the Zoom desktop client. Click on the upward arrow to the right of this button to invoke a number of other sound-related options, including testing your speaker and microphone.
Chat	Sends a message to other webinar attendees, a panelist, or everyone on the call.
Raise Hand	Indicates that you require attention. This action notifies the panelist host or co-host. If you change your mind, then click on Lower Hand.
Q&A	Asks the host a question. Zoom displays two tabs: Open and Answered.
Leave	Exit stage left and remove yourself from the webinar.

Sharing and annotating your screen

Say that your webinar is going swimmingly well. For example, attendees are enthusiastically asking you pointed questions about what your software product can do and how to do it. As the host, you want to demonstrate a specific feature as clearly as possible.

REMEMBER

Zoom's screen-sharing and annotation functionality mirrors that of its Meetings & Chat service, discussed in Chapter 4.

Follow these directions to annotate your screen for all webinar attendees:

1. **After you launch the meeting, choose Share Screen from the menu.**

2. **Select the specific screen on your computer that you want to share with webinar attendees.**

   Zoom displays that screen with everyone on the webinar.

3. **Mouse over the black menu and click on the Annotate icon.**

   Zoom displays a separate annotation menu.

Table 8-3 lists the webinar-annotation options that Zoom provides for hosts:

TABLE 8-3   **Zoom Webinar Host-Annotation Options**

Name	Description
Mouse	Click here to revert to using your mouse. That is, you'll temporarily disable all of the other formatting options in the menu.
Select	Click and drag here to create a box that engulfs your other annotations, allowing you to easily move them as a group.
Text	Enter text over any part of your screen.
Draw	Draw whatever you like with your mouse or touchpad. Zoom also lets you insert a number of basic shapes.
Stamp	Place any number of stamps. Examples include an arrow, checkmark, X, star, heart, and question mark.
Spotlight	Click here to make your computer's cursor more visible. You can turn it into a red circle or a rightward arrow.

Name	Description
Eraser	As its name states, click on this button to erase prior annotations or parts of them.
Format	Click here to change the color, line width, and font of your annotation.
Undo	Reverse your previous annotation.
Redo	Repeat your previous annotation.
Clear	Click here to invoke three options: Clearing All Drawings, Clearing My Drawings (the ones that you have created), and Clearing Viewers' Drawings (the ones — if any — that they have created).
Save	Click here to save entire screen markup as a local file on your computer.

REMEMBER These icons largely overlap with the ones for Zoom meetings covered in Chapter 4. This fact shouldn't surprise you. Webinars are special types of Zoom meetings.

Figure 8-10 shows how I marked up the *Zoom For Dummies* manuscript during a practice webinar.

FIGURE 8-10:
Annotating your screen during a webinar.

Interacting with webinar attendees

More than 10 million people purchased and presumably read Stephen Covey's 1990 book *The 7 Habits of Highly Effective People* (Free Press). The text didn't impress me all that much when I read it 25 years ago, but one of his recommendations always stuck with me: Begin with the end in mind.

Think about that oft-quoted adage in the context of holding a successful webinar. More specifically, it's critical to consider the following questions well before starting your webinar:

» What should attendees be allowed to do during the webinar?

» In both positive and negative ways, how could attendees' actions affect the webinar?

» How many strikes do offending attendees get?

» Do you want to limit how attendees ask questions and interact with others?

» Based on the answers to the previous questions, which permissions will allow co-hosts and panelists to manage the webinar most effectively?

By thinking through these issues ahead of time, you maximize the chance of a smooth webinar.

REMEMBER

There's no one right recipe for holding a successful webinar. Much hinges upon the size and demographics of your audience, their level of inquisitiveness, and even the topic itself.

TIP

Bounce ideas off of more experienced colleagues, especially if you're new to hosting webinars.

Disabling attendee annotation

Webinar attendees run the gamut. In my experience, most act in a professional way. Never confuse most with all, though. It takes only one troll to disrupt a webinar and ruin it for everyone.

One simple way to thwart potential trolls is to disable attendees' ability to annotate the screen. Just follow these steps:

1. **After starting the webinar, share your screen.**

2. **From the black menu bar, click on the More icon on the right-hand side.**

    Zoom displays the webinar-specific menu in Figure 8-11.

3. **From the drop-down menu, choose Disable Attendee Annotation.**

FIGURE 8-11:
Disabling
attendee
annotation.

TIP

Of course, you may want to keep this option enabled if you trust your attendees and there's a legitimate need for them to annotate the host's screen.

Dismissing attendees' questions

Panelists and co-hosts typically want to save interesting attendee queries for the host to answer at the end of the webinar. Sometimes, however, attendees ask redundant, previously answered, or downright silly questions. In such cases, the webinar co-host can easily dismiss them as follows:

1. **During the webinar, click on the Q&A icon in the menu.**

2. **Click on the Open tab and mouse over an attendee's question.**

3. **Click on the gray X Dismiss text that appears over the question.**

   Zoom moves the question to the Dismissed tab in the Q&A panel, as Figure 8-12 displays.

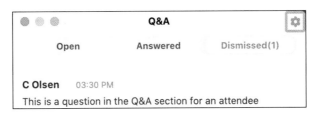

FIGURE 8-12:
Zoom attendee
questions
dismissed by
webinar panelist
or co-host.

Answering attendees' questions

Sometimes the host has already answered an attendee's question. As such, why should a panelist or co-host leave it open for the host to address again?

To mark an attendee's question as answered, follow these steps:

1. **During the webinar, click on the Q&A icon in the menu.**

2. **Click on the Open tab and mouse over the attendee's open question.**

3. **Click on the Type answer button and enter your response.**

4. **(Optional) Select the Send privately checkbox.**

   If you leave this box unchecked, then all webinar attendees can view your answer.

5. **Click on the blue Send button.**

   Zoom moves the question to the Answered tab and updates the number to its right. For example, if you answer eight questions, you see Answered (8).

Reopening dismissed attendee questions

Perhaps a panelist or co-host dismissed an attendee's question too early. To reopen a dismissed question, follow these steps:

1. **During the webinar, click on the Q&A icon in the menu.**

2. **Click on the Dismissed tab and go to the dismissed question.**

3. **Underneath the question, click on the Reopen button.**

   Zoom moves the question back under the Open tab. From here, you can respond to the attendee's query.

Allowing attendees to upvote others' questions

Attendees sometimes pepper the host with questions. The co-host or panelist may not know or want to decide which ones are most important to the audience. To this end, the host can enable question upvoting. (Reddit users are intimately familiar with this feature.)

1. **During the webinar, click on the Q&A icon in the menu.**

   Zoom launches a new window.

2. **In the upper right-hand corner of the Q&A window, click on the Settings icon.**

   Zoom displays additional options, as Figure 8-13 shows.

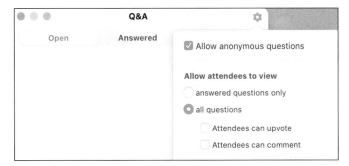

FIGURE 8-13:
Zoom Q&A
options.

3. **Select the All questions checkbox and then select the Attendees can upvote checkbox.**

   Now attendees can mouse over others participants' questions and click on the thumbs-up icon. Zoom tracks the number of likes and places the ones with the most votes at the top of the list.

Attendees can respond to others' questions by following these directions:

1. **During the webinar, click on the Q&A icon in the menu.**

   Zoom launches a new window.

2. **Click on the Open tab.**

   Zoom displays attendees' open questions.

3. **Click on a specific question.**

4. **(Optional) Click on the thumb-ups icon to upvote the question.**

5. **(Optional) Type a comment and click on the white Comment button.**

REMEMBER

As of this writing, many popular webinar tools pale in comparison to Zoom's attendee functionality. For example, WebEx, GoToWebinar, ON24, and Brightalk currently do not allow webinar attendees to upvote or comment on questions.

Responding when webinar attendees raise their hands

When attendees raise their hands, panelists and co-hosts can view new activity by clicking on the Participants tab during the webinar. Zoom displays Figure 8-14.

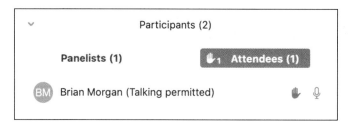

FIGURE 8-14:
Zoom notification
of participant
activity.

Performing other attendee-related actions

Zoom allows co-hosts and panelists to do a number of other things with individual participants:

1. **During the webinar, click on the Participants tab.**

2. **Click on the name of the attendee in question.**

3. **From the menu that appears, select the action(s) that you want to perform.**

   Figure 8-15 displays the following attendee-related options:

   ● Allow the attendee to talk to fellow attendees and disable that ability if already enabled.

   ● Send them direct chat messages.

   ● Promote to panelist.

   ● Rename.

   ● Remove the attendee from the webinar.

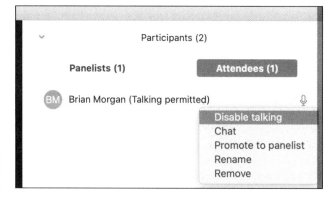

FIGURE 8-15:
Zoom attendee
options.

ADVICE ON HANDLING ATTENDEE Q&A FROM AN EXPERIENCED WEBINAR PROFESSIONAL

I've been around webinars for many years. Here's some advice on making the most out of them.

Understand the user experience from host to attendee — and everyone in between

If you want to run a smooth webinar in Zoom, then you need to understand each user's experience.

Great, but where to begin? How about by first testing your webinar with three to five participants? As the host, you can change each person's role by scrolling your mouse over her name and assigning her a new one. Encourage all participants on the test webinar to click around and kick the tires. What they discover by just clicking around may well surprise you.

For example, say that you share your screen during your webinar — a nearly ubiquitous activity. Not only does Zoom move the black toolbar to the top, but it presents additional menu items. Consider New Share, a tool that lets presenters seamlessly sharing different screens and documents with their audiences. Also, disable participant annotation so that participants can't interfere with your presentation. Do the same for their ability to share their computer sound, especially if you plan on showing a video.

Test these out ahead of time — not on the fly.

The Q&A box is not as simple as it seems

Host, co-hosts, and panelists can see and respond to all attendees' questions. Great, but what do the attendees see? Remember: Webinars are for attendees, not for hosts.

Some attendees send questions expecting them to be private. In your test webinar, make at least two attendees ask questions in the Q&A box. Respond in every way you can: Answer live, type your answer, or dismiss their questions outright. Attendees can share what they see as you respond in these different ways. Next, play around with Zoom's different options. For example, it's generally wise to allow attendees to upvote and comment on submitted questions.

Parting thoughts

The more that you understand how the attendee Q&A box works in advance, the more that attendees will get out of your webinar.

Melissa Turk is the Associate Director of Alumni Engagement at Carnegie Mellon University.

TIP

For more information on managing attendees' questions, visit `bit.ly/zfd-manq`.

Options for managing attendees' specific questions remain after they leave the webinar. That is, they don't need to be present for co-hosts and panelists to answer or dismiss them.

REMEMBER

As the nearby sidebar illustrates, an experienced webinar co-host is worth her weight in gold.

Practice for your webinars. Unprofessional or underprepared hosts usually get only one bite at the apple. Attendees can always leave with a few mouse clicks.

TIP

Concluding Your Webinar

To state the obvious, by recording your webinar, Zoom provides you with more options than if you had not. For example, after you conclude your webinar, you can do each of the following things:

>> Follow up with registrants and attendees.

>> Access and/or edit the webinar recording.

>> Share it on your website, YouTube, or wherever you like.

>> Run reports and analyze data from your webinar.

Accessing your recorded webinar and sharing it with the world

All your preparation paid off. The webinar killed, and you're glad that you recorded it. You want to access it and share it with people who couldn't attend the live event via Facebook, Twitter, LinkedIn, and more.

Zoom makes performing these actions very easy.

1. **In the Zoom web portal, under the Personal header, click on Recordings.**

2. **In the main area of the screen, locate the recorded webinar and click on the Share button.**

3. **In the window that appears, indicate what you'd like to do by sliding the appropriate toggles.**

Figure 8-16 displays your related webinar-sharing options, including whether you want to:

- Enable a password for the webinar.
- Allow people to view the webinar on-demand without registration.
- Let the link to the webinar expire on a certain date.

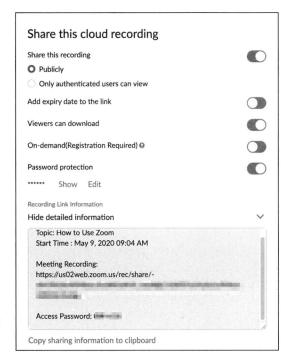

FIGURE 8-16:
Zoom webinar-
sharing options.

4. **Make whatever changes you like from the options in the previous step.**
5. **Copy the sharing information to your computer's clipboard.**

Pay special attention to the webinar's unique URL.

6. **Click on the white Done button.**

You can share the link however you want, with whomever you want, and as often as you want.

Downloading your recorded webinar

Another popular distribution channel is YouTube. After uploading the webinar there, it takes all of about eight seconds to embed the webinar on your company's website. By doing this, you keep users on your site and hopefully encourage them to interact even more.

1. **In the Zoom web portal, under the Personal header, click on Recordings.**

2. **On the right-hand side of the screen, locate the recorded webinar and click on the More button.**

3. **From the drop-down menu, choose Download (2 files).**

4. **Select where on your computer you want to save the video file.**

    Zoom's default video-file format is .mp4.

5. **Click on the Save button.**

6. **(Optional) Select where on your computer you want to save the audio file.**

    Zoom's default audio-file format is .m4a.

7. **(Optional) Click on the Save button.**

    Figure 8-17 displays both the audio and video files.

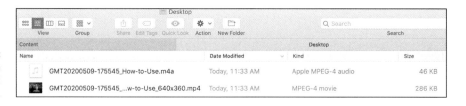

FIGURE 8-17:
Zoom
downloaded
webinar files.

REMEMBER

Just like with meetings (covered in Chapter 4), Zoom provides transcriptions when you record your webinar to the cloud, but not locally.

8. **(Optional) Edit the audio and video files with whatever program you like.**

    Visit `bit.ly/zfd-edit` to read an informative post about some of Zoom's file-editing options.

TIP

9. **Upload the audio and video files to whatever service you like.**

Soundcloud is a popular audio destination. Along with YouTube, Facebook and Vimeo are obvious choices for videos.

Running webinar-related reports

Who exactly who attended your webinar? How did attendees respond to your poll questions?

As long as your formal Zoom role permits you (and not your webinar-specific role), you can answer these types of questions by running reports:

1. **In the Zoom web portal, under the Admin header, click on Account Management.**

2. **Under Usage Reports, click on Webinar.**

    Account admins and regular members will see the word Reports instead of Usage Reports.

3. **Select a reporting option.**

    Underneath the Step 1 heading, Zoom provides the following five reporting options:

    *   **Registration Report:** Displays a list of webinar registrants and related information.

    *   **Attendee Report:** Presents information on webinar attendees. (Remember that this data stems directly from the questions that you required them to answer upon registering for the webinar.)

    *   **Performance Report:** Provides information on attendee registration, attendance, and feedback.

    *   **Q&A Report:** Displays attendee questions and answers during the webinar.

    *   **Poll Report:** If you conducted polls during the webinar, displays attendee responses.

4. **In the top part of the screen, select the checkbox to the left of the report that you want to run.**

5. **(Optional) Underneath the Step 2 heading, restrict your available reports by date range and/or by webinar-ID filters.**

    For example, I selected the attendee report option. From here and as Figure 8-18 shows, Zoom displays the reports that I can run.

6. **Select the radio box to the left of the specific report that you want to run.**

    For example, I am running a report from May 9, 2020 at 9:04 a.m.

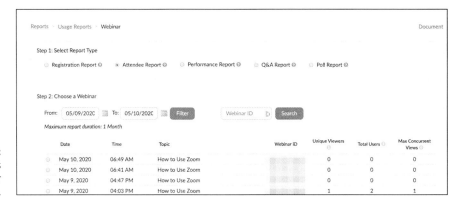

FIGURE 8-18:
Available reports on webinar attendees.

TIP

7. **Under the Step 3 heading, select your report options.**

   Note that report options hinge upon the specific one that you want to run.

   If you prefer simple, structured data, you probably want to leave these options blank.

8. **Click on the blue Generate CSV Report button.**

   CSV here stands for comma-separated values.

9. **Download the file to wherever you like on your computer.**

10. **Open the file in whatever data-analysis program you like.**

    I chose Microsoft Excel, as Figure 8-19 displays.

    Note that I hid a few of the report fields and formatted the header record in Figure 8-19 to improve its visibility for the book.

FIGURE 8-19:
Zoom webinar attendee report.

Chapter 6 goes much deeper into the subject of Zoom reports.

For more information on Zoom's webinar-specific reports, visit `bit.ly/zfd-webrep`.

TIP

Deleting your recorded webinars

After a while, you may decide that you no longer need to store a copy of the webinar in your account, especially if you've already taken the steps in the previous section.

Delete your webinar by following these instructions:

1. **In the Zoom web portal, under the Personal header, click on Recordings.**

2. **On the right-hand side of the screen, locate the recorded webinar and click on the More button.**

3. **From the drop-down menu, choose Delete.**

   Zoom displays a prompt confirming that you want to delete your files.

4. **Click on the blue Yes button.**

If you change your mind, you can recover your deleted webinar as follows:

1. **In the Zoom web portal, under the Personal header, click on Recordings.**

2. **On the right-hand side of the screen, click on the word Trash.**

3. **To the right of the deleted webinar, click on Recover.**

   Zoom displays a prompt confirming that you want to recover the deleted webinar.

4. **Click on the blue Yes button.**

   Zoom briefly displays a green message acknowledging its successful recovery at the top of the screen.

Just like with meetings (discussed in Chapter 4), you can store your webinars as long as you like with one caveat: You need to stay within your plan's data storage limit. As Chapter 2 describes, Zoom provides 1GB of free storage per account user on its Pro and Business plans.

TIP

Zoom emails the account owner when a user reaches 80 percent of his storage capacity. If a host reaches his storage limit during the webinar, Zoom graciously continues the recording until it finishes.

4

Deploying Zoom in the Organization

Dig deeper into Zoom's privacy and security settings.

Garner a greater understanding of Zoom's conference room tools.

Discover how to use Zoom Phone in lieu of your organization's current phone system.

Predict how Zoom will improve its offerings in the future.

Chapter **9**

Protecting Your Communications in Zoom

You may be familiar with the concept of a first-world problem. For example, say that you're routinely bored at work. That's frustrating, but at least you're employed and collecting a paycheck. Hundreds of millions of other people can't say the same thing, even in a good economy. They would love to have your problem.

Zoom has experienced an equivalent quandary. On one hand, its suite of tools allows hundreds of millions of people to communicate in a seamless way. *To Zoom* became a verb, the holy grail of marketing. It has helped solve or at least alleviate critical business and social problems, especially in the wake of COVID-19.

On the other hand, though, Zoom's popularity has attracted plenty of flies in the form of bad actors. The situation forced its management to face some existential questions. What if organizations, school teachers, and other folks couldn't secure their sensitive conversations from prying eyes, disgruntled exes, and black-hat hackers? What if any troll could show grade-school children pornographic images during a math class?

Without substantial safeguards in place, organizations and employees alike would be justifiably loathe to hop on the Zoom train. They would find alternative communications tools and, in due time, Zoom's popularity would wane.

Fortunately, you need not abandon Zoom to secure your communications. You do, however, need to understand its most important security and privacy controls. And that, in a nutshell, is the objective of this chapter.

Putting Zoom's Challenges into Proper Context

I'm a big fan of quotes. One of my favorites comes from the American historian and former Case Western Reserve University professor Melvin Kranzberg. Among his six laws of technology is the following: "Technology is neither good nor bad; nor is it neutral."

If anyone has ever uttered a truer statement, I have yet to hear it.

Think about it. The rise of the web around 1995 birthed a slew of new industries, companies, and types of jobs. Before then, the idea of a *web developer* didn't exist, nor did do-it-yourself (DIY) travel sites, such as Travelocity, Priceline, and Expedia. Good luck trying to find a social-media influencer or a YouTube celebrity in 1994.

Understanding creative destruction

Plenty of winners emerged from this era, but which formerly massive industries have suffered? How about travel agents, newspapers, 24-hour photo development shops, and bookstores? Automated teller machines (ATMs) meant that banks didn't need to employ nearly as many tellers as they once did. The ubiquity of email resulted in far fewer fax machines. A few enthusiasts aside, typewriters have largely died thanks to computers, email, and word-processing programs.

It turns out that the advent of the web is just part of a larger trend: As technology creates some jobs, companies, and even entire industries, it concurrently destroys others. In 1942, the Austrian economist Joseph Schumpeter coined a colorful phrase for this phenomenon that remains popular nearly a century later: *creative destruction.* (See `bit.ly/zfd-disr` for a fascinating data visualization on how quickly successful companies have fallen from grace.)

TIP

For more on this subject, check out *The Innovator's Dilemma: When New Technologies Cause Great Firms to Fail* (Harvard Business Review Press) by the late Clayton Christensen.

Compounding matters further, the rate at which people adopt new technologies has been intensifying for decades, a trend that shows no signs of abating. (See `econ.st/2KuPw9w` for more here.)

Case in point: Consider Pokémon GO, an augmented-reality game for smart-phones. In September 2016, Niantic released the app in collaboration with The Pokémon Company. Remarkably, just a few weeks later, the creators reported that people had downloaded the app more than 500 million times. Not long after that the number exceeded 1 billion.

Managing the double-edged sword of sudden, massive growth

Consider Amazon, Facebook, Google, eBay, Reddit, Uber, Airbnb, Twitter, Netflix, Craigslist, Nextdoor, and Zoom.

What do they all have in common?

Many things. Most important here, though, one is that their founders weren't following tried-and-true playbooks that guaranteed success. That is, it's not like these folks were starting Subway or McDonald's franchises circa 2012. As such, they understandably failed to think about every possible use — and misuse — of their products and services along the way.

From the onset, it's essential to understand two things. First, Zoom is a not fundamentally insecure set of communications tools. Second, it is not a repeat privacy offender à la Facebook, Google, and Uber. Still, Zoom's unprecedented growth unearthed some fundamental issues that its management and software engineers hadn't considered, much less fully appreciated. You may have even heard of the most severe problem that the company has encountered to date.

Zoombombing

I often draw analogies and use metaphors to drive home my points, especially between Zoom communications and their brick-and-mortar counterparts. Here's another one.

Gordon is meeting with a group of Japanese investors in his office. Young buck Bud has weaseled his way into Gordon's waiting room. (In case you're curious, I'm referencing the 1987 film *Wall Street*. What can I say? I'm a cinephile.) After a while, Bud becomes impatient and storms into Gordon's office. He starts screaming at Gordon about a high-stakes deal involving his father's airline gone bad.

Think of Zoombombing as the digital equivalent of this scenario. Unknown and unwanted intruders entered countless Zoom meetings and started bothering participants and acting inappropriately. Think of it this way: For years, one of Zoom's most valuable features was letting people quickly meet with others all across the globe. Within a few weeks, you could argue that that feature suddenly morphed into a bug.

Prior to March 2020, the term *Zoombombing* effectively didn't exist. (To be fair, though, trolls have long crashed many of the other videoconferencing tools that I reference in Chapter 1.) Don't take my word for it, though. Figure 9-1 displays a Google Trends graph that proves my point.

FIGURE 9-1:
Google Trends searches for Zoombombing over time.

TIP

Play around with Google Trends yourself at `bit.ly/zfd-bomb`.

General trends are certainly informative, but by definition they mask individual stories. Tales of rampant Zoombombing pervaded local and national media precisely because Zoom exploded. For example, on April 6, 2020, the New York City Department of Education cited Zoombombing in its decision to ban its schools from using Zoom for remote learning. A few days earlier, the Federal Bureau of Investigation (FBI) had issued a formal warning about criminals who were effectively hijacking classrooms across the country. A few litigious folks even filed lawsuits against Zoom.

In hindsight, the advent and rise of Zoombombing stemmed from several interrelated factors. I briefly touch on them in Chapter 1, but it's critical to explain them more fully here.

By way of background, at the end of 2019, 10 million people regularly used Zoom's suite of communication tools. As former *Bloomberg Technology* cohost Cory Johnson used to say on air, "That ain't nothing." The vast majority of these people qualified as enterprise customers. That is, they happily used Zoom to communicate with colleagues, partners, subordinates, vendors, job applicants, and other businessfolks.

Then, in late 2019, coronavirus shook the world.

Despite adequate time to get ready for the inevitable, relatively few American institutions and companies were prepared for the end of normal life as they knew it. On the business front, even retail behemoths Amazon and Walmart experienced significant problems meeting customer demand. For its part, Zoom suddenly had to deal with two interrelated issues:

» A flurry of new users

» Fundamentally different types of users than those from its existing customer base

There are decades where nothing happens, and there are weeks where decades happen.

— Vladimir Lenin

It's impossible to overstate the enormity of Zoom's challenge. One day, Zoom supported 10 million people, almost all of whom were enterprise customers. A few months later, it was providing critical services to 20 times as many folks across the globe from all walks of life. Very few companies have experienced anywhere near that type of exponential increase in such a compressed period of time.

The qualitative shift in Zoom's customers and users was just as important as the quantitative one, if not more so. The nearby sidebar serves as a reminder that enterprise tech and consumer tech are two very different types of animals, a fact that many people failed to appreciate.

Unfortunately, some of Zoom's most vocal critics disregarded this critical distinction: The communication needs of large for-profit firms dramatically differ from those of school teachers, religious organizations, and the countless other decidedly nonbusiness groups that adopted Meetings & Chat in droves. Sadly, social media and outrage culture don't lend themselves to nuance and facts.

Before detailing the specific changes that Zoom has made to date, it's instructive to think about them in a different context. (For a car-related analogy of the daunting task that Zoom suddenly faced, read the nearby sidebar.)

WHY THE IPHONE WASN'T AN INSTANT HIT EVERYWHERE

In 2013, Luke Cocalis started a new job as an in-house attorney at TaylorMade Golf Company in Carlsbad, California. He received the standard accoutrements: an office, an employee badge, an email account, a computer, and the like. His company's choice of phones surprised him: TaylorMade issued him an iPhone. "The only people I knew who used iPhones and Apple tools for work were graphic designers and employees at marketing agencies," he told me when we spoke. "Everyone else had an iPhone because they purchased it on their own." (Read an interesting *Wall Street Journal* article about the topic at https://tinyurl.com/y8zluhw2.)

By way of background, you were far more likely to see an iPhone than Bigfoot circa 2014. Apple launched what turned out to be the most successful product in the history of the world way back on June 29, 2007. People of a certain age, however, remember that the iPhone was an instant consumer sensation. TaylorMade Golf Company and the vast majority of businesses, however, generally ignored this new tchotchke for years.

Chuckle now, but BlackBerry maker RIM, Palm, Microsoft, and Nokia were serious players back then. These reigning champions continued to dominate the enterprise-cellphone market long after iPhone's debut. These firms dismissed Apple's newfangled smartphone. In this way, they echoed the sentiments of Microsoft's excitable CEO at the time, Steve Ballmer. A few months before the iPhone's proper release, Ballmer boldly predicted, "There's no chance that the iPhone is going to get any significant market share." (Watch the video yourself at bit.ly/zfd-iph.)

With a mind-boggling 2.2 billion iPhones sold worldwide since 2007, people today laugh at the absurdity of his statement. To be fair, though, Ballmer wasn't entirely wrong — at least for a few years and specifically about one large group of customers.

As influential venture capitalist Benedict Evans noted on his popular blog, the iPhone did not portend the instant death of Palm Pilots, BlackBerrys, and other cellphones now relegated to tech museums. (I'm not kidding.) Case in point: BlackBerry unit sales actually rose for four consecutive years after the iPhone's launch. In fact, they increased by 600 percent. (Visit bit.ly/zfd-bevans to read Evans' insightful post on the subject.)

Steve Jobs and company needed a few years to build the software features that its business customers demanded. Fred Vogelstein sheds light on this subject in his excellent 2013 book *Dogfight: How Apple and Google Went to War and Started a Revolution* (Sarah Crichton Books). Near the top of the list were enterprise-grade security and app and device management tools. Once Apple checked these boxes, the iPhone quickly left its enterprise competitors in the dust.

IF ZOOM WERE AN AUTOMOBILE. . .

Dave is an environmentally conscious college professor who drives a Chevrolet Bolt. Every day, he hops in his modest electric vehicle and travels 15 miles to and from the university. His car is reliable and, even better, it lets him save time by legally driving in the HOV lane. Upon returning home, he dutifully plugs his Bolt into to battery charger, makes dinner, watches Netflix, and goes to bed.

Life is good — until it isn't.

Dave loses his job, catching him completely off guard. Without a financial safety net, he needs to find work — fast. He knows that Amazon is hiring delivery drivers. After interviewing, he quickly lands a gig there dropping off packages.

Sitting at a traffic light one day, he contemplates how his life has changed. He now finds himself in his Bolt for ten consecutive hours at a time. He straps televisions and other large items to his car's roof with elastic cords. He puts small boxes on his lap and in his car's dashboard. He even jimmies a few smaller ones into his Bolt's glove compartment.

Despite his best efforts, though, Dave cannot keep up. His Bolt simply isn't built for his new gig. He's constantly worried about running out of juice and being stranded in the middle of nowhere. If he wants to continue making deliveries for Amazon, then he'll need to acquire a proper van or truck to stay sane.

Interestingly and as an aside, Zoom's tools held up just fine as its user base mushroomed. That is, its suite of tools experienced only a few minor hiccups. This remarkable achievement is a testament to Zoom's modern technological underpinnings. (For more on this subject, see Chapter 1.)

Gauging Zoom's Response

Here's the good news: Zoom's management didn't not pooh-pooh Zoombombing. On the contrary, its top brass took a number of immediate and bold steps to staunch the bleeding. It's even fair to say that CEO Eric Yuan and company overcorrected. In this way, the company's actions parallel Johnson & Johnson's famous 1982 Tylenol recall, a case study that remains a staple in most MBA programs nearly four decades later.

On April 8, 2020, Zoom announced it had hired Facebook's former security chief Alex Stamos as an advisor. (Read his Medium post at bit.ly/zm-adpt.) Zoom also formed a security council to carefully guide its eagerly awaited next steps. What's more, Yuan began holding weekly "Ask Eric Anything" webinars — via Zoom, of course. He used that time to update customers, users, employees, partners, and investors on Zoom's progress and future plans. Rare is the organization that responds to a crisis in such a rapid, consequential, and transparent manner.

As Stamos doubtless counseled Zoom's head honchos, hiring consultants, hosting information sessions, and forming committees presented respectable initial responses. By themselves, however, words alone wouldn't put Humpty Dumpty back together again. Zoom would have to act quickly to shore up its wares, restore trust, and change the narrative.

Zoom quickly proved that it was up to the task.

Exhibit A: On April 2, 2020, Zoom announced that it was enacting a 90-day feature freeze. (See `bit.ly/zfd-freeze` for more information.) In laymen's terms, Zoom had suspended the development and deployment of new functionality. Instead, the company shifted its focus to making its existing tools and features as secure as possible.

Bringing Zoom's privacy and security settings to the forefront

Less than a week after Zoom announced that it was enacting a 90-day feature freeze, the company started pushing updates to its desktop client and mobile apps that put security front and center. Along these lines, Zoom added a new Security icon to the desktop client's user interface or UI. With a single click on its in-meeting menu, users could now access these essential security-related options:

- **Lock Meeting:** Prevent others from entering the meeting.
- **Enable Waiting Room:** For more information on this topic, see Chapter 4.
- **Allow participants to share screen:** Enable or disable this ability for all meeting participants.
- **Allow participants to chat:** Prohibit participants from exchanging text messages during the call or allow them to do so.
- **Allow participants to rename themselves:** As Chapter 4 details, both options offer benefits and drawbacks.

REMEMBER

The April 2020 update also removed the Zoom meeting ID from the title toolbar. Some unruly meeting participants were distributing that number to uninvited guests.

Zoom had already offered many of these features. The UI change made it easier for users to access them. Other enhancements, however, required much more than just hiding an important field from meeting participants and moving options around.

Enhancing its encryption method

Laypeople generally don't know or care much about arcane security matters, such as application encryption. I certainly understand the sentiment, but I'd be remiss if I didn't provide at least a little technical detail about this essential topic.

TECHNICAL STUFF

On April 25, 2020, Zoom announced that it was upgrading Meetings & Chat to the AES 256-bit Galois/Counter Mode (GCM) encryption standard. For its part, Zoom Phone uses Secure Real-time Transport Protocol (SRTP). This method allows Zoom to encrypt and protect customers' phone conversations in transit to — and from — its data centers.

Zoom now secures its users' video, voice, and text communications more securely than it has at any point in its history. Still, for the time being, Zoom falls short of the industry's gold standard: end-to-end encryption or E2EE. As the nearby sidebar illustrates, tools that use this industrial-strength method restrict messages to only intended senders and recipients.

HOW E2EE ENSURES USER PRIVACY

Pete and Ian are exchanging ideas via WhatsApp, Facebook's popular mobile messaging app that provides E2EE. Mark is curious about their ideas and knows a thing or six about hacking. He intercepts some of their messages midroute — that is, while they are in transit from one person to another.

Should Pete and Ian start panicking?

Not at all.

Unfortunately for Mark, Whatsapp's E2EE prevents him from reading those intercepted messages. Specifically, WhatsApp translates all users' messages into an indecipherable series of random characters, letters, numbers, and/or symbols. Security experts refer to this gobbledygook as *ciphertext*. In other words, Mark cannot make heads or tails of the messages that Pete and Ian have exchanged. He may as well never have stolen them in the first place.

TIP

If you're curious about what ciphertext actually looks like, check out the Zimmermann Telegram from World War I at `bit.ly/zfd-ciph`.

Waiting for E2EE

You may be wondering, "When will Zoom deploy E2EE?"

I'd bet my house that you'll see it sooner rather than later.

As I did my research and wrote this book, two events in particular stood out that helped me read the tea leaves.

On May 7, 2020, Zoom announced that it had acquired Keybase, the maker of a niche chat tool lets its users easily and securely share messages and files. Critically, Keybase offered its users end-to-end encryption or E2EE. The timely Keybase acquisition marked the first one in Zoom's storied nine-year history. (To read more about it, visit `bit.ly/zfd-acq`.)

In a related strategic move, consider what Zoom did on May 22, 2020. On that day, the company published its cryptographic design for peer review on the über-popular code repository GitHub. Put simply, Zoom's management wants other techies, advocacy groups, customers, and academics to do the following:

>> Identify any potential flaws in its proposed security framework.

>> Suggest improvements.

Trust me: Rare is the company that does such a thing. (See `bit.ly/zfd-crypt` for more information about this topic.)

Protecting your devices and communications

Even when Zoom builds E2EE into its offerings, you can and should increase your security by doing one critical, simple, but oft-neglected thing.

Drumroll.. . .

I'm talking about regularly using a *virtual private network* (VPN) on all your devices. They are downright essential when connecting to public Wi-Fi networks at coffee shops, airports, bookstores, and gyms. VPN providers accomplish this task by rerouting all of their users' Internet traffic through their own secure servers.

Ignore using a VPN at your own peril.

WARNING

TIP

For years I've happily paid for a single Encrypt.me subscription. I've used it to secure communications on my laptop, tablet, and smartphone. (For more information, visit `bit.ly/zfd-enc`.)

Enabling default passwords and waiting rooms for all meetings

Sure, Zoom has made a heap of critical product changes since March 2020. That's not to say, however, that Zoom was the wild west before that time. On the contrary, the company had long provided its customers with ample security controls. For example, Zoom had long allowed its users to create passwords for each of the following meetings:

>> Newly schedule meetings

>> Instant meetings

>> All meetings that participants joined via the host's meeting ID

The rise of Zoombombing forced senior management to rethink its default meeting options. To this end, in April 2020, Zoom enabled passwords and waiting rooms for all meetings by default. Put differently, hosts now have to actively disable these features for their meetings.

Increasing the length of meeting and webinar IDs

In Chapter 4, I describe how you can give your PMI to a friend or loved one without much concern. For other types of meetings, though, you probably want to use a disposable, randomly generated ID number.

In April 2020, Zoom announced that those random numbers would consist of 11 digits — up from 9. Here's some math to help you get your head around this change. There are now 100 billion different possible unique meeting numbers. Every person on earth could concurrently host 14 different meetings if Zoom ever allowed it. (Remember that you can host only one meeting at a time per account.) What's more, Zoom tracks these meeting numbers and recycles them intelligently and in an attempt to minimize fraud.

TECHNICAL STUFF

Zoom uses the popular CAPTCHA method to thwart hackers' attempts to join meetings and webinars to which they're not invited. CAPTCHA is a contrived acronym — or backronym — for "completely automated public Turing test to tell computers and humans apart." You have certainly seen a CAPTCHA in the form of typing letters or identifying stop signs when signing in to your online accounts.

Configuring Zoom for Maximum Privacy and Security

So far, this chapter has introduced Zoombombing and described how Zoom responded by overhauling its security and privacy settings. Kudos to the Zoomies for all of their hard work. The ones I know have been burning the midnight oil.

Now it's time to shift gears and talk about you. What specific steps should you take to protect your communications in Zoom as much as possible?

>> Keep Zoom up to date.

>> Enable two-factor authentication.

>> Authenticate user profiles.

>> Intelligently use passwords.

>> Follow Zoom's best security practices.

>> Use your brain.

Keeping Zoom up to date

Like just about every software vendor today, Zoom updates its products on a regular and sometimes weekly basis. (This reality makes writing *For Dummies* books especially challenging, but I digress.) To be sure, Zoom has followed this practice from its early days. Since March 2020, however, Zoom has increased the frequency with which it pushes new versions. A 30-fold increase in users in a matter of months tends to alter any company's standard operating procedure.

At a high level, Zoom updates typically fall into the following five buckets:

>> **Changes to its user interface:** Zoom modifies its menus, icons, navigation, and the like. Collectively, these tweaks affect how all users interact with Zoom. Because it does not want to confuse or alienate its users, the company does not shake things up too often and too drastically in this vein. Radical UI changes typically result in chaos and mass user defections.

>> **Improved or entirely new functionality:** Zoom introduces an enhanced or brand new feature. For example, as Chapter 4 describes, Zoom didn't always let users apply virtual backgrounds to their video meetings.

- » **Bug fixes:** Zoom fixes a feature that should have worked from day one. Alternatively, the company triages a feature on a specific operating system, such as MacOS or Microsoft Windows.

- » **Security enhancements:** Zoom understands both that hackers are a sophisticated lot and trolls are shameless. To this end, the company makes regular security-related front- and back-end changes to minimize the chance that bad actors wreak havoc.

- » **Back-end or underlying code changes:** In some cases, Zoom doesn't alter what its software does as much as how its software does it. While invisible to users and customers, these types of changes can significantly improve how a program or application performs. (For example, consider Slack's much-heralded 2019 application rewrite. Industry analysts praised its new version as much faster and resource-efficient than its predecessor.)

TECHNICAL STUFF

Software engineers refer to this process as *refactoring*. At a high level, although end-users ultimately perform the same tasks, the new code usually allows them to run in a smoother, more reliable, and more efficient manner than before.

On occasion, Zoom may push a new version with a single and critical change or fix. The vast majority of the time, however, the company bundles a series of changes and goodies into a new release. In this way, Zoom follows the industry's best practices.

Locating your version of Meetings & Chat

With rare exception, you should always use Zoom's most current version. Fine, but how can you tell? Follow these steps to find out:

1. **Go to the Zoom desktop client and select the zoom.us menu.**

2. **From the drop-down menu, choose About Zoom.**

   Zoom displays the version number in a new window. For example, as of this writing, I am running the latest version of Zoom: 5.0.5.

3. **Click on the white Done button to return to Zoom.**

TIP

When you follow these steps, Zoom tells you if you are using the current version. If so, then you are gold.

Updating your software

Unless someone in your IT department explicitly tells you otherwise, update all Zoom tools to their most recent versions on a regular basis. Failure to do so robs you of new features. More important, lagging behind puts you, your colleagues, and even your entire organization at risk.

To update to the latest version of Meetings & Chat, follow these steps:

1. **Go to the Zoom desktop client and choose the zoom.us menu.**

2. **From the drop-down menu, choose Check for Updates.**

   Zoom informs you that you're either

   - Running its latest version; or

   - An updated version is available.

   Assuming that the latter is true, continue following these directions.

3. **Click on the blue Update button.**

   Zoom begins its update process while a green progress bar steadily moves from left to right at the bottom of the screen.

4. **Click on the white Install button.**

   Zoom displays a wizard similar to Figure 9-2.

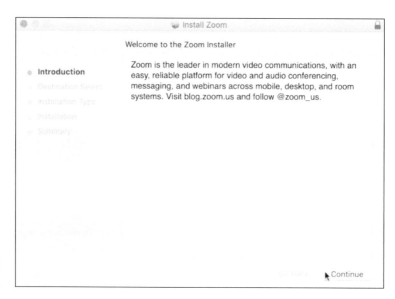

FIGURE 9-2:
Zoom installation wizard for Macs.

5. **Click on Continue.**

   Depending on your computer's settings, you may need to specify whether you're installing Zoom for all user accounts or for only your own user account.

6. Click on Continue again.

7. (Optional) Change the folder in which you want to install the new version of the Zoom desktop client.

8. (Optional) Depending on your computer's settings, enter your computer's master password.

Don't confuse this password with your Zoom one.

9. Click on Install Software.

Zoom completes the upgrade process.

10. When finished, Zoom reverts to the desktop client's user interface.

WARNING

At the risk of stating the obvious, updating your Zoom desktop client does not do the same for your tablet and smartphone apps, much less Zoom Rooms (discussed in Chapter 12). You'll have to separately update those apps if you use them.

Dealing with forced upgrades

Despite the myriad reasons to upgrade their software and the ease of doing so, far too many organizations and individuals invariably forget to stay current — or actively resist doing so.

In response, software vendors occasionally compel people to upgrade to more current versions. Failing to move to a contemporary version may render the program inoperable. More bluntly, the old version stops functioning altogether.

The reasons for forced upgrades vary, but the usual suspects include when a company:

» Forgoes supporting a legacy technology

» Introduces key enhancements to its products

» Patches a critical security flaw

» Responds to new regulatory requirements

Again, Zoom plays by the same rules as most software vendors. For example, on April 27, 2020, Zoom released version 5.0 of Meetings & Chat. It included a slew of new security features, most notably enhanced encryption. (Read the release notes at bit.ly/zfd-new5.) At that point, the clock started ticking on its predecessors, specifically version 4.6.

As the nearby sidebar describes, running outdated software poses significant risks to all concerned.

YOUR LOCAL ATM MAY BE RUNNING A 20-YEAR-OLD OS

To this day, some banks still refuse to upgrade their ATMs from an antiquated and unsupported operating system: Microsoft Windows XP, originally released on October 25, 2001. (See `bit.ly/zfd-atm` for more information on this terrifying reality.)

Interestingly, the problem is particularly acute in India. If you think that laggards' inaction ultimately harms themselves and others, trust your instincts. As you may expect, newer versions of Windows offer superior network security than a 20-year-old operating system does.

Enabling two-factor authentication

There are two types of companies: those that have been hacked, and those who don't know they have been hacked.

— John Chambers

Say that you are one of the billions of Gmail or Facebook users. You may think that setting a complex password for each account guarantees that you and only you can access it.

And you'd be spectacularly wrong.

Black hats all too often pierce or circumvent organizations' intricate security measures. In this vein, the quote from former Cisco Systems' CEO John Chambers is spot-on. That's not to say, however, that users and customers remain helpless against hackers. Nothing could be further from the truth. To that end, this section covers one of the most effective steps that Zoom users can take to protect their accounts and their communications.

Zoom is one of a boatload of tech companies that provides *two-factor authentication,* or 2FA. (Rare is the bank, social network, ecommerce site, or popular tech service that hasn't offered this option for years.) In a nutshell, 2FA requires users to authenticate their true identities on a separate device — typically a smartphone. In so doing, 2FA provides users with an additional layer of security beyond their account passwords. In the event that hackers obtain users' passwords, 2FA usually stops them in their tracks.

Activating 2FA at the organizational level

To activate 2FA for users under your organization's Zoom account, follow these directions:

1. **In the Zoom web portal, under the Admin header, click on Advanced.**

2. **Click on Security.**

3. **Slide the Sign in with Two-Factor Authentication toggle button to the right so that it turns blue.**

4. **Select the checkbox to the left of the option that you want to enable throughout your organization.**

    Zoom provides three options:

    *   **All users in your account:** This self-explanatory option is also the most powerful. If you click on it, then also click on the blue Save button. If you select this option, then the next two are moot.

    *   **Users with specific roles:** Zoom lists its three default roles, plus any custom ones that you created. (See Chapter 3 for more detail on user roles.) By selecting desired roles here, you are requiring the members with these roles to set up 2FA.

    *   **Users belonging to specific groups:** Zoom lists the user groups that you have created. (See Chapter 3 for more information on this topic.) If you select a user group here, then you force all of its members to set up 2FA.

Congratulations. You have now required some, or even all, members in your organization to turn on 2FA. This move is wise. Still, specific users must activate it based upon your selection(s) in Step 6 in the preceding list.

TIP

Say that your organization did not enable 2FA for all employees when it rolled out Zoom. It's best to let them know that you've done so. As usual, a little common sense and communication typically minimizes user confusion and help desk calls.

REMEMBER

Zoom's 2FA works only when users access the web portal — not the desktop client. I suspect that Zoom will address this limitation in the near future.

Turning on 2FA for yourself

Your account admin or owner has enabled 2FA for your user group or even the entire organization. Now it's time for individual users to set it up for their specific

Zoom accounts. Pick up your smartphone, get your popcorn ready, and follow these steps to secure your Zoom account with 2FA:

1. **(Optional) Open a web browser, go to** `https://zoom.us,` **and make sure that you've signed out of your Zoom web portal.**

2. **Sign back in to your Zoom web portal.**

   Zoom displays a screen that walks you through the 2FA process.

3. **Open the Google Authenticator app on your smartphone.**

   If you have not downloaded and installed this app, then do both.

   Although the precise steps may vary, you can also use the Microsoft Authenticator, FreeOTP, and Authy mobile apps.

   TIP

4. **In the Google Authenticator app, click on the blue plus icon in the top right-hand corner of the screen.**

   You're indicating that you want to add 2FA for another site, app, or service.

5. **Press Scan barcode with your finger.**

6. **Point your phone at your computer until it recognizes the QR code.**

7. **In the Google Authenticator app, click on the blue plus icon in the top right-hand corner of the screen.**

   As Figure 9-3 displays, a six-digit verification code appears in your smartphone's Google Authenticator app.

FIGURE 9-3: Partially redacted Zoom six-digit verification code in the Google Authenticator app.

Note the timer in the lower right-hand corner of Figure 9-3. If it expires, then the Google Authenticator app automatically generates another six-digit code and resets the clock.

8. **Returning to the Zoom web portal, enter the six-digit code from the app under the Enter the verification code header.**

9. **Click on the blue Continue button.**

HOW 2FA COMES TO THE RESCUE WHEN A MARRIAGE BREAKS BAD

Walter is happily married to Skyler. They share no secrets, and he freely gives her his Zoom password. In fact, the two of them consider it a joint Zoom account. Walt and Skyler use their home computer to log in to the Zoom web portal.

Then things break bad.

Walt discovers that he has terminal lung cancer and months to live. Determined to provide for his family after his death, he starts doing untoward things.

Skyler eventually finds out that he's been lying to her for months about all sorts of things. She forces him to move out of their home on 308 Negra Arroyo Lane in Albuquerque, New Mexico. She files for divorce and starts seeing her boss Ted. Walt purchases a new laptop and a new condominium to boot. (*Breaking Bad* fans will recognize the plot twists.)

After he settles into his new digs, Walt enables 2FA on the family's Zoom account. Now, when he attempts to log in to the Zoom web portal, Zoom dutifully forces him to enter the six-digit code that it sends to his smartphone's Google Authenticator app.

Because Walt has activated 2FA, Skyler cannot log in to the web portal on their joint Zoom account, even though she knows their current Zoom password. (Walt has not changed it yet.) She can, however, access the Zoom desktop client provided that she never logged out of it.

A few days later, Walt finally changes the password on the Zoom account. As a result, Zoom automatically signs him out on all devices to which he had logged in — including the desktop client on the computer in his old house. As a result, Skyler can no longer access the Zoom account. Walt can now hold private meetings with Jesse, Gus, Mike, and Saul.

You may already be using 2FA for other services, such as Twitter, Facebook, LinkedIn, and Gmail. If not, then you really should. For those of you who are curious about how 2FA works, the nearby sidebar provides a detailed example.

Remaining vigilant, even with 2FA enabled

Yes, activating 2FA adds some friction to Zoom's sign-in process, but the juice is well worth the squeeze. You'll considerably reduce the odds that someone hacks your Zoom account.

Note my phrasing in the preceding sentence: Reduce the odds. Lest you think that 2FA negates the possibility that hackers will be able to gain access to your account, be warned. Bad actors are devilishly clever.

Among the tools that hackers routinely employ in their attempts to circumvent 2FA is the *SIM swap*. (SIM stands for *subscriber identification module*.) They call phone carriers pretending to be you, often using data readily available on the Dark Web. Equipped with your mother's maiden name, the make of your first car, your social security number, or just about anything else you can imagine, they call AT&T and Verizon. They are often able to convince call center reps to switch your phone number over a SIM card that they own and control.

TIP

Chapter 6 provides covers the reports that Zoom owners and admins can run. In some cases, those reports can help identify suspicious account activity.

Authenticating user profiles

Mary-Kate and Ashley are 19-year-old college students who decide to venture out to a bar one Friday night. At the door, a gruff bouncer asks for their IDs. The two try to flirt their way in, but he isn't having any of it. He can see from their licenses that they aren't legally old enough to drink. Mary-Kate and Ashley will have to try their luck somewhere else.

The preceding example is a decidedly low-tech version of user authentication. In a way, a bouncer verifying college students' ages is the same as an enterprise system ensuring that a specific user can access sensitive employee and company data. Along the same lines, it's not a stretch for Zoom to make reasonably certain that people are who they claim to be prior to allowing them to enter webinars and meetings.

Up until December 2019, Zoom provided some degree of user authentication, but not nearly the same level that it does as of mid-2020. Put another way, Zoom used to allow people to join meetings and webinars without formally authenticating users. In this example, Mary-Kate and Ashley would have had a better chance of pounding shots of whiskey despite being legally prohibited from drinking.

Zoom now allows hosts to restrict who can attend meetings in two ways:

>> Users must use the email addresses tied to their Zoom accounts.

>> Users can register only if their email address contains a specific domain.

WARNING

Zoom disables user authentication by default.

For starters, Zoom requires owners or admins to enable authentication at the account level. Follow these steps to kick-start this process:

1. **In the Zoom web portal, under the Admin header, click on Account Management.**

2. **Click on Account Settings.**

3. **Slide the Only authenticated users can join meetings toggle button to the right so that it turns blue.**

   Zoom displays a message asking you to confirm your decision.

4. **Click on the blue Turn On button.**

   Zoom lets you know that it has updated your settings.

REMEMBER

User authentication is just as useful for one-to-many webinars as it is for intimate meetings.

The first authentication option involves making meeting participants sign in to Zoom. Remember that, by default, Zoom does not require participants to have registered for Zoom accounts; they can join calls anonymously. (Forget about waiting rooms for the time being — a subject broached in Chapter 4.)

Enabling this authentication method means that only people with valid Zoom accounts can join your meeting or webinar. In other words, under this scenario, Zoom permits users to join irrespective of the email domains linked to their accounts.

Say that Elliot hasn't created a valid Zoom account. (I'm referencing *Mr. Robot* here in case you're curious.) Still, he discovers your meeting's URL or PMI. In this example, when he attempts to join, Zoom displays the authentication message in Figure 9-4.

FIGURE 9-4:
Zoom user authentication message.

Problem solved, right?

Not necessarily.

Within minutes, Elliot registers for a Zoom account with his Gmail address. He then attempts to join your meeting. Other than the waiting room, what's to stop you from letting him in?

Absolutely nothing.

For this very reason, Zoom offers an additional and more powerful authentication option. The following example demonstrates the benefits of using it.

Say that your work at Spotify and you're holding a sensitive company meeting. Maybe you're finalizing Joe Rogan's jaw-dropping $100-million podcast deal. You want to do more than just restrict participants to people who have created verified Zoom accounts. You allow people to join only if their Zoom accounts are attached to one specific email domain: spotify.com.

Zoom lets meeting and webinar hosts impose this more restrictive authentication level as follows:

1. **In the Zoom web portal, under the Admin header, click on Account Management.**

2. **Click on Account Settings.**

3. **To create another authentication method, under Only authenticated users can join meetings, click on the white Add Configuration button.**

    Zoom displays the form in Figure 9-5.

4. **In the first text field, enter the name of the custom configuration that you're creating.**

    For example, I am calling mine Spotify.

5. **Enter the email domain(s) that you want to approve in the Select an authentication method box or upload a comma-separated value (CSV) file in lieu of typing multiple domains.**

    Think of this list as a whitelist; only accounts tied to the email domains that you enter here can join your meeting or webinar.

    Uploading a CSV file can save you a good deal of time and data entry.

6. **(Optional) If you want to set this authentication option as your default, then select the checkbox.**

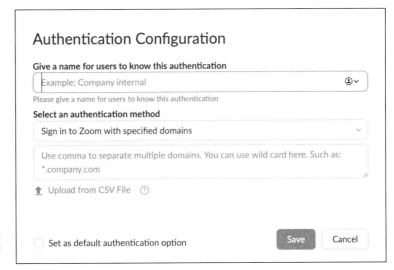

FIGURE 9-5:
Zoom form
to create
domain-specific
authentication.

Authentication Configuration

Give a name for users to know this authentication

Example: Company internal

Please give a name for users to know this authentication

Select an authentication method

Sign in to Zoom with specified domains

Use comma to separate multiple domains. You can use wild card here. Such as:
*.company.com

⬆ Upload from CSV File ⓘ

◯ Set as default authentication option   Save   Cancel

7. **Click on the blue Save button.**

    Zoom confirms that you've successfully completed this process. Now, Zoom
    users won't be able to participate in the meeting unless their accounts are tied
    to the email addresses that you specified. Zoom will block those who try.

REMEMBER

You can create personal Zoom accounts to go with your employer-issued one. To
this end, say that you used the former to log in to the Zoom desktop client. Simply
sign out and sign back in with the credentials tied to your employer's Zoom
account. You should be good to go for your business meeting.

TIP

Zoom provides a bevy of additional authentication options. For example, Zoom
doesn't force an all-or-nothing approach. Firms can customize authentication
options for both groups and even individuals. For more on what you can do in this
regard, visit `bit.ly/zfd-auth`.

Intelligently using passwords

As you may expect, Zoom offers a number of password-related protections:

>> Set a password for an individual upcoming meeting.

>> Set other password-related options for your Zoom account.

>> Apply different security options for different user groups.

>> Require more complex meetings and webinar passwords.

Setting a password for an individual upcoming meeting

George and Jerry are planning a meeting to discuss an idea for a TV show about nothing. It's all very hush-hush. As the meeting's host, Jerry should follow these directions to password-protect the meeting:

1. In the Zoom web portal and click on Meetings.

2. Click on the blue Schedule a New Meeting button.

3. Enter the information about your meeting.

Chapter 4 covers this topic in considerable depth.

4. Select the Meeting Password checkbox and enter a password.

5. Click on the blue Save button at the bottom of the screen.

Setting other password-related options for your Zoom account

Zoom allows people to use passwords in a variety of significant ways.

REMEMBER

The availability of these features hinges upon your role and your organization's Zoom plan. For example, if your company subscribes to Zoom's Enterprise or Education plan, then an administrator may have locked some of the options in this section. As such, you may be unable to change them.

Follow these directions to invoke other password-related options:

1. In the Zoom web portal, under the Personal header, click on Settings.

2. Slide the toggle button next to the password options that you want to enable.

Zoom provides the following password-related options:

- **Require a password when scheduling new meetings:** Generates a password when you schedule a meeting. Participants will need to enter the password to join the meeting. Note that this option excludes meetings held via users' Personal Meeting IDs (PMIs).

- **Require a password for instant meetings:** Generates a password for your instant meetings.

- **Require a password for Personal Meeting ID (PMI):** Enable this option only for meetings with the Join Before Host activated or for all meetings using the PMI. Regardless of the one that you select, you'll need to enter a password.

- **Embed password in meeting link for one-click join:** Appends a code to the end of the invitation's URL that eliminates the need for attendees to use a password.

- **Require password for participants joining by phone:** Requires participants to enter a numeric password. If you created an alphanumeric meeting password, Zoom provides callers with a numeric version of it.

Zoom confirms that you have successfully changed that option.

Applying different security options to different user groups

Chapter 3 details the benefits of creating and populating user groups — a valuable feature for customers on premium Zoom plans. User groups allow organizations to easily apply, change, restrict, and lock a variety of different settings to different users. Customizing users' security settings represents possibly the best application of user groups, as the following example illustrates.

Ricky, Shelley, Blake, George, and Dave sell residential real estate for Premiere Properties in Chicago, Illinois. (I'm alluding to the exceptional 1992 film *Glengarry Glen Ross* here.) When these five realtors hold Zoom meetings with their prospects, they sometimes forget to enable certain securing settings. Their inattention to detail rankles John, their nominal boss and the company's Zoom account owner. For example, they schedule meetings without requiring user authentication. John wants to lock down their settings such that they can't forget to do these important things.

John starts by creating a new user group called Realtors. He then places the five of them in it. Finally, he follows the following directions to customize the new group's security settings:

1. In the Zoom web portal, under the Admin header, click on User Management.

2. Click on Group Management.

3. Click on the name of the user group whose settings you want to change.

4. Under the Meeting tab, slide the toggle button next to the option(s) that you want to enable.

   For example, some of the choices include requiring members of the group

   - Use their PMIs when starting instant meetings or scheduling meetings

   - Use a password when holding meetings via their PMIs

   - Restrict their meetings' participants to authenticated users

Depending on the option that you select or enable, Zoom may prompt you with a confirmation window asking you to confirm your choice. Alternatively, Zoom may display a message in green at the top of the screen that reads, "Your settings have been updated."

Zoom confirms your selection with an email similar to the one displayed in Figure 9-6.

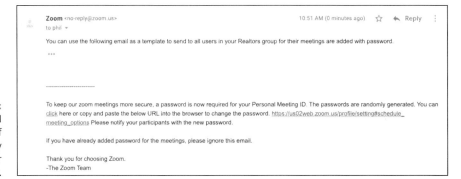

Zoom <no-reply@zoom.us>   10:51 AM (0 minutes ago)   ☆   ← Reply   ⋮
to phil ▾

You can use the following email as a template to send to all users in your Realtors group for their meetings are added with password.

• • •

To keep our zoom meetings more secure, a password is now required for your Personal Meeting ID. The passwords are randomly generated. You can click here or copy and paste the below URL into the browser to change the password. https://us02web.zoom.us/profile/setting#schedule_meeting_options Please notify your participants with the new password.

If you have already added password for the meetings, please ignore this email.

Thank you for choosing Zoom.
-The Zoom Team

FIGURE 9-6: Zoom email confirmation of new security settings for user group.

Here's an example of this new security setting in action. John enables the Use a password when holding meetings via their PMIs setting for the Realtors user group. John notifies the group of this change in the #Announcements channel, but Shelley ignores it. He attempts to schedule a meeting with his prospects Bruce and Harriet Nyborg, once again without setting a meeting password.

Shelley now has no choice but to use a password when he schedules a meeting. It's a required field. As Figure 9-7 shows, Zoom won't let Shelley uncheck the Password box. In other words, John has disabled all realtors' ability to hold password-free meetings.

Requiring more complex meeting and webinar passwords

Generally speaking, people leave themselves susceptible to hackers in all sorts of ways. As but one example, the collective inability to understand — never mind follow — basic password protocols never ceases to amaze security experts. (Check out `bit.ly/zfd-worst` for a list of the 100 worst passwords from 2018. I'm sure that you can guess at least a few of them.) To nudge people in the right direction, many companies compel their users to create complex account passwords that include numbers, symbols, and/or minimum-length requirements.

Schedule Meeting

Topic

Shelley Levine: Nyborg Meeting

Date

5/22/2020 ⌄ | 4:30 PM ⌄ | to | 5/22/2020 ⌄ | 5:00 PM ⌄

☐ Recurring meeting   Time Zone: Arizona ☽

Meeting ID

○ Generate Automatically   ● Personal Meeting ID :

Password

☑ Require meeting password | 566985

Video

Host ● On ○ Off   Participants ● On ○ Off

Audio

○ Telephone ○ Computer Audio ● Telephone and Computer Audio
Dial in from United States Edit

Calendar

○ iCal   ○ Google Calendar   ○ Outlook   ● Other Calendars

Cancel   **Schedule**

FIGURE 9-7:
Scheduling a
meeting now
that password
field is required.

Zoom allows account owners and admins do the very same thing. That is, they can force members in their organization to create more intricate passwords for meetings and webinars in two ways:

>> Mandate a minimum password length.

>> Require all passwords to contain letters, numbers, and/or special characters.

To require members on your account to use strong passwords, follow these directions:

1. **In the Zoom web portal, under the Admin header, click on Account Management.**

2. **Click on Account Settings.**

3. **Click on Schedule Meeting.**

4. **Select the Meeting password requirement options that you want to turn on.**

   Your options here include

   - Establishing a minimum password length (Zoom's current maximum is ten characters)

   - Including at least one letter

- Including at least one number

- Including at least one special character or symbol

- Only allowing a numeric password

5. **After making your selections, click on the blue Save button.**

Zoom confirms that it has successfully updated your settings.

Following Zoom's best security practices

Your scientists were so preoccupied with whether or not they could they didn't stop to think if they should.

— Jeff Goldblum as Dr. Ian Malcolm, *Jurassic Park*

As Chapter 4 describes, Zoom offers a bevy of robust features for meetings. (Short version: Thanks to Zoom, hosts and participants *can* perform many useful tasks.) There's a chasm, though, between could and should. Put simply, just because Zoom lets you enable or disable a feature doesn't mean that you should do it.

With that in mind, here are some tips on minimizing the chance that someone Zoombombs your meeting. More generally, follow the advice in this section to protect the privacy and security of your Zoom communications as much as possible.

Keeping your PMI private

Again, as Chapter 4 discusses, you wouldn't give a stranger a key to your home. The same principles apply to your PMI. Giving it to your spouse or mother is benign. Sharing it on social media is a recipe for disaster.

Using waiting rooms

Yes, Zoom lets users with sufficient permissions disable waiting rooms for their meetings — and possibly for others employees in the organization. I'd advise against it, however, especially on a permanent basis. Visit `bit.ly/zfd-diswr` for directions on how to effectively make your meetings less secure.

Preventing removed meetings participants from rejoining

John is acting like a putz during the company Zoom meeting, a fact not lost on the other participants. You have warned him a few times to knock it off, but he's incorrigible. As host, you finally boot him from the meeting. Everyone applauds.

By default, Zoom prevents John from jumping back in, even if he retained the host's PMI or the meeting's ID and password.

Again, depending on your formal Zoom role, you can change this setting. Still, I'd leave it as is. What's more, if you're a Zoom account owner or admin, then you may want to lock this setting such that non-administrative members cannot change it for themselves.

To do so, follow these directions:

1. **In the Zoom web portal, under the Admin header, click on Account Management.**

2. **Click on Account Settings.**

3. **Click on In Meeting (Basic).**

4. **Slide the Allow removed participants to rejoin toggle button to the left to turn it off.**

5. **Click on the gray lock icon to the right of the toggle button.**

   Zoom displays a message asking you to confirm your decision.

6. **Click on the blue Lock button.**

   Zoom confirms that it has successfully updated your settings.

Limiting who can control the main meeting screen

As Chapter 4 explains, Meetings & Chat offers a bevy of powerful screen-sharing features. If you want to dial back those options a bit, you certainly can. For example, say that you'd like to prevent participants from sharing their screens. Just follow these directions:

1. **Launch the Zoom desktop client.**

2. **Start your meeting.**

3. **Mouse over the bottom of the screen so that Zoom displays a menu.**

4. **Click the up arrowhead (^) next to Share Screen.**

5. **Select Advanced Sharing Options from the pop-up menu.**

6. **Underneath Who can share?, select the Only Host checkbox.**

7. **Close the screen and return to your meeting by clicking on the red circle in the top left-hand corner of the screen.**

Using your brain

The history of technology teaches its students many important lessons. Perhaps at the top of the list is that even the smartest cookies cannot predict every conceivable problem that a software product, feature, or version may cause. First, the law of unintended consequences is alive and well.

Second and just as important, bad actors are a clever lot. They invariably employ sophisticated tactics to circumvent even the most thoughtful security and privacy controls. In this way, Zoom has had to confront some of the very same challenges that have plagued Facebook, Twitter, Google, Amazon, and other firms of consequence. All of this is to say that managers and software engineers can do only so much to mitigate the problems that invariably arise with massive usage.

At least you always take with you one of your most effective weapons to combat attendee mischief and malfeasance. I'm talking about the organ that lies between your ears. Think carefully and critically about what you're doing in Zoom and with whom. Always be skeptical.

Exhibiting a healthy skepticism

Say that your son is a sophomore at a small northeastern university in a different part of the country. You and your spouse eagerly await your weekly Zoom call with him every Sunday afternoon at 4 p.m. You shared your PMI with him a year ago and thought nothing of it.

On Saturday, you receive an email from an unrecognized sender who purports to be your son. Still, something about the situation just rubs you the wrong way. This individual asks you to provide your PMI because he lost it.

What do you do?

Maybe nothing untoward is really taking place here. Maybe not. In this case, I would call your son or send him a text message explaining the situation. Based upon his response, your next step should be clear: Provide the PMI or report the email as the phishing attack that it appears to be.

TECHNICAL STUFF

Phishing perhaps represents bad actors' most effective means of obtaining sensitive information from their targets. They are often able to acquire others' credentials and other pieces of vital information by fraudulently posing as friends and loved ones.

TIP

Always err on the side of safety. If that means making it a tad more time-consuming for participants to join your Zoom meetings, then so be it. To quote a famous Russian proverb, "Trust, but verify."

Keeping privacy in mind during Zoom meetings

Regularly using your brain doesn't just make it harder for hackers to wreak havoc; it can protect you from putting your foot in your mouth in front of others. Remember that meeting hosts can easily generate chat logs, subject to a few disclaimers. They just need to follow a few simple steps:

1. **Launch the Zoom desktop client.**

2. **Start your meeting.**

3. **Mouse over the bottom of your screen to invoke Zoom's in-meeting menu.**

4. **Click on the Chat icon.**

5. **In the lower right-hand corner, click the ellipsis icon.**

6. **From the prompt, click on Save Chat.**

For example, Michael Bluth is hosting a meeting with his brothers Gob and Buster. During the meeting, at any point Michael can produce a chat log file because:

>> He's the meeting host.

>> Michael has enabled participants' ability to chat.

About five minutes into the meeting, Michael does this very thing. Zoom dutifully saves a simple text file to the default location on his computer. This file includes the following data from the meeting:

>> All participants' public chat messages

>> Any private chat messages that Michael exchanged with Gob and Buster

>> Any private chat messages that Gob and Buster exchanged with Michael

Michael's log file looks something like Figure 9-8.

REMEMBER

Note that Zoom omits from these log files all private messages that participants exchanged with each other during the meeting that excluded Michael. In other words, Michael won't know that Gob sent Buster a message calling him a chicken and Buster agreed with his brother.

```
12:39:42      From Michael Bluth : Hey brother.
12:39:44      From Michael Bluth : Gob?
12:40:45      From Gob Bluth : Come on.
12:41:29      From Michael Bluth to Buster Bluth (Privately) : Come on.
12:41:53      From Buster Bluth : Hey Brother. Where's Mom?
12:42:12      From Buster Bluth to Michael Bluth (Privately) : She always makes everything about her.
12:42:29      From Buster Bluth to Michael Bluth (Privately) : She gets off on being withholding.
```

FIGURE 9-8:
Zoom log file of chat activity during meeting.

Against this backdrop, keep the following privacy-related facts in mind as you use Meetings & Chat:

» Unless a host actively hits the Record button during a meeting, Zoom does not store video, audio, or chat content. That is, Zoom records nothing by default.

» When the host begins recording, Zoom provides both video and audio notifications to all meeting participants. If participating on a recorded meeting makes you uncomfortable, then you can always tell the host as much. You can also exit the meeting.

» Think of each Zoom meeting as a quasi-private forum. If you want to slam your boss or mock your colleagues mid-meeting, then have at it. Zoom can't stop you from exercising poor judgment. No tool can. Just remember that meeting participants are likely to notice inappropriate actions. When they do, prepare to suffer the consequences. In this way, Zoom is just like Slack, Microsoft Teams, email, and any other contemporary communications tool.

WARNING

Whether you're the host or not, think carefully about what you disclose both publicly and privately. There's no guarantee that those messages from Zoom meetings will ultimately stay private. Say that you privately chat with colleagues, partners, customers, or other meeting participants. Someone could easily take screenshots of those private messages with a third-party tool and release them after or even during the meeting.

For more information on Zoom's privacy policy, see `bit.ly/zfd-priv`.

Looking toward the Future

As I write these words, Zoom has nearly completed its self-imposed 90-day feature freeze. During this time, it has confronted a clear existential threat and made enormous progress. I'm hard-pressed to think of another company that has made such rapid, significant, and transparent changes to its product in such a short period of time — all while experiencing phenomenal growth. Brass tacks: Zoom's current version (5.0.5) is its most secure yet. It has solidified the foundation of its products and paved the way for significant safety and privacy enhancements down the road.

It follows, then, that Zoom will never encounter another security- or privacy-related issue again, right?

Wrong.

I'm no soothsayer, but I do know this much: From time to time, every organization occasionally makes a blunder. I'm referring to both acts of commission and acts of omission. When any company drops the ball, the key questions to ask are

- » How big is the gaffe?
- » Whom does it affect, and how?
- » What specific steps is its management taking to remedy the situation and prevent its recurrence?
- » Did those steps ultimately work?

In the context of these questions, it's impossible not to recognize and even applaud Zoom's recent actions. Think about how it has responded to the legitimate security issues that prompted its 90-day feature freeze. Making the changes outlined in this chapter was no small endeavor. As someone who has studied consumer and enterprise technology for the last 25 years, I cannot recall seeing such decisive action and results from a software vendor under comparable circumstances. Zoom's level of focus and execution put it in rarefied air indeed.

And I'm hardly the only person to take note. In fact, to say that many people noticed Zoom's rapid response is the acme of understatement. Don't take my word for it, though.

Early in this chapter, I mention that the NYC Department of Education banned teachers from using Zoom in their classrooms on April 6, 2020. Only a month later, the DoE reversed its decision. It determined that Zoom had fully addressed all of its security and privacy concerns. In fact, CEO Eric Yuan worked with the New York City school district himself. (See `bit.ly/zfd-nyc2` for more details on this story.)

Zoom will forge ahead with impressive product improvements and valuable new features. Many of these updates and upgrades will rely upon cutting-edge technologies. (Chapter 13 describes some the specific ones that Zoom is using to enhance its offerings.) Expecting true product innovation from any company without the occasional bump in the road is a fool's errand.

IN THIS CHAPTER

» Understanding immersive-telepresence technology

» Covering the basic features of Zoom Rooms

» Reviewing hardware, software, and lighting considerations

Chapter **10**

Taking Group Meetings to the Next Level with Zoom Rooms

Meetings & Chat serves a valuable purpose: It allows individuals to hold videoconferencing calls with anyone on the globe with their computers, tablets, and smartphones. Put differently, meeting hosts and participants just install Zoom software on their existing devices and get to work.

But what if an organization's videoconferencing needs exceed letting people dial in from their own individual devices? That is, a company wants to hold its video meetings with groups of people in the same physical location. Doing so would let remote attendees feel like they're in the same room as their peers.

For this reason, Zoom offers a popular service that takes Meetings & Chat up several notches: Zoom Rooms.

Revisiting the Early Days of Immersive-Telepresence Technology

It turns out that the idea of fusing high-tech software and hardware together to provide ginned-up conference rooms, corporate meetings, and training sessions isn't exactly new. In fact, the idea behind contemporary immersive-telepresence technology dates back to the early 1990s.

REMEMBER

While you're unlikely to hear the term around most water coolers, *immersive telepresence* refers to an integrated set of visual, audio, and network conferencing technologies and services. Together, they deliver a communications experience that resembles real-world ones.

Put it this way: Say that one group of suits was in São Paulo, Brazil while the other was in Montreal, Canada. If both groups were using immersive-telepresence technology, then people in each cohort would feel like they were actually in the same physical room.

How does the magic behind immersive-telepresence technology happen? I asked that very question to Jeff Fillbrandt of Utelogy, a company that builds tools that let people manage their audio-visual setups. The two of us spoke in early April 2020 — via Zoom, of course. Fillbrandt told me that Lifesize, Polycom, and other early immersive-telepresence vendors created this effect by installing three large, high-tech video screens next to each other. At the risk of oversimplifying, those screens and the software behind them created the illusion that people in Room A were sitting across from the people in Room B.

TelePresence by Cisco Systems

Arguably the highest profile product launch in the category took place in October 2006. Cisco announced the release of TelePresence, a suite of products that linked two physically separated rooms in a tighter way than people previously thought possible. Ideally, thanks to TelePresence, two conference rooms would resemble a single, integrated one despite their disparate locations.

To be sure, the idea behind TelePresence made plenty of sense. After all, the web had been around for more than a decade at that point. Generally speaking, new technologies were starting to make the impossible possible or, if you like, flatten the world. Thomas L. Friedman makes that point in spades in his 2005 book *The World Is Flat: A Brief History of the Twenty-first Century* (Farrar, Straus and Giroux).

Brass tacks: The time was ripe for Cisco Systems and other large technology vendors to take their first-generation immersive-telepresence tools to the next level. Cisco's execs envisioned the company's TelePresence in organizations' boardrooms and classrooms across the globe.

In 2008, Cisco claimed that it had outfitted 2,000 rooms with its wares. Beyond its paid customers, the company used the tool itself and commendably donated dozens of units to philanthropic organizations.

Unfortunately for Cisco, TelePresence never caught on as a mass-market tool. In retrospect, it's not hard to understand why adoption wasn't universal or even prevalent. Many executives found its costs exorbitant. The 2009 book *Cisco TelePresence Fundamentals* (Cisco Press) quotes the starting price back then for a single room at $250,000 plus additional maintenance and installation fees. Needless to say, a company couldn't just buy purchase TelePresence for a single room. It would have to sign up for at least two of them. Add in costs for bandwidth, switches, and other services, and the price tag could easily exceed seven figures.

Believe it or not, a large firm could spend even more money if it wanted to purchase and deploy best-of-breed immersive-telepresence technologies back then.

Halo by Hewlett-Packard

Many millennials have never heard of Hewlett-Packard (HP). Not that long ago, however, HP was just as influential as Google or Apple is today.

The iconic Silicon Valley technology company first dabbled in high-tech video-conferencing with its launch of Halo Collaboration Studios (HCS) on December 12, 2005. It did not take the world by storm. The company launched its successor to HCS a few years later. On March 18, 2008, Halo Collaboration Center (HCC) purported to "delive[r] an immersive collaboration experience for executives or small groups." (Read the press release at `bit.ly/zoom-hp`.) The price tag? Oh, not much. Just a cool $349,000 for a single room.

Perhaps because of its higher price and sagging consumer brand, HP's Halo remained an also-ran to Cisco Telepresence and others. On July 22, 2009, Justin Scheck and Ben Worthen of *The Wall Street Journal* reported that, in the first quarter of the year, Cisco sold two-thirds of the 520 telepresence units purchased worldwide. By way of comparison, that number was only 51 percent in 2008, according to estimates from Wainhouse Research. During that time, HP's share dropped to 10 percent from 11 percent.

The underwhelming results of early immersive-telepresence technology

In theory, installing a state-of-the-art telepresence system of the 2000s would ultimately pay for itself. I'm certain that these vendors' salespeople included this claim in their standard pitch to their prospects back in the day.

Sure, organizations would have to fork over princely sums, but consider the savings. Telepresence systems weren't just cool tchotchkes that illustrated a company's level of tech-savvy. These tools could save them millions of dollars per year. Say goodbye to hundreds of airline tickets, hotel bills, physical conference rooms, food, and other travel- and meeting-related expenses. Telepresence systems practically paid for themselves!

Despite their utility, the immersive-telepresence tools of the aughts remained niche tools. The obvious question is why. Three reasons come to mind, although I suspect that there are others.

First and to state the obvious, few companies outside of the Fortune 500 could afford them. Second and on a related note, the financial crisis of 2008 and 2009 thwarted most of the momentum behind their widespread adoption. Organizations needed to slash their internal IT budgets, not expand them. (I should know because I was there. I worked as an enterprise-systems consultant during that time.)

Finally, management at most firms decided that it was more important to connect everyday employees via affordable — if less chic and powerful — desktop video-conferencing tools. That is, ultimately it just didn't make sense to reserve this collaboration and communication technology exclusively for a company's top-20 bigwigs in their cordoned-off conference rooms.

THE EARLY DAYS OF IMMERSIVE-TELEPRESENCE TECH

My first, albeit indirect, exposure to immersive-telepresence tech took place in 1998. Back then, I worked at Merck & Co., the pharmaceutical giant based out of rustic Whitehouse Station, New Jersey.

During my Merck tenure, from time to time I mingled with company muckety-mucks. Executives often lunched in a private dining room equipped with a waitstaff and requiring an access card to enter. They also could hold virtual meetings with other Merck executives, government officials, and media members. The setup was pretty advanced, at least for the technologies of the day.

Introducing Zoom Rooms

Here's the best way to think about Zoom Rooms. As Chapter 3 describes and as more than 300 million people know, Meetings & Chat works exceptionally well for individuals and their personal and employer–issued devices. For group meetings and events, however, it's often not practical for everyone to huddle around Steve's laptop or Joni's iPad, much less Aimee's smartphone. If you intend to hold group training or brainstorming sessions online in this manner, you most likely won't be pleased with the result.

For this reason, Zoom Rooms is a popular choice. The product allows organizations to augment their physical conference, huddle, and training rooms with powerful technology that simulates more expensive immersive–telepresence solutions. Put differently, through the combination of software and hardware, Zoom Rooms lets groups of people in the same physical space communicate and collaborate effectively with others who are somewhere else.

Conceptually, Zoom Rooms shares a great deal in common with its ancestors. That is, with Rooms, Zoom has done what vendors such as Polycom, Cisco, and Lifesize did. At a high level, all these companies' solutions allow their clients to turn their relatively low–tech conference rooms into far more immersive ones.

Features of Zoom Rooms

Generally speaking, people can do the same things in Zoom Rooms that they can in Meetings & Chat, but together in the same room. Highlights here include

- » **Screen-share a camera:** Users are not limited to just sharing their computer's screen with others. They can also share a second camera — the one in the physical room.

- » **Pin a video:** Individuals can disable the active-speaker view and just focus on one attendee.

- » **Spotlight a video:** The meeting host can disable the active-speaker view so that everyone in theory focuses on a single attendee or speaker.

- » **Control different aspects of the meeting:** Options include recording, stopping the video, managing the participants, and much more.

- » **Use voice commands:** It's not quite Alexa or Siri yet, but you can say "Hey, Zoom: Start meeting." As I describe in Chapter 13, expect more voice-initiated options in the future.

- » **Chat with others in Zoom Room via text:** In this way, Zoom Rooms resemble the functionality that I cover in Chapter 5.

>> **Invite others to your Zoom Room meeting:** You can easily let internal and external contacts join the party.

>> **Schedule meetings in Zoom Rooms:** By synchronizing Zoom Rooms with your organization's calendar system, scheduling is a breeze.

Check out the informative webinar "5 Things You Didn't Know About Zoom Rooms" at bit.ly/zfd-webinar. (Note that you'll have to register to view it.)

Visit bit.ly/zmrmfeat to learn more about the specific features of Zoom Rooms and how to deploy them.

Cost and functionality

Say that you're in the market for a new car. Few people would confuse a 2020 Lamborghini Aventador S with a modest electric car. Sure, both qualify as automobiles, but that's where the similarities end. The price of the latter is a rounding error in comparison to the price of the former. Few people can drop $400,000 on a premium sportscar.

You can lay the same claim about Zoom Rooms with respect to Cisco TelePresence and other ultra-upscale offerings. Six-figure, immersive-telepresence solutions remain far beyond the budgets of the vast majority of organizations, even in good economic times. Zoom Rooms represents an affordable, powerful, and user-friendly option. It allows individuals and companies to realize many of the benefits of more expensive tools at a fraction of the cost. For example, the Dell Optiplex, HP EliteOne, and other entry-level models start at roughly $1,000.

The types of environments that typically benefit from Zoom Rooms

Today many organizations deploy Zoom Rooms in the following environments:

>> Executive conference rooms

>> Huddle rooms

>> Lounge areas

>> Theaters

>> Classrooms

Setting up a Zoom Room in your 8-x-8-foot cube at work probably doesn't make sense. Outside of the office, though, personal Zoom Rooms are becoming increasingly common in home offices and studios.

Setting Up Your Zoom Room

At a high level, a Zoom Room requires two things: hardware and software. While entirely optional, a little lighting does wonders as well.

Software

Someone in your organization will have to purchase a Zoom Room software license, available at $49 per month per room. (For more on pricing, see Chapter 2.) Once you do, download and install the Zoom Rooms app, displayed in Figure 10-1.

FIGURE 10-1: Zoom Room iPad app.

The Zoom Rooms app differs from other Zoom mobile apps. Visit bit.ly/zr-app to download it.

TIP

Hardware

I'll bet that, at some point, you have attended a conference. If so, then you may have noticed that the speaker was wearing a headset or using a microphone. If she looked down from time to time, odds are that she was looking at a confidence monitor. Through a clicker, she was advancing her PowerPoint slides. The audience could see the slides on the projection screen when they looked up from their own devices. And without those speakers, you wouldn't hear a thing unless you were in the front row.

In this sense, Zoom Rooms works the same way as traditional audio/visual (A/V) systems. It requires a number of different, integrated components in order to function properly. Fortunately, Zoom provides plenty of hardware options.

All-in-one appliances

Zoom's management has forged partnerships with a number of popular hardware vendors to make all-in-one appliances. These devices make installing and configuring Zoom Rooms far easier than trying to piece together hardware components from different manufacturers.

As of this writing, Zoom's recommended appliances include:

>> **Neat Bar by Neat:** This device looks like a Sonos Playbar and goes for $2,500. It includes an on-table controller. (See https://neat.no.)

>> **Poly Studio X Video Bars:** Poly's offering also resembles a Sonos Playbar. It plays nice with Microsoft Teams, BlueJeans, and GoToMeeting. I found the X30 model on Amazon for $1,500 as of this writing. (See amzn.to/2MJ7vdr.) Note that you need to purchase a separate controller to make it work.

>> **DTEN All-in-One Video Conferencing Device:** DTEN's touchscreen-enabled model looks like a large flat-screen television, but does so much more. I found the 55-inch model available for $4,300 as of this writing. (See amzn.to/37iKFD8.) Because it's a touchscreen, you don't need to purchase a controller. Figure 10-2 shows a picture of this model.

In June 2020, the company launched its little brother, the 27-inch DTEN Me.

TIP

For more information on suggested appliances for Zoom Rooms, see bit.ly/zm-app.

FIGURE 10-2:
55-inch DTEN
All-in-One Video
Conferencing
Device.

Bundles

Bundles represent a second hardware option. Other vendors make very slick video screens that work seamlessly with the Zoom Rooms software. For example, consider Urben, a maker of interactive, modular, movable, customizable, and affordable hardware enclosures. In effect, they stitch together the devices from Zoom-approved vendors into an all-in-one solution. Figure 10-3 displays a three-screen version of the Urben Immersive Datapresence (ID) product.

Individual components

If appliances and bundles don't float your boat, then feel free to purchase and configure other third-party hardware to work with Zoom Rooms. For the best experience, you'll need each of the following components:

- **Computer:** The device that powers the main visual display.

- **Main display:** A large monitor that others in the room can view.

- **Controller:** A device that remotely powers the Zoom Rooms software. Typically, Zoom's customers use a tablet for this purpose.

FIGURE 10-3:
Urben Frame ID
for a three-
screen, 55-inch
Zoom Room
setup.

>> **External camera:** This device allows others to view the meeting attendees in the physical room and vice versa.

>> **Speaker/microphone:** This device allows in-person meeting attendees to speak to the remote participants and vice versa.

Zoom Rooms for Touch

Employees who seek an even more interactive experience for their Zoom Rooms are in luck. Zoom Rooms for Touch lets organizations add large touchscreens to their Zoom Rooms. With it, meeting attendees can concurrently touch the Zoom app on a large video display.

TIP

See bit.ly/zfd-tch for more information about Zoom Rooms for Touch.

Deployment options

People who want to deploy Zoom Rooms can go in a number of directions:

>> Buy the hardware and install it themselves — the DIY option.

>> Hire a certified, third-party integrator.

>> Use Zoom's professional services.

But do you have to buy new hardware to make Zoom Rooms sing? As I briefly mention in Chapter 2, not necessarily.

Zoom Conference Room Connectors

Say that your organization has already purchased specific hardware and configured it to work with a competing immersive-telepresence product. Along comes Zoom Rooms. Understandably, your management doesn't want to underwrite yet another series of expensive hardware purchases.

You might be in luck. That is, your company may be able to link its existing proprietary hardware to a Zoom Room using a gateway product called Zoom Conference Room Connectors. These devices let employees make Zoom video calls using their organization's existing conference-room hardware. Put differently, employees can to take advantage of Zoom's intuitive UI and port their existing, on-premises videoconferencing systems to the cloud.

TIP Before junking your company's existing hardware, talk to an experienced professional about integrating your company's current monitors, speakers, and other devices with Zoom Rooms.

TIP To find out more about Zoom Connectors, see `bit.ly/zfd-connect`. For much more about its technical specifications, visit `bit.ly/zoom-connector`.

As the nearby sidebar on Drew University illustrates, Zoom Rooms allows organizations to meet business needs that Meetings & Chat simply cannot.

UNDER THE HOOD OF CONFERENCE ROOM CONNECTORS

Zoom Conference Room Connectors support third-party calling systems from Cisco, Poly, and others. There's just one caveat: Those systems rely upon one of the two most popular standards for audio-, video-, and data-transmission interoperability: H.323 and Session Initiation Protocol (SIP).

Both protocols manage the voice, data, and control aspects of calls. They only differ in their approach to achieving these goals. H.323 uses Voice over Internet Protocol (VoIP). For its part, SIP uses an Internet-based approach. In other words, Connectors allow companies to link Zoom Rooms to their existing *endpoints*.

In its simplest form, an endpoint is a remote-computing device that communicates with other endpoints on a connected network. Typical examples include laptop and desktop computers, mobile phones, tablets, servers, and even virtual environments.

For more on this subject, see Chapter 1.

HOW DREW UNIVERSITY ROLLED OUT ZOOM ROOMS

Located in the leafy suburb of Madison, NJ, Drew University is home to more than 2,000 undergraduate and graduate students. The university consists of three different schools, including the Drew Theological School (DTS). Historically, DTS has appealed to older students, some of whom were in their 60s, and many of whom held part- or full-time jobs. To this end, DTS held many of its classes remotely. (Researching this book, I interviewed Shawn Spaventa, the school's Director of Instructional Technology.)

Faculty in Drew's Doctor of Ministry (DMin) program had been using videoconferencing technology for more than a decade. Back in 2009, it relied upon Breeze, a clunky and expensive tool that Adobe purchased and fused with its Connect offering. After that, the school paid for a Webex subscription for a few years with mixed results.

Moving to Meetings & Chat

Spaventa had heard good things about Zoom. In 2015, he signed Drew and the DMin program up for Meetings & Chat. Students and faculty and loved it. They didn't need a great deal of training. In fact, Spaventa told me that the number of tech-support tickets dropped from two or three per week under previous videoconferencing programs to two total for an entire semester.

In July 2014, Javier Viera joined Drew as the Vice Provost and Dean of the Drew Theological School (DTS). When it came to technology, Viera and Associate Dean Melanie Johnson-DeBaufre wanted to do more — especially with teleconferencing technology. They were interested in conducting on-campus virtual meetings. Like quite a few universities at the time, DTS had fiddled with hybrid classes: those that professors could concurrently hold in-person and online. Viera envisioned location-independent, synchronous learning via small classes that would appeal to the school's older students with long commutes and full-time jobs.

As it turned out, Spaventa identified a few prospects for these virtual meetings: two small classrooms at Drew that faculty had rarely used. Because Drew's faculty had already seen the benefits of Meetings & Chat, Spaventa decided to up the ante with Zoom Rooms.

To review its different configuration options, Drew brought in Captus Systems, a New York-based firm that designs and builds A/V frameworks. Drew and Captus personnel reviewed hardware requirements for setting up the rooms, and Drew launched Zoom Rooms in 2018.

Results and lessons

Zoom Rooms has been an unequivocal success at Drew. Specific highlights include

- Students immediately took to the new Zoom Rooms. They routinely reported that they felt like they were in a physical classroom.
- In the span of a single semester, the primary Zoom Room went from barely being used to professors holding more than five hours of instruction in it per day.
- Tech support for Drew's Zoom Rooms is minimal. Professors simply walk in, fire up the iPad, and activate the room with a single touch.

Sure, Drew experienced a few bumps along the way, as Spaventa candidly admits. For example, he recommends that organizations considering Zoom Rooms explore the specific functionality that they want to make available to their employees. That discussion will form the organization's choice of specific hardware, such as which camera, microphone, and video display to select.

Also, remember to consider the physical dimensions of a potential Zoom Room. For example, Spaventa described to me a small conference room at Drew with a wall-mounted 75-inch monitor and large, U-shaped table. That setup seemed fine in theory. In practice, though, building and testing the room yielded slightly different results. Positioning the camera and microphone might require several bites at the apple.

Finally, aim for simplicity, especially at first. "We tried to shoehorn in a lot of things in there that we probably didn't need," Spaventa tells me.

Lighting

To be sure, your firm can spend thousands of dollars on hardware. Don't be surprised, though, if the people who use the new Zoom Room don't look as good as they would like. After all, the DTEN and its ilk aren't dedicated lighting units.

In other words, lighting matters. As the nearby sidebar illustrates, it's wise to equip your Zoom Room with professional lighting.

I'm a fan of Brightline's cMe2 Huddle Room Light, displayed in Figure 10-4. I mounted it above my DTEN, and it has done wonders for my personal Zoom Room. It's the difference between night and day, if you'll excuse the pun.

LIGHTS. CAMERA. ACTION!

You've probably heard this expression before, but far too often people forget the lights part of it.

Inadequate light means that cameras can't see the action. It's that simple.

Without getting too technical, a camera sees differently than the human eye does. The latter processes light and its associated color through a narrower spectrum.

Professional lights promote enhanced video imaging in two important ways. First, they automatically direct light where it's needed. Second, and just as important, they shield light from unwanted areas, such as physical whiteboards or presentation screens.

Lighting professionals are intimately familiar with the term *color rendering index*. CRI quantifies the ability of a light source to faithfully reveal the colors of different objects in comparison with an ideal or natural light source. The higher the CRI of a light source, the more accurate its color reproduction.

Brass tacks: If you're going to purchase an immersive-telepresence system, it's downright silly to ignore professional lighting. After all, you want to look like a professional, not an amateur.

Kathy Katz is the managing partner at Brightline, a maker of energy-efficient lighting fixtures for television broadcast-studio, videoconference, e-learning, and government applications based in Pittsburgh, Pennsylvania.

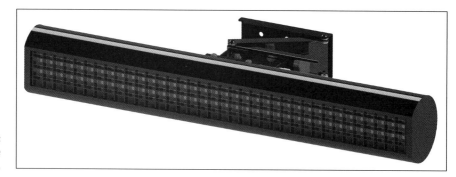

FIGURE 10-4:
cMe2 Huddle
Room Light.

Chapter **11**

Making Calls with Zoom Phone

For several reasons, odds are that you don't give much thought to the idea of a traditional work phone. First, depending on your vocation, they might as well just not exist. Maybe you're a grade-school teacher, a digital nomad, a freelancer, a touring musician, or a Lyft driver. Second, your employer might provide traditional landlines at the office, and the technology behind these phones doesn't matter to you at all. Third, your company may provide you with a dedicated smartphone that you're supposed to use for business purposes only. Ever see someone packing two iPhones? Make no mistake, though: The explosion in technology has not resulted in the death of dedicated office phone numbers — at least, not yet. Oodles of enterprises possess a legitimate need to outfit their employees with them. The options for employers in this regard, however, are a far cry from their counterparts in the 1950s and 1960s. In this vein, companies such as Vonage, Nextiva, RingCentral, and others have offered powerful and affordable business phone systems for decades. Although new to the field, Zoom's offering compares favorably with those of established players. This chapter provides an overview of Zoom Phone, a service that seamlessly integrates with Zoom's desktop client.

Getting Started with Zoom Phone

Zoom Phone arrived on January 22, 2019. (Go to `bit.ly/zoom-prph` to read the press release.) The service represents an add-on to customers' existing Zoom subscriptions. Note that people using Zoom's Basic Meetings & Chat plan can add Zoom Phone. At present, Zoom Phone is not a standalone service that organizations can purchase independently. (Zoom will be changing this policy by the end of 2020.) Like much of its competition, the technology behind Zoom Phone relies upon Voice over Internet Protocol (VoIP). For more on the technology behind making calls over the Internet, see Chapter 1. Largely due to space considerations, this chapter focuses on the basics of Zoom Phone. Of course, organizations may want to configure Zoom Phone with separate, dedicated, physical phones. (See `bit.ly/zm-ph-hw` for more information on configuring Zoom Phone with recommended third-party devices.)

WARNING

Also, to keep this book at a reasonable length and cost, I cover only the most popular features of Zoom Phones. (Fans of the cult 1999 flick *Office Space* may even say that I'm doing the bare minimum here.) Trust me: One could scribe a separate 200-page *For Dummies* book on a robust system such as Zoom Phone, especially as the company continues to add new functionality to it.

Adding Zoom Phone to your existing plan

Just like with Zoom Webinars, a Zoom account owner can always add Zoom Phone to the organization's existing Zoom subscription. Note, however, that Zoom Phone isn't a binary. In fact, you can customize it in myriad ways to meet the specific needs of your organization and avoid paying for licenses that it doesn't need. Brass tacks: The exact sign-up process and monthly or annual cost differs depending upon the following factors:

>> **Your current Meetings & Chat plan:** Zoom may provide quantity discounts to organizations that need multiple phone numbers and hundreds or even thousands of extensions.

>> **The number of phone numbers that you need:** This number usually hinges upon the number of employees in your organization.

>> **The specific types of phone numbers that your employees need:** Zoom charges extra for toll-free numbers.

>> **The countries that employees in your organization call:** Zoom charges vastly different rates to call different countries.

>> **The chattiness of your employees:** Again, the cost depends on the plan and add-ons that your organization selects. Still, all things being equal, employees who make and take more calls pay more than their reticent counterparts.

>> **An à-la-carte or an all-you-can-eat calling plan:** Employees who call exotic places on a piecemeal basis will run up larger bills than their brethren who don't pay by the call. Against this backdrop, I'm going to keep it as simple as possible here. For example, say that you already pay for the popular Zoom's Pro Meetings & Chat plan. What's more, you want to add a single phone number to it. Two limitations apply:

- Only account owners and admins can provision Zoom Phone licenses to existing users in an account.

- Along these lines, your current role may prohibit you from adding Zoom Phone to your account.

In the event that these limitations don't apply to you, follow these directions:

1. **In the Zoom web portal, under the Admin header, click on Account Management.**

2. **Click on Billing.**

   Zoom displays your current plans and add-ons.

3. **Next to Zoom Phone, click on the white Add button.**

   TIP

   As with all Zoom subscriptions, accounts with fewer than 50 licensed users can add additional ones via the web portal. For larger accounts of 50 and more, Zoom requires organizations to contact its sales department.

4. **Select whether you to want to subscribe monthly or annually.**

5. **Choose the type of calling plan to which you want to subscribe.**

   Zoom provides a number of different options here depending on your calling needs. For example, an individual who intends to make a small number of calls within the United States may opt for an entirely different plan than a jetsetter who expects to call people in 80 countries over the course of a month.

   For more information on the available add-ons and options for Zoom Phone, see Chapter 2.

   TIP

   With Zoom Phone, employees are always connected. They can make and take calls from anywhere on the planet.

6. **Click on the blue Continue button at the bottom of the page.**

   Zoom takes you to a page that allows you to verify both your forthcoming purchase as well as your payment information.

7. **Click on the blue Buy Now button.**

   Zoom presents an order summary screen.

8. **Click on the orange Confirm button.**

Voilà! Zoom emails you an invoice for your purchase.

Setting up Zoom to receive inbound calls

Say that you are an account owner or admin, and you already have subscribed to Zoom Phone. The next step is to select a phone number for incoming calls:

1. **In the Zoom web portal, under the Admin header, click on Phone System Management.**

2. **Click on Setup.**

   At the top of your screen, choose your main company number.

3. **From the first drop-down menu, select your country or region.**

4. **From the second drop-down menu, choose your state, province, or territory.**

   Zoom displays different area codes that correspond to your choice. For example, selecting California as your state results in different options than selecting Oregon.

5. **Select the area code and city of your new Zoom phone number.**

TIP

   Zoom allows customers to change their company numbers after setup as long as they possess the rights. That is, as the account owner or administrator, you can make the change. For obvious reasons, people who lack this role cannot.

6. **Select your phone number from the Choose Number menu.**

   Zoom may not be able to accommodate your selection here. If that's the case, return to the previous step and select a new combination of area code and city.

7. **Enter a three- to six-digit number under Specify Extension Number for Owner.**

   Zoom requires this field.

8. **Click on the blue Next button.**

   Zoom presents a confirmation window asking whether you're sure that you want (123) 456-2112 or whatever as your company number.

9. **Click on the blue Yes button.**

   Zoom asks you to verify your company's address in the event of an emergency.

10. **Enter your country address, city, state or province, and zip or postal code.**

11. At the bottom of the screen, select the following checkbox: **By setting your company's emergency address, you agree to Zoom Phone Emergency Calling Customer Notification.**

12. Click on the blue **Done** button.

Zoom sends you an email indicating that you have successfully activated your Zoom Phone number. Figure 11-1 displays the new Phone icon that appears at the top of the Zoom desktop client.

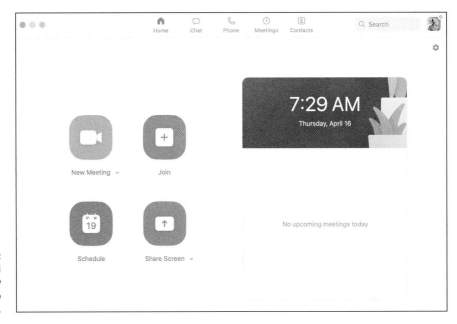

FIGURE 11-1:
Zoom updated UI after successfully subscribing to Zoom Phone.

Note how Figure 11-1 is relatively spartan at this point. That's because I haven't used Zoom Phone to call anyone and no one has called me — yet. As you use Zoom Phone, however, you can view your call history, access your voicemails and recordings, dial out, and do a whole lot more.

TIP

If you do not see the new Phone icon in Figure 11-1 appear, then simply sign out of the Zoom desktop client. After you sign back in, it should appear.

REMEMBER

You can set up different Zoom accounts with different email addresses and add different subscriptions to each account. Keep this fact in mind. For example, say I have set up two separate Zoom accounts: phil@marillion.com and phil@ptree.com. I add a Zoom Phone subscription to the marillion.com account, but not the ptree.com account. As a result, I won't see the Phone icon if I log into Zoom with the latter credentials.

Setting up Zoom to make outbound calls

Before employees in your organization can use Zoom Phone to make outbound calls, you'll have to assign them a calling plan.

WARNING

If you want your employees to call other people, then this process is essential. For example, say that I run Nakatomi Corporation. (Yeah, I'm a big fan of the original *Die Hard*.) I assign myself a calling plan to make outbound calls. However, I forget to do the same for Holly. As a result, she will not be able to use Zoom Phone to call anyone. Period. To allow the employees in your organization to make outbound calls over Zoom Phone, follow this admittedly lengthy process:

1. **In the Zoom web portal, under the Admin header, click on Users & Rooms.**

   Zoom shows the users in your organizations, as Figure 11-2 displays.

FIGURE 11-2:
Zoom users and rooms prior to plan assignment.

2. **Select the user(s) to whom you'd like to assign calling plans.**

   The available plans are the one(s) that you selected when you subscribed to Zoom Plans as an add-on. (See the section "Adding Zoom Phone to your existing plan," earlier in this chapter.)

TIP

You need not assign an outbound calling plan to every employee in your organization. As long as you are an account administrator or owner, Zoom allows you to select a subset of employees to whom you want to grant this option. (See Chapter 3 for more information about roles in Zoom.)

3. **Click on the Assign Number drop-down list on the right-hand side of the page.**

   Zoom displays the plan(s) that you have previously selected.

4. **Select an outbound calling plan for the user(s).**

5. **Click on the Assign Number drop-down list on the right-hand side of the page.**

   Zoom displays the plan(s) that you have previously selected. Zoom prompts you to choose an outbound calling number, as Figure 11-3 shows.

FIGURE 11-3:
Zoom Phone first
prompt to choose
an outbound
calling number
from unassigned
numbers.

Choose from Unassigned US/CA Numbers

| Search | Number Type (All) | Get Numbers |

No Data

Cancel   Confirm

6. **(Optional) Select a number type from the drop-down list to restrict your forthcoming search.**

   You can also just click on the Get Numbers button the right-hand side of the screen. Zoom displays the screen in Figure 11-4.

7. **Enter a state, providence, or territory from the drop-down list.**

   The options hinge upon the countries that appear at the top of Figure 11-4. For example, since I selected a US/CA number, I can select only states and provinces in the United States and Canada, respectively.

8. **Enter your desired area code.**

   Yes, your options hinge upon your selection in the prior step.

9. **Click on the Search button.**

   Zoom attempts to display available outbound numbers in your desired area code. If Zoom cannot locate any, then you may still be in luck. Zoom displays the following message:

   ```
   Please fill out this form to obtain numbers that are not available in Zoom
       Web Portal.
   ```

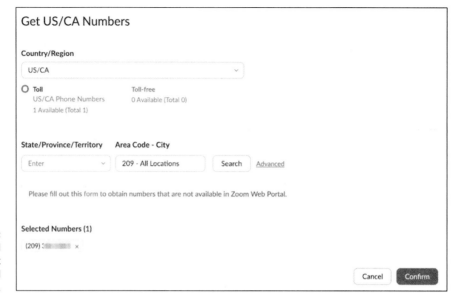

FIGURE 11-4:
Zoom's second
prompt to select
an outbound
calling number.

10. **If Zoom didn't locate any numbers and you want to proceed, click on the word "form" in the message that appeared.**

Zoom takes you to a web page in which you can order a phone number in your desired area code.

11. **(Optional) Click on the word Advanced for a separate prompt.**

Zoom allows you to enter a string of numbers that you'd like to include in the outbound number. For example, say that you want to use a phone number with 2112 in it. Enter those four numbers consecutively and then click the Search button. Zoom returns results that match your criterion.

12. **Select the checkbox next to the area code and phone number that appeals to you.**

Zoom places the number or numbers selected at the bottom of the screen.

13. **Click on the blue Confirm button in the bottom right-hand corner of the screen.**

Zoom confirms that you have added the phone number to your subscription. Zoom also sends you a confirmation email, such as the one presented in Figure 11-5.

Now, when you call others, they will see the number that you have selected. If you want to change this selection, see the section "Changing your default calling number," later in this chapter. You may find Zoom's process of assigning outbound calling numbers a bit laborious. That position is certainly understandable. As the nearby sidebar illustrates, though, Zoom's deliberate design choice is a feature, not a bug.

FIGURE 11-5:
Email confirming assignment of a new Zoom Phone number.

WHY ZOOM (PROBABLY) DOES NOT DEFAULT OUTBOUND CALLING PLANS TO USERS

I'll come clean: I've never spoken to Zoom CEO Eric Yuan. Sure, we're connected on LinkedIn, but that fact and $4 will get me a latte at Starbucks.

I'm speculating here, but I'm not venturing too far out of my areas of expertise. I know a thing or six about enterprise technology. Beyond that, my first full-time job out of college was at SONY Electronics in Park Ridge, New Jersey. I worked as a call center rep, answering easily more than 100 calls per day from less-than-happy customers. Because of my background, I've got a pretty good idea about why Zoom separates inbound and outbound calling numbers. (Only licensed Zoom Phone users can make outbound calls and receive inbound calls.)

Think about it this way: Say that Zoom fused outbound and inbound calls. That is, companies could not pick which calls employees could make or receive using Zoom Phone. As a result, management would have a difficult time policing their phone activity.

Sure, the occasional five-minute call from California to Canada on the company dime may not matter. But what if hundreds or even thousands of employees called exotic locations? For example, consider Bushwood Country Club, a company on a pay-as-you-go Zoom calling plan. Bushwood can expect to pony up 54 cents per minute when its employees call Algeria. Similar calls to Morocco cost 41 cents per minute. If you think that these charges can add up, trust your judgment. What's more, many call centers allow their reps to receive only inbound calls, not make outbound ones. (Yes, this process typically frustrates customers who have to wait 20 minutes or more to speak with a human being.) Bottom line: Zoom has made this decision for a valid business reason. Every employee in every type of organization doesn't need to make and receive traditional phone calls.

Reviewing the Basic Features of Zoom Phone

Say that you never heard of Zoom Phone prior to purchasing this book. You are aware, though, of the concept of the telephone, an invention that harkens back to 1876. Congratulations. You already understand the central idea behind Zoom Phone: At the risk of stating the obvious, it lets you talk and listen to other human beings in real time, even if they are somewhere else. After adding Zoom Phone to your existing plan, customers can access their new bells and whistles from a number of places:

>> The Zoom desktop client

>> The Zoom tablet app

>> The Zoom smartphone app

>> The phone section of the Zoom web portal

The calling features of Zoom Phone work on every device: on all mobile apps, on the desktop client, and through off-the-shelf VoIP desk phones. For example, say that you want to listen to your voicemail. You can perform this action wherever you like. Note, though, that you can only perform certain administrative Zoom Phone functions via certain mediums. A few examples clarify what I mean:

>> You want make and receive phone calls. You can use whatever app you like, but you cannot make calls in the Zoom web portal.

>> If you want to configure your voicemail settings, then you will have to use the Phone section of the Zoom web portal. In other words, you can perform certain functions in Zoom Phone only over the web.

In this vein, Zoom Phone resembles other popular mainstream communications products, namely Slack and Microsoft Teams. Say that you mostly work in an office or at home in front of your computer. You'll probably spend most of your time in the Zoom desktop client. Figure 11-6 displays it along with the specific features of Zoom Phone.

REMEMBER

If you or your organization has not subscribed to Zoom Phone, then you will not see the Phone tab at the top of the Zoom desktop client — or on any Zoom app, for that matter. Again, changing other settings requires customers to access the Zoom web portal. Figure 11-7 displays the Phone section of the Zoom web portal.

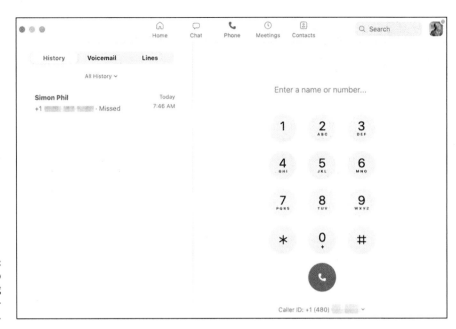

FIGURE 11-6:
Zoom desktop
client displaying
new phone-
related features.

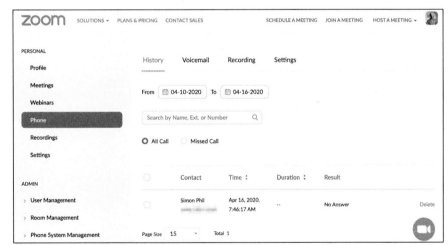

FIGURE 11-7:
Phone section of
the Zoom web
portal.

Before distributing your Zoom Phone number

Zoom offers dozens of ways for its customers to configure and tweak Zoom Phone to their liking. This section provides some highlights, but it hardly provides a comprehensive list of features and settings.

Configuring your voicemail

To set up your voicemail, follow these steps:

1. **In the Zoom web portal, under the Personal header, click on Phone.**

2. **Click on the Settings tab at the top of the screen.**

WARNING

Fight the urge to click on the Voicemail tab here. Doing so displays your existing voicemails, if you have any.

3. **(Optional) Scroll down and select what action you want to occur when you don't answer a call.**

You can select one of the following options:

- **Forward to voicemail:** This default option is self-explanatory, and, I suspect, the most common among Zoom customers.

- **Play a message, then disconnect:** Again, this option provides a bit more information to the caller before hanging up.

- **Disconnect:** Choosing this option terminates the call. This option is a bit more abrupt than the previous one.

- **Forward to another extension:** If you select this option, then Zoom provides the additional prompts in Steps 5 and 6. Select the option and/or extension that reflects what you want Zoom to do.

4. **(Optional) Underneath Blocked List and to the right of Voicemail, click on Set.**

5. **(Optional) Select another Zoom Phone user in your organization who can access the voicemails for your phone number and extension.**

Here you can let other Zoom Phone users access the voicemail associated with your number and/or extension.

6. **After selecting another user, click on the blue Save button.**

WARNING

If you're the only one in your organization subscribed to Zoom Phone, then understandably you won't see any options here.

7. **(Optional) Under PIN Code, display or edit your original PIN.**

By default, Zoom displays a series of asterisks below your PIN. To display your original PIN, click on Show or Edit.

8. **(Optional) Click on the blue Save button.**

Setting your business hours

After you distribute your Zoom Phone number to others, expect others to call it. By default, your Zoom app(s) will ring during all hours of the day and days of the week. If Jesse is up at 2 a.m. your time and rings your number, then Zoom will put your call through. After all, you didn't tell Zoom to do otherwise. Of course, your brick-and-mortar or digital business may not abide by a 24/7 schedule. As such, Zoom offers its customers the ability to set custom time frames in which outbound calls reach them. To do so, follow these steps:

1. **In the Zoom web portal, under the Personal header, click on Phone.**

2. **Click on the Settings tab at the top of the screen.**

3. **Scroll down the page to where you see Business Hours and click on Edit.**

    Zoom by default displays 24 Hours, 7 Days a Week.

4. **From the prompt, click on Custom Hours.**

5. **Select the checkboxes next to the days of the week to indicate that you accept calls during those days.**

    Zoom displays the grid displayed in Figure 11-8.

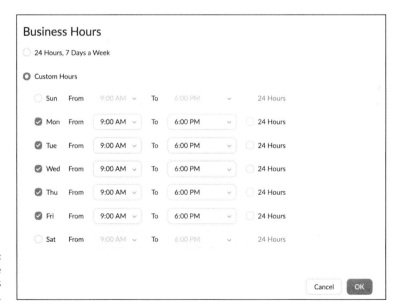

FIGURE 11-8:
Setting available business hours in Zoom.

6. **From the drop-down lists, select the hours for each day that you want to receive calls.**

7. **Click on the blue OK button.**

Talking to people via Zoom Phone

As is the case with traditional landlines, you can use Zoom Phone to both make calls to — and receive calls from — others. In both cases, whether call participants use Zoom Phone themselves or not is immaterial. It just works. Also, rest assured, the inbound and outbound calling features in Zoom Phone are remarkably easy to understand and operate.

Placing outbound calls

To call another person or organization, simply follow these steps:

1. **Launch the Zoom desktop client.**

2. **Click on the Phone icon at the top of the screen.**

3. **Call a number.**

   You can use any of the following methods:

   - Dial a number using the number pad, just like you would on your smartphone or an old-school landline phone.

   - Paste a previously copied phone number into the text field.

   - Type a name or phone number in the text field. Zoom will attempt to identify the individual based upon any matches in your contacts.

4. **Click on the blue Phone icon after you enter a valid name or phone number below the number 0.**

5. **(Optional) Click on the drop-down list underneath the Phone icon to enable or disable caller ID.**

   Take advantage of this option if you want to hide the number from the person you're calling. Of course, in this era of pervasive robocalling, realize that many people these days are wary of answering calls from unknown numbers.

TIP

You can make Zoom calls from apps on your tablet and phone as well. The process is very similar to the one described placing outbound calls as described in the preceding steps. However, it may vary slightly based upon your specific device and operating system.

Receiving inbound calls

You'll get the hang of making calls in Zoom quickly. As for receiving others' calls, the process is just as simple. Follow these steps:

1. **Launch the Zoom desktop client.**

   Zoom notifies you that you are receiving a call.

TIP

   Chapter 5 covers how you can set your status in Meetings & Chat. If you set yours to Do Not Disturb (DND), then Zoom won't bug you. As a result, your call will go to voicemail or your delegate, depending on the option that you selected.

2. **Assuming that you are accepting calls from the outside world, decide what you want to do with the call.**

   You can select from one of the following options.

   - **Accept the call:** You can then start talking with the caller(s).

   - **Decline:** Zoom routes your call to voicemail or your delegate, depending on which option you selected. (For more on this subject, see the section "Configuring your voicemail," earlier in this chapter.)

   - **Close icon (x):** The Zoom call continues to ring on the other devices on which you have installed the Zoom app.

   - **(Optional) Dismiss:** You can skip the call alert and remove yourself from the queue. Zoom attempts to route the call to other people in your organization who belong to its call distribution list. Think call-center reps or sales agents.

3. **(Optional) If you're currently talking to someone via Zoom Phone and you receive another Zoom call, then decide what you want to do.**

   Zoom displays the following three options:

   - **Hold & Accept:** By clicking here, you answer the incoming call and concurrently put the current one on hold.

   - **Send to Voicemail:** In this epic phone faceoff, the current call wins. You send the incoming caller to voicemail and continue your chat with the current caller.

   - **End & Accept:** This scenario is the reverse of the previous one. The incoming caller wins the phone faceoff, and you terminate the call with the current caller.

Performing in-call actions

Regardless of who called whom, once you're on a Zoom call, you've got plenty of options. Figure 11-9 displays the in-call controls that you see when using the Zoom desktop client.

TIP

Zoom has wisely standardized its in-call controls. That is, you can expect to see the same menu regardless of whether your call takes place on a Windows, macOS, Android, or iOS device. Pretty cool.

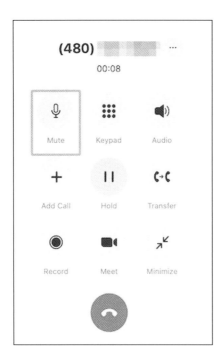

FIGURE 11-9:
Zoom Phone
in-call controls.

Table 11-1 lists each icon and describes what it does. If you think that Zoom's icons resemble the ones for making calls on your smartphone, trust your instincts.

TABLE 11-1   **In-Call Options for Zoom Phone Calls**

Icon	Description and Purpose
Mute	This option lets you mute and unmute your device's microphone.
Keypad	Click here to show a dial pad during the call. Perhaps you're calling a 1-800 number and need to make a selection from the menu.
Audio	Click here to change the audio settings or the volume of your computer's speaker or microphone. (Note that this icon appears as Speaker if you're using the Zoom smartphone app.)
Add Call	Again, much like your smartphone's functionality, you can add another person to your current call. You can only engage in a three-way call after you have successfully connected to the second person.
Hold	Nothing new here. If you need to place your fellow caller on hold, then click here. To resume the call, click on Unhold.
Transfer	You can send the call to another number or to voicemail.
Record	If you'd like to record the call for future use, then click on this button.

Icon	Description and Purpose
■◖ Meet	Say that you called Saul via Zoom to discuss a complex legal matter. You decide that you should move this call over to video in Meetings & Chat.
↗↙ Minimize	Hitting this button minimizes the in-call icons.
☎	Press or click here to hang up the phone.

Performing other call-related actions

Zoom Phone wouldn't be terribly useful if it only let you perform actions *while on calls*. Fortunately, you can do a number of things that you'd expect from a phone system after your calls conclude and just in general for that matter.

Listening to your voicemails

Say that Steve calls you. You decline the call and send him to voicemail. He actually leaves a message. By default, Zoom sends you an email message with his voicemail attached as an .mp3 file. Figure 11-10 displays a typical email.

FIGURE 11-10:
Zoom email message indicating new voicemail.

WARNING

Don't expect perfection in Zoom's current voicemail transcriptions. They are works in progress in English, let alone in other languages. Although they are improving, it's best to take them with a bit of salt for now. From the Zoom desktop client, follow these steps to listen to your voicemails:

1. **Launch the Zoom desktop client.**

2. **Click on the Phone icon at the top of the screen.**

3. **Click on the Voicemail tab.**

You see something resembling Figure 11-11.

4. **Click on the Play icon to the right of the call.**

Zoom plays the message over your computer.

FIGURE 11-11:
Accessing your voicemails in the Zoom desktop client.

Accessing your recorded calls

Say that you recorded your conversation with a colleague and want to listen to it. Follow these steps:

1. **Launch the Zoom desktop client.**

2. **Click on the Phone icon at the top of the screen.**

3. **Click on the History tab.**

By default, Zoom shows you all of your call history. You can hunt and peck for your recorded calls if you like, but it's easiest to just filter on recorded calls.

4. **Underneath the three tabs in the top left-hand corner of the desktop client, select Recording from the drop-down menu.**

   Zoom now displays only your recorded calls.

5. **Click on the Play icon to the right of the call.**

   Zoom plays the recorded call over your computer.

Viewing your call history and returning your calls

To view a history of your calls, follow these steps:

1. **Launch the Zoom desktop client.**

2. **Click on the Phone icon at the top of the screen.**

   Zoom Phone presents a list of calls on the left-hand side of the screen underneath the History tab in reverse chronological order. If you want to return a missed call, simply mouse over the missed call and click on the Phone icon that appears to the right of the call. Zoom then redials that number. If you want to view only your missed calls, simply click on the drop-down menu underneath the Voicemail tab and select Missed.

   Zoom displays only your — wait for it — missed calls.

Changing your default calling number

Say that you have two Zoom numbers at your disposal — the main one associated with your company and your personal one. What's more, you want to change the one that appears on recipients' caller IDs. Simply follow these steps:

1. **Launch the Zoom desktop client.**

2. **Click on the Phone icon at the top of the screen.**

3. **Click on Caller ID underneath the blue Phone icon.**

4. **From the drop-down list that appears, select how you want Caller ID to display.**

   Zoom Phone displays the three options shown in Figure 11-12.

   - The direct number that you assigned yourself. (For more on this subject, see the section "Setting up Zoom to make outbound calls," earlier in this chapter.)

   - The main company number.

   - Hide Caller ID.

   Zoom then redials that number.

TIP

Play around with Zoom Phone's individual and organizational settings.

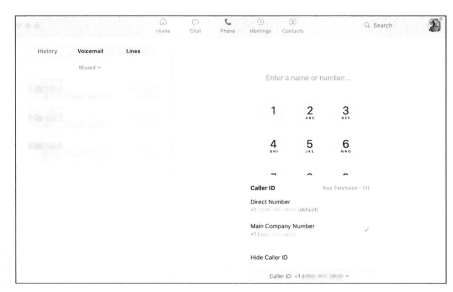

FIGURE 11-12:
Zoom Caller ID
option.

SIZING UP ZOOM PHONE

In the course of researching Zoom Phone for this book, it didn't take long for me to discover Rebekah Carter. Carter is a respected tech reporter for *UC Today*, a leading Unified Communications (UC) publication. I asked her to size up Zoom Phone in comparison to its more established competition. "Zoom Phone is an extremely accessible cloud-calling solution, designed to echo the simplicity and convenience of Meetings & Chat," she told me. "Perfect for those conversations that don't demand video, Zoom Phone adds an extra layer to the rapidly evolving Zoom UC portfolio. With Zoom Phone, the company competes with other major-league players like Microsoft and Cisco, looking to provide a single pane of glass for productivity."

For her complete review of Zoom Phone, check out `bit.ly/zm-rev1`.

Chapter **12**

Getting Everyone to Zoom Together

'm going to go out on a limb here: The chapters in this book have energized you.
You're now thinking about all the ways that Zoom can improve how your
colleagues, friends, and others collaborate and communicate.

Good.

There's just one small problem, though. Success with Zoom is not only or even
primarily about you. To realize its benefits within your team and throughout your
organization, your coworkers and friends need to embrace it as well. Make no
mistake: Zoom does not exist in a vacuum — and therein lies the rub.

This chapter offers advice on how to get your colleagues to share your excitement
about Zoom. Ideally, this feeling will translate into widespread usage. As a
result, everybody wins. Your organization, employees, colleagues, customers, and
partners will reap its significant rewards.

Understanding the Relative Ease of Zoom Adoption

In my years, I've learned quite a few things about how technology and people intersect. The following truism lies at the top of the list: When it comes to technology, people generally hate change.

Although usually understandable, this mindset is still maddening. For four intertwined reasons, however, it's unlikely that you'll have to twist your colleagues' arms to get them to regularly use Meetings & Chat. Trust me: You can't say the same thing about every new enterprise technology.

Zoom is remarkably easy to use

I'll start with the elephant in the room: The Zoom desktop client is easy to install, configure, and use. Sure, like any program, users often ignore some of its nuances and most valuable features. (Hopefully, this book shines a light on them, but I digress.)

Put differently, Zoom passes what some people call *the Grandma test*. It's easy to explain Zoom to someone who lacks a strong technical background.

Zoom doesn't step on email's toes

Go back to early January 2020. Assume that hundreds of millions of decidedly nontechnical people already had at their disposal a user-friendly group videoconference tool. Examples include teachers, small business owners, and senior citizens. They used this magical videoconferencing app daily to conduct a variety of video-based meetings, classes, and the like.

Then a global pandemic broke out.

In this alternative scenario, teachers and professors would not have had to scramble to find a tool that would allow them to teach something resembling a normal class. Ditto for Pilates instructors, rabbis, priests, and countless other professionals. Why? They already possessed a user-friendly, affordable, and reliable videoconferencing tool.

Unfortunately, the vast majority of state and local governments, companies, universities, hospitals, institutions, supply chains, and citizens were wholly unprepared for COVID-19 on many levels. In a critical way, Zoom's tools fulfilled urgent professional needs. For this very reason, Zoom's already sizeable customer base ballooned 2,000 percent in the first quarter of 2020.

After all and in hindsight, educators under the gun didn't have too many other viable options. (To be fair, I'm sure that Skype and Facetime usage increased during that horrifying period. Google Classrooms also experienced meteoric growth.) It's not as if Microsoft Outlook, Gmail, or another email program allowed educators to simulate in-person classes. Those familiar applications simply did not allow people to easily hold videoconferences. Other asynchronous communication tools weren't going to cut it either.

Take away that crisis for a moment. Today Zoom would still be a popular tool, but nowhere near as ubiquitous as it is right now. Say what you will about the ethics of forcing people to adopt new technologies, but COVID-19 proves that it often works.

REMEMBER

Claiming that Zoom's offerings don't directly compete with email isn't entirely accurate. Chapter 5 covers how to use Meetings & Chat to send text-based messages and files. If you think many people use email for the same purpose, trust your instincts.

Zoom doesn't require people to rethink how they work

Consider the following two tasks under normal — that is, nonpandemic — circumstances:

>> Nudging someone in your organization to use Meetings & Chat, but just for videoconferences.

>> Convincing a coworker to abandon his email fetish. Instead, you want him to use Slack or Microsoft Teams.

By and large, the first chore is relatively easy to accomplish. The second, however, can be downright maddening. Here's the obvious question: why the distinction? After all, aren't all of those preceding tools communication and collaboration applications?

The short answer is that people often lack the time and desire to learn new things — especially when it comes to new work-related technologies and apps. For the longer, more nuanced answer, see the nearby sidebar.

Brass tacks: You will rarely encounter people who are anywhere near as defensive about switching to Zoom from another videoconferencing tool. Relative to other tools, Zoom doesn't cut nearly as close to the bone.

WHY EMPLOYEES OFTEN RESIST ADOPTING NEW WORK-RELATED COMMUNICATION TOOLS

You probably know someone who routinely resists new technologies at work. Maybe you know dozens who fall into that category.

I'm no psychiatrist, but three obvious reasons come to mind.

First, it's not uncommon for busy professionals to spend three hours per day in their inboxes. Imagine repeating this activity every workday for 15 or 20 years. You, too, would master the art of inbox management. You would develop, refine, and perfect an email-centric productivity system that works for you.

In this all-too-common scenario, there's no point in minimizing the time that you spend in your inbox because your system isn't broken in the first place. What's more, you will probably resent someone implying as much.

Second, skeptics of new collaboration tools aren't exactly bored while on the clock, nor are they hurting for software applications. On the contrary, they already use a slew of other productivity and business-oriented tools. (See the section "Consolidate your tools" later in this chapter for more here.) Many people struggle trying to keep up with new features, updates, and user interface (UI) tweaks.

Finally, forced adoption may work during pandemics, but it rarely applies to Slack and Microsoft Teams under normal circumstances. To be sure, managers, colleagues, consultants, and productivity experts may encourage oodles of employees to use new communication tools. Rarely, however, are those groups of people able to compel their audiences to use them. Most of the time, they can only make recommendations.

Put these reasons together. Is it any wonder that so many workers view these newfangled collaboration apps with suspicion? Many skeptics have been burned before by promises of a pot of gold at the end of the rainbow. As such, they tend to focus on the downsides exclusively of learning new tech. Specifically, these tools have the potential to do each of the following things:

- Upset the applecart.
- Waste time that they probably don't think they can spare.

- Make them feel even more overwhelmed than before.

- Above all, make them confront the bruising reality that they have been missing out on a better way of doing things for a long time.

As a result, cynics often blithely dismiss Slack, MS Teams, and their ilk as email 2.0.

Are they right?

No, not at all. Still, try telling them that. (Maybe the related *For Dummies* books will change a few of their minds.) Regardless, their reluctance to fundamentally change their established work routines is formidable.

Zoom benefits from network effects

Imagine for a moment that you're the only person in the world on Facebook.

In this scenario, Facebook is effectively worthless. After all, no one can connect with you — and vice versa. You can share a meme or funny story, but no one will see it. In a way, a single-member version of Facebook may as well not exist.

Add just one more person to the social network, though, and its value increases. You now can communicate with that other person. (By the way, you can say the same thing about a fax machine, a telephone, an email address, an Internet connection, or any other communications medium.) Now add a million more members to Facebook or a billion. The network is now exponentially more powerful and useful than before.

I've just demonstrated the concept of a *network effect*. At its core, think of network effects simply as elusive yet powerful and virtuous cycles that offer major benefits to companies and users alike. When a company is able to create a vaunted network effect, the value of its product or service grows exponentially. (According to Metcalfe's Law, it increases in proportion to the number of people using it.)

Zoom is no exception to this rule. More people started using Meetings & Chat because, reflexively, an increasing number of people were already using it. Facebook, Twitter, LinkedIn, Amazon, eBay, Microsoft, and Netflix are just a few of the other companies that have benefited enormously from network effects.

To wit, starting in February 2020, a buzz started building around Zoom. Tens of millions of people were willing to give it a shot, even though many, if not most, of them already used Skype, FaceTime, or another tool. Now that Zoom has become the *de facto* standard for videoconferencing, convincing newbies to use it isn't difficult.

Put differently, say that there's an obscure but objectively better, more secure, cheaper, more reliable, and more user-friendly videoconferencing app out there. Call it *Marzipan*. (Yes, this name is yet another nod to the band Marillion.) Unfortunately, because of its obscurity, no one uses Marzipan. Jane and John Q. Public have never heard of it. Beyond that, IT departments are reluctant to sanction it in the workplace. After all, it could pose a security risk to the enterprise.

Again, Zoom doesn't face this problem. Holding a meeting via Zoom is commonplace these days. In fact, you're more likely to face resistance by recommending a tool other than Meetings & Chat for your next videoconference.

Applying Different Types of Techniques

Make no mistake: Anticipating little employee resistance to Zoom is not the same thing as facing no resistance at all. To that end, here's some advice for how to maximize the chance that Zoom takes root in your organization. I've broken the tips into two buckets: organizational and individual.

Organizational techniques

At a high level, employers can do a number of things to prioritize Meetings & Chat over similar videoconferencing tools.

Retire similar videoconferencing apps

Say that people in your organization have used some of the videoconferencing tools described in Chapter 1 for years — sometimes a decade or more. For example, newly hired Marvin and Paul in sales love Zoom, but Jules and Jody in accounting count themselves among the Webex crowd. Vince and Butch in HR prefer GoToMeeting. For their part, Marsellus and Mia in marketing refuse to wean themselves off of Google Hangouts Meet. (Apropos of nothing, these names refer to *Pulp Fiction* characters.)

Marvin and Paul need to bring the whole team together for a companywide virtual meeting. Forget agreeing on times and dates: The group can't even decide which tool to use. No one wants to back down.

I've seen this movie before in my days as an enterprise-systems consultant. Employees are busy with their day jobs; they often don't want to devote the necessary time to learn a new application. As a result, different groups use their own tools. They want others to bend to their wishes, not the other way around.

The solution is simple: A senior person at the company should make an executive call. That individual may be the president, founder, or chief technology officer (CTO). Regardless, the company needs to pick a lane.

Such a move doesn't just eliminate carping among departments and groups. Relying upon a single tool confers additional benefits to the organization and ultimately its employees.

Consider two companies:

» **Company A:** It subscribes to only Zoom.

» **Company B:** It subscribes to a slew of comparable videoconferencing tools, including Zoom, Webex, and GoToMeeting.

Which one do you think spends less money on software licenses?

Second, it's far easier to secure a company when employees use a single app or suite of apps than myriad ones from different software vendors. Anyone who has spent a few months working in IT knows as much.

WARNING

Note that your organization may not be able to completely eliminate its use of Zoom's competitors. For example, say that your company's sales reps routinely hold calls with prospective clients, some of which use Webex. Insisting that they use Meetings & Chat in lieu of their preferred application may be a deal-breaker.

Warn first-time offenders

Never attribute to malice that which can be adequately explained by stupidity.
— Hanlon's Razor

I remember when videoconferencing tools began to make inroads in the mid- to late-1990s. Back then, few employees used laptops. (I knew a few executives who used them as expensive paperweights, but that's an entirely different discussion.) Most employees found themselves figuratively chained to theirs desks and their clunky beige boxes. Contemporary smartphones didn't exist, never mind apps.

Those days are long gone. For more than a decade, people have been living in an era of *bring your own device* (BYOD) and *Shadow IT*. The latter term simply means that untold numbers of workers routinely use software applications not sanctioned by the IT department while on the clock.

In case you're curious, blocking network access to specific apps at work usually fails. Employees can simply use their phones' personal data plans from AT&T,

Verizon, or T-Mobile. Confiscating employee phones will cause far more problems than it will solve.

What to do?

At the risk of being heavy-handed, it behooves management to explain to employees the benefits of using Zoom's tools, such as those described in the prior section. In the event that an employee or group of employees ignores the new Zoom-only policy, it's best to politely sit them down and cover it again.

Part ways with repeat offenders

Employees who routinely ignore the Zoom-only policy may not be evil. They may just be stubborn or too lazy to learn a new tool. Regardless, letting them slide sends a dangerous message to everyone else in the organization: These folks are special. The rules don't apply to them.

If you are comfortable setting such a dangerous precedent, then don't be surprised when more and more employees ignore your firm's rules. If you're not, then it may be time to show recalcitrant folks the door.

Encourage employees to use Zoom's powerful third-party apps

Although Microsoft Excel gives it a run for its money, the killer business app of the last 25 years is email.

Where would you be without it?

Thanks to email, you can communicate with just about anyone in the world — and vice versa. (See the section "Zoom benefits from network effects," earlier in this chapter, for more information here.)

Over the last quarter-century, untold numbers of employees have improved and expanded how they use email. For their part, software vendors have added to their email programs new features such as read receipt, recall messages, better spam detection, focused inboxes, and countless others.

Think of Zoom as a continuation of this evolution. Employees can install third-party apps that connect Zoom not only to Gmail and Outlook, but to many other valuable services. Examples include Slack and Microsoft Teams, among others. Doing so can facilitate scheduling meetings, effective business communication, and save employees a great deal of time. (Chapter 7 discusses third-party apps in far more detail.)

Offer Zoom training

Meetings & Chat wouldn't be nearly as popular if it were difficult to use. Although very similar in concept to legacy videoconferencing tools such as Webex and GoToMeeting, differences still persist. If management wants all employees to use Meetings & Chat and nothing else, then ideally it will offer training and ensure that employees attend. Period.

If your organization isn't equipped to hold in-person Zoom training sessions for thousands of employees, fear not. I cover some of the excellent online resources in Chapter 16.

Individual techniques

Organizations can do only so much. At some point, you are ultimately responsible for the applications that you use at work — and how you use them.

Consolidate your tools

Does the following scenario ring too close to home?

At work, you routinely use a panoply of tools, including

>> Email: Lots and lots of email

>> A powerful collaboration app, such as Slack or Microsoft Teams

>> Videoconferencing tools, such as Zoom and Webex

>> An internal wiki

>> A project or task management app, such as Todoist, Trello, or Microsoft Project

>> LinkedIn and other social networks, mostly for work-related purposes (wink-wink)

>> Dropbox, Box, or OneDrive for file sharing

>> Productivity suites, such as Microsoft Office and Google Drive

>> Mainstream enterprise systems, such as Workday, Salesforce, and others

Oh, and you often access these programs on your laptop, tablet, and smartphone.

Does reading the preceding list exhaust you or describe your day to a tee? At least I can report some good news: You're not alone in feeling overwhelmed.

It turns out that *tool fatigue* is real and even harmful. A good deal of research has proven that multitasking is a misnomer. Rather, you are multichanging. (Big difference.) Constantly shifting back and forth among different programs and devices hinders productivity and rewires brains in ways that neurologists don't completely understand yet.

TIP

For more on this important subject, see the 2011 book *The Shallows: What the Internet Is Doing to Our Brains* (W. W. Norton & Company) by Nicolas Carr.

What to do?

First, take a page from Marie Kondō, author of the bestseller *The Life-Changing Magic of Tidying Up* (Ten Speed Press). For the vast majority of employees, I doubt that using PowerPoint or Excel sparks anything close to joy.

Fair enough, but workers can often take Kondō's decluttering idea to the digital world. Say that your employer, department, or manager allows employees to hold meetings via every videoconferencing tool under the sun. Fine, but you don't have to use them all. Rather, it's best to pick a lane (Meetings & Chat) and stay in it as much as you can.

Consolidate your conversations

Say that you're working on a marketing project with your colleagues Larry, Kent, Doug, Mandy, and Greg. Sometimes you exchange emails and text messages with them. Most of the time, you ask them questions in Slack channels. Occasionally, however, you find yourself using Meetings & Chat.

The day before the project's due date, you forget a key decision that the group made. You're certain that it's out there, but where exactly is it?

>> In your inbox?

>> On your phone's messages app?

>> WhatsApp or Snapchat?

>> In a comment in a Google Doc or Word Document?

>> In Zoom?

>> In the Slack workspace?

>> In more than one of these apps?

>> None of the preceding tools?

You frantically scramble to find that key piece of information.

Again, Meetings & Chat does not necessarily portend the end of email and other full-fledged collaboration tools, such as Slack and Microsoft Teams. You'll probably continue to use a number of applications to communicate with others inside and outside of your company's walls. As of this writing, there's no one mega-search app that scans disparate tools and documents for key pieces of information.

To this end, do yourself a favor: On group projects, decide from the get-go which communication tool you'll use and, most important, stick with it. If people begin deviating from your agreed-upon program, use memes, emojis, and other good-natured ways to gently remind them about the group's decision. Escalate if these techniques don't work.

Embrace Zoom channels

One of the biggest frustrations of heavy email users is the never-ending inbox.

For years, power users have embraced folders, rules, filters, and tags — depending on their email client of choice. Doing so has allowed them to more quickly locate key correspondence and files.

Zoom lets you do the same thing. Take advantage of the functionality. Specifically, channels — covered in Chapter 5 — address this very issue. They take just a few seconds to set up. By consistently using them, you'll keep Zoom organized. In the process, you'll dramatically reduce the time required to find key conversations.

Chapter **13**

Zooming toward the Future

The history of business is littered with examples of successful and complacent companies that famously fell from grace: Kodak, Blockbuster Video, Yahoo!, and BlackBerry maker Research in Motion are just a few.

It's folly to think that Zoom will rest on its laurels. It simply can't. After all, many deep-pocketed competitors are ready to pounce should Zoom fall from glory. Beyond that, should another company build a fundamentally better mousetrap, Zoom can expect mass customer defections. After all, the very same thing began happening to Webex after new videoconferencing tools started lapping it.

Over the course of its storied history, Zoom has significantly improved its flagship offering and introduced new ones as well. And this trend won't abate. That is, Zoom will get smarter and even more useful in the coming years, especially now that it has largely revamped its security.

Against this backdrop, this chapter does two things. First, it predicts some of the specific features that Zoom will add in the years ahead. Second, it describes the technologies that Zoom will use to achieve these ends. At a high level, I put on my swami hat and cover what Zoom is likely to do and how Zoom is likely to do it.

Cutting-Edge Technologies

For the last decade or so, Amazon, Apple, Facebook, Google, and Microsoft have placed a number of massive but eerily similar bets. Specifically, these power-houses have been fixating on the same group of promising technologies. The reason is obvious: Each company recognizes their current and future significance.

Make no mistake: Zoom does as well.

Augmented reality

Zoom held its first ever annual conference in September 2017. At the inaugural Zoomtopia, the company's senior leadership laid out some of its plans to incorporate augmented reality (AR) into its products.

At its core AR fuses physical environments with slick, interactive, and digital elements. Examples of AR include the following:

>> Stunning, high-tech visual overlays of real-world objects

>> Buzzy haptic feedback, also known as three-dimensional (3D) touch

>> Other sensory projections

Imagine that you're in Paris, France marveling at the Eiffel Tower. You launch an app from your smartphone and point it at the iconic building. Within seconds, your phone recognizes it and beams related information next to it.

Is this scenario is a pipe dream or scene out of the 2002 film *Minority Report*? It is neither. In fact, depending on your particular smartphone brand and model, you may be able to see AR in action right now. (To watch a cool video of AR in action involving the U.S Army, see `bit.ly/ar-army2`.)

Virtual reality

You may never have stepped inside an entirely computer-generated world. If you have, though, then you have experienced virtual reality (VR). If not, then maybe you know someone who owns an Oculus, the VR headset that enthralled Facebook CEO Mark Zuckerberg so much that he ponied up a cool $2.3 billion for the company in 2014.

To be fair, tech analysts and leaders have been hearing the VR hype for the better part of the last 30 years. (For an early attempt to represent VR on the big screen, check out the 1992 film *The Lawnmower Man*.) The day that it arrives in earnest, however, may finally be approaching.

TIP

Are you struggling to get your arms around VR in a typical corporate setting? For an example of what a VR-enabled presentation may look like, see this fancy demo of a future version of Microsoft PowerPoint at `bit.ly/vr-pptz`.

Zoom's management is clearly — and justifiably — excited about the mind-blowing possibilities of both AR and VR. As but one example, imagine a high school science teacher by the name of Walter White. In the near future, Mr. White takes his students on simulated, Zoom-powered spaceflights. One day, they land on Mars and walk around. At key points, a hologram of famous astrophysicist Neil deGrasse Tyson appears to discuss the solar system. Perhaps they visit some of Jupiter's moons later that week. For their part, students don't need to own or even use any special equipment.

Zoom is already making this dream a reality. Exhibit A: In 2017, it started integrating the technology of one pioneering AR company into Meetings & Chat. Meta View (formerly Meta) created a headset that would allow teachers to do exactly what I describe in the preceding example. (Read more at `bit.ly/-meta`.)

It's also easy to envision a souped-up version of Zoom Rooms predicated on AR and VR. I'm talking about one that would put today's immersive-telepresence technology to shame. (See Chapter 10 for more on this subject.) Garden-variety corporate training classes and presentations may actually excite their audiences.

Artificial intelligence and machine learning

Beyond AR and VR, tech heavyweights are betting even bigger on artificial intelligence (AI) and machine learning (ML). In each case, the reason is obvious: These companies want —nay, *need* — their products and services to become smarter.

Again, Zoom's management feels the same way.

Definitions of AI abound. One of my favorites comes from Andrew Moore, Dean of the School of Computer Science at my alma mater — Carnegie Mellon University. (Go Tartans!) Moore succinctly defines AI as "the science and engineering of making computers behave in ways that, until recently, we thought required human intelligence."

For its part, ML is the study of how to train computers to do things that humans presently do better. Although many people mistakenly conflate the two terms, ML is actually a subset of the larger field of AI.

What do AI and ML mean for Zoom's product roadmap?

I don't know for certain, but I'll hazard a few intelligent guesses.

More efficient meetings

The politics of the university are so intense because the stakes are so low.
— Wallace Stanley Sayre

Everyone has sat in a meeting at some point and marveled at its utter meaninglessness. For example, during my days as a college professor, I frequently watched my colleagues incessantly debate moot points. More than once I grimaced and asked myself, "What am I doing here?" I was certainly not alone.

Imagine wasting even five minutes per meeting per day. Throughout the year, that number would translate to days or even weeks of lost time. (For some interesting survey results on how meetings sap employee productivity, see `bit. ly/zfd-ai`.)

What if Zoom used AI to politely suggest critical questions during rambling meetings? What if it could keep attendees focused on the issue at hand?

Timely and unexpected recommendations

What if Zoom could do more than transcribe meetings and your sync with calendar via third-party apps? Much more. What if Zoom asked you interesting questions? I'm talking about queries such as the following:

>> You haven't checked in with Tobias, your head of sales, this month. Would you like Zoom to automatically schedule a call with him for you?

>> You hold regular team meetings with Michael, Lindsay, Tobias, and Franklin. Tobias hasn't been participating as much over the past month. Might there be something wrong with him?

>> What if Zoom could subtly recommend relevant documents and resources at key points?

>> The last call between George and Lucille started to get a little heated. Is it wise to involve HR now about a potential conflict? (Sentiment analysis is a burgeoning field.)

>> During your last call with Michael and Buster, the latter asked for information about open houses in the Sudden Valley development. Do you want to send him a brochure?

Answers to these questions would help businesses be more efficient and suss out hidden issues and opportunities.

Better reporting and analytics

Chapter 6 describes some of the simple statistics and reports available to Zoom customers. To be sure, data on basic Zoom usage, the devices that people used while accessing Zoom, their departments, locations, and the like can be helpful. I can think of many scenarios in which each report could address a business issue or identify a previously unknown need.

Rest assured, though: Zoom's tools will provide far more sophisticated analytics down the road. For example, imagine Zoom answering the following questions:

>> Which popular third-party apps are the most popular in an organization and why? What's the trend?

>> Which attendees were engaged during sexual harassment training class?

>> What are users' unstated communication preferences? When is a quick text exchange preferable to a phone or video call?

>> Which students were really paying attention during a professor's lecture?

>> What are prospects' most common questions of salespeople or call-center reps?

>> Which employees are discussing sensitive topics, using profanity, or making racist or sexist jokes on Zoom?

>> What is the ideal time to schedule a call with a person or group?

Given its high-profile privacy and security challenges, Zoom must walk a fine line here. Still, it's tough to overstate Zoom's potential in this area. The answers to the preceding questions could profoundly improve how Zoom's customers communicate.

Voice

Zoom's current voice capabilities are admittedly somewhat limited. In this way, it's fair to compare Zoom to the early days of Apple's Siri. Sure, the latter still makes laughable and frustrating errors, but it is objectively more accurate and powerful than it was when Apple launched it way back in 2011.

The following sections describe three ways in which Zoom will up its voice game. Each enhancement will arrive; it's just a matter of when.

Better voice transcriptions

At present, Zoom's customers can view automated meeting transcripts as long as they meet the following two conditions:

>> The organization subscribes to a Business, Education, or Enterprise plan.

>> Individual users record their calls to the cloud.

To be sure, this feature is certainly useful. It eliminates the need for notetakers and, even better, creates searchable transcripts. Finally, there's the obvious benefit for hearing-impaired individuals.

I have recorded my fair share of Zoom meetings and subsequently viewed the transcripts. Although they certainly weren't perfect, they represented a vast improvement over early speech-to-text efforts. Expect Zoom's accuracy in this area to vastly improve as its technology does, and as the company analyzes troves of voice data.

More useful commands

As of this writing, Zoom Rooms supports a number of relatively simple voice commands. In five years, Zoom will have zoomed past its current functionality.

Zoom and its developers will create tools that let people invoke a greater variety of voice commands, and in more languages to boot. In this vein, Zoom will start to resemble Amazon Alexa, Google Home, Microsoft Cortana, and other digital assistants.

The applications are almost limitless, but here's one practical scenario.

Imagine that you and Newman have been brainstorming from the start of your 9:30 a.m. meeting. Unfortunately, your 30-minute window is rapidly drawing to a close. Each of you has another meeting scheduled at the top of the hour, but the two of you clearly need to cover more ground. What if you could say, "Hey, Zoom. Can you schedule a one-hour meeting with Newman?" Zoom then scans both of your calendars, finds a mutually convenient time, books it, and sends you both confirmation messages in Meetings & Chat.

Real-time language translation

Say that you're the top salesperson at a niche widget manufacturer in Boston. The company president needs you to take a meeting with a big Chilean prospect. Although you used to be fluent, it's been more than a decade since you could *habla español.* You think about it. It's not an ideal situation, but you decide to dust off your Spanish dictionary, study for a few days, and give it a go.

What if Zoom could bridge the language barrier with automated, real-time translation? In this case, that feature might help you land a big account.

The idea is not that far-fetched. Consider Google's Pixel Buds. These wireless earphones include that very capability, although its reviews are decidedly mixed. There's also interpreter mode for the Google Assistant app, an absolute godsend during my recent trips to Montreal, Canada and Porto Alegre, Brazil.

I suspect that Zoom will soon roll out a similar feature for Meetings & Chat, starting with a few languages and expanding from there.

TIP

In the interim, you may be in luck if your company subscribes to a premium Zoom plan. You could designate a meeting or webinar participant as a formal interpreter. (Read how at `bit.ly/zfd-inter`.)

Other Developments and Enhancements

Zoom will rely upon its developer ecosystem and strong financial position to bolster its services even more. It will also continue to make security tweaks.

More robust third-party apps

As Chapter 7 covers, the Zoom App Marketplace currently sports more than 200 third-party apps. Expect that number to balloon over the next few years. Beyond the quantity of available apps, developers will conceive of innovative and valuable uses for Zoom's different services. In many cases, those coders will use and even extend the very technologies already discussed in this chapter: VR, AR, ML, AI, and voice recognition.

Beyond these forthcoming advancements, expect Zoom's offerings to integrate with even more popular services — and with existing ones in tighter ways. Absent some type of catastrophe or new legislation, the history of technology teaches us as much.

REMEMBER

Chapter 7 provides one of the many examples of how Zoom's partners add to its core capabilities. Zoom has forged a partnership with Otter.ai, an AI-powered transcription company.

Key acquisitions and partnerships

Zoom's legions of talented developers constantly make its services better and safer. Over the last five years, those improvements have generally taken the form of new features. In other instances, they have enhanced a tool's performance by tweaking its underlying code or thwarting hackers. That's not to say, though, that all future Zoom enhancements will stem exclusively from the efforts of its own coders.

Zoom's stock has exploded since the end of 2019. Today, the company is downright flush with funds. At the end of April 2020, it sported more than $1.3 billion in cash and short-term investments on its publicly filed balance sheet. (View the company's financial statements at on.wsj.com/2N6uZcw.) Even if you halved that number, Zoom would remain financially solvent.

Before continuing, I don't possess any insider information. I just pay close attention to how companies navigate future technology trends and current events. For what it's worth, some of my predictions in *Slack For Dummies* have already come to pass.

With that disclaimer out of the way, I'd be astonished if Zoom did not make several targeted, strategic acquisitions in the near future. Perhaps a startup has created a particularly cool tchotchke that falls into one of the buckets mentioned in this chapter. Maybe some developers have created an interesting, complementary, or tangential app with a loyal following. These deals are often as much about a startup's engineering talent as the product itself. Businessfolks today refer to these moves as *acquihires*. Brass tacks: Sometimes it's easier for a company with oodles of cash and a healthy stock price to buy an app and the team behind it rather than try to build it independently.

Increased security

Eric Yuan conceived of Zoom as an enterprise service, not a consumer one. (For more on this subject, see Chapters 1 and 9.) It's hardly a semantic distinction. The massive explosion in Zoom's consumer users in February and March 2020 took the company by surprise. It also forced Zoom's management to seriously rethink its approach to security.

Preconfiguring default settings for different customers and environments

Different organizations in different countries need to abide by different pieces of legislation. For example, U.S. financial institutions must follow different regulations than their counterparts in the European Union do. Colleges and universities have to navigate their own set of laws. Ditto for hospitals and other healthcare organizations.

I expect Zoom to offer simple installation wizards that easily allow IT departments, college professors, hospital administrators, and other folks to easily configure their environments when they first install the Zoom desktop client. This move would represent a tacit admission that one size does not fit all.

Intentionally introducing additional friction

On April 9, 2020, I was cranking out the *Zoom For Dummies* manuscript. On that day, I received a timely *New York Times* newsletter from Shira Ovide titled "Zoom is easy. That's why it's dangerous."

Plenty of smart cookies have noted that Zoom's lack of friction no doubt makes it simple to use. (As someone who struggled with some of the early videoconferencing tools, Meetings & Chat was and remains markedly more user-friendly than many of its predecessors.) In hindsight and as Ovide points out, perhaps Zoom made its Meetings & Chat service too easy for people use.

Expect Zoom to experiment with different levels of friction over the coming months and years. Like Goldilocks, it may take the company a few attempts to get the porridge temperature just right.

WHAT ABOUT FACIAL RECOGNITION?

Given Zoom's recent privacy and security issues, I suspect that the company will hit pause on integrating facial recognition into its products — at least for the time being. To be sure, Zoom would not be alone in taking a step back here. In light of widespread social protests in the United States, Microsoft, IBM, and Amazon are reconsidering their positions in this multibillion market.

Progressive regulators (particularly those in the European Union) may view facial recognition as a bridge too far under the current circumstances. I'd bet my house, though, that the topic has been on Zoom's radar for years.

5

The Part of Tens

Chapter **14**

Ten Great Zoom Tips

This chapter provides some quick advice on getting started with Zoom, maximizing its benefits, and minimizing the issues that you experience with it. No, the following pages do not represent a comprehensive list of what to do and not to do, but I have condensed my suggestions into a snackable list.

Try Before You Buy

Just about every popular software vendor has embraced the freemium business model to one extent or another. Zoom is no exception to this rule. As such, anyone can begin using Meetings & Chat and many of its features within minutes and at no cost. Employees can unlock additional goodies when their employers upgrade their plans with useful add-ons. (Chapter 2 covers Zoom's different plans and their features.)

Consider Grohl Records, a fictitious company new to Meetings & Chat. I can see Grohl's rationale to kicking the tires, especially on a small scale. For example, Grohl purchases a few licenses for employees in its sales department. For whatever reason, though, the sales reps and customers struggle with Meetings & Chat. (Remember that no technology sports a 100-percent success rate.) After a few months, Grohl can then search for another videoconferencing tool with minimal cost and disruption.

Consider Upgrading Your Firm's Existing Zoom Plan

To be sure, Zoom's Basic Meetings & Chat plan offers robust features and generous limits on call length, the number of meeting participants, and more. Plenty of individuals and businesses find this plan sufficient for their relatively limited needs. I don't fault them if they choose to take advantage of the company's no-cost Meetings & Chat offering, especially in difficult economic times.

For two reasons, there comes a point for most companies when upgrading just makes sense. As I describe in Chapters 3, 4, and 9, Zoom's additional features often more than justify their nominal costs. Companies on the Basic plan cannot use roles, user groups, and IM groups. They also lack the ability to record meetings to the cloud, receive meeting transcriptions, and tighten up security. Although many garden-variety Zoom users may not fully appreciate the significance of these features, IT folks worth their salt certainly do.

If that argument doesn't sway you, then perhaps this one will. By upgrading, you cease being a Zoom user and become a Zoom customer. Trust me: The difference is more than a matter of semantics.

By way of comparison, if you consider yourself a Facebook customer, then you're sadly mistaken — unless you pay the social network to advertise on it. Google Hangouts, Facebook's new Messenger Rooms, and other free videoconferencing alternatives may seem sexy. Just remember, though, that if you pay nothing for a company's product, then its product is you. You are merely a means to an end.

Take Security Seriously

I'll be the first to admit that many of Zoom's security- and privacy-related features broached in Chapter 9 add friction. That is, they collectively make it harder to sign in, communicate, and collaborate. For example, enabling 2FA takes time, as does having to find and enter a six-digit verification code when you log in to the Zoom web portal. Ditto for enabling meeting waiting rooms and requiring meeting passwords.

Zoom doesn't compel its users and customers to enable many of these features, including the preceding three. Depending on your role in the organization, someone above you may have already set those options globally, ultimately making moot your choice to activate them.

Brass tacks: You and your colleagues would be wise to err on the side of caution. Your business and personal communications are far too important to do anything else. Unfortunately, far too many people have historically acted as if hackers would never care about them, only to find their sensitive messages and photos on 4chan or the Dark Web.

Whoops.

To paraphrase Cher, "If they could turn back time. . . ."

Keep Zoom Updated

In the mid-1990s, software vendors typically released new versions and upgrades once every year or so via snail mail no less. Installation involved inserting floppy or compact discs into your computer. The manual process could take an hour or more.

Today, it's a much different story. Software vendors routinely release new versions, upgrades, and patches at lightning speed. (This trend has made writing *For Dummies* books challenging, but that's a conversation for a different day.)

Bottom line: It's incumbent upon Zoom users and customers to keep abreast of software updates. Ignore those red badges on your devices at your own peril.

Create a Personal Zoom Account

Chuck is a partner at HHM, a prestigious law firm based in Albuquerque, New Mexico. HHM has purchased a Zoom license, and Chuck uses Zoom frequently to hold videoconferences with clients when he has to work from home.

Could Chuck use HHM's Zoom account for decidedly non-HHM matters, such as when he holds video chats with his ex-wife Rebecca and his brother Jimmy? Sure, and he may even get away with it. Still, it would behoove him to create a separate Zoom account for his personal use.

REMEMBER

Zoom admins and owners can easily run a variety of member-usage reports. Historically, many firms have terminated employees for using company property and services for their own personal ends. I'm no labor lawyer, but you're unlikely to find a sympathetic judge if you use Zoom's services in this way.

Explore Zoom's Advanced Features

As I wrote in the Introduction, *Zoom For Dummies* cannot cover every feature of any Zoom offering, let alone all of them. Trust me: Chapters 3, 4, 5, 6, 8, 11, and 12 could easily be full-length books by themselves. I deliberately chose what I consider to be Zoom's most important functionality for the majority of its hundreds of millions users.

It's wise to keep digging, though. Just because I didn't mention a specific bell or whistle doesn't mean that Zoom doesn't offer it — or will by the time this book hits the shelves.

Measure Twice and Cut Once

Say that you're about to noodle with Zoom functionality with which you're not familiar. Perhaps it's a large group meeting or your first Zoom webinar. In both cases, a trial run is in your best interest.

Case in point: In April 2020, I held a webinar for my alma mater Carnegie Mellon University on remote work. It went smoothly for a few reasons.

First, after I agreed to do the webinar, I connected with webinar emcee Melissa Turk. Over the course of a few weeks, the two of us exchanged basic information via Slack and Google Docs. (She shares my aversion to incessant email threads.)

Second and most germane here, a few days before showtime, we held a trial webinar for 30 minutes in Zoom. (Turk's knowledge of Zoom webinars is extensive; she penned a sidebar in Chapter 8.) We worked out the audio, video, and screen-sharing logistics and kinks beforehand, not in front of hundreds of attendees.

Develop a Contingency Plan for Important Meetings

Better to have, and not need, than to need, and not have.

— Franz Kafka

Say that you're going to be using Zoom to interview for your dream job. Maybe you're pitching a prospect on your own company's products and services. For good reason, you don't anticipate any technical issues. After all, in your experience, Meetings & Chat has been remarkably reliable for such a popular tool.

Would you bet your life, though, that your call will take place without incident?

More specifically, what happens if you lose power? What if Zoom isn't available, or the call latency is surprisingly high? How about if a key call participant can't figure out Zoom or her computer crashes? What do you do? Think quick. The clock is ticking.

After hundreds of Zoom calls, I've yet to experience any of these catastrophic scenarios. If they ever do occur, though, my blood pressure won't double because I'm already armed with a suitable backup. Long before I started using Meetings & Chat in earnest, I relied upon Free Conference Call, an (obviously) free service that lets its users hold individual group audio calls, record them, and save and distribute them at will. (By the way, plenty of similar tools exist.)

Make no mistake: My default preference these days is to hold all of my audio and video calls via Meetings & Chat, and not just because I'm researching Zoom for this book. It's downright silly, though, not to have a backup communications tool at the ready in case things break bad. I always keep my credentials for the service Free Conference Call handy just in case.

Expect Some Resistance to Zoom at Mature Firms

If I've learned one thing in my years around enterprise technology, it's that people typically hate change.

Say that your work at a large, successful, and conservative pharmaceutical company. Call it Hogarth Drugs. Its 40,000 employees have used Webex as its primary videoconferencing tool for a decade or more. Immediately forcing all of them to use Zoom because Hogarth purchased an Enterprise license is likely to ruffle some feathers. Odds are that Roger, Syd, and at least a few other curmudgeons will find a minor difference between Webex and Zoom and make a fuss about it. Organizational politics at its finest.

Should Hogarth hold off on Zoom because a few squeaky wheels have made some noise? Of course not, but its management should expect at least a little employee disaffection.

Avoid Zoom Fatigue

Zoom has simplified and improved the process of holding videoconferences. Coupled with its innovative tech, robust features, and superior call quality, you may be tempted use video for every meeting and conversation with your customers, colleagues, friends, and family members.

Don't.

Dr. Jeremy Bailenson is a bestselling author, virtual-reality expert, the founding director of Stanford University's Virtual Human Interaction Lab, and an overall smart dude. His extensive research suggests that defaulting to videoconferences results in what he terms *nonverbal overload*. (Read his insightful *Wall Street Journal* op-ed at on.wsj.com/3bH5rxE.)

Occasionally, unplugging your webcam gives your brain much needed respite.

Chapter **15**

Ten Common Myths about Zoom

In this chapter, I dispel some of the most common myths about what Zoom can do and how to make it stick inside your organization.

Note that these myths apply to Zoom's most popular offering: Meetings & Chat.

Zoom Is No Different than Legacy Videoconferencing Tools

Say that your organization continues to rely upon a 1990s-era videoconferencing application. You think it is just as good as Zoom. By that rationale, when it comes to basketball, I am as skilled as LeBron James.

Those last two statements are patently ridiculous. I couldn't hold a candle to King James on the court when he was 15 years old, never mind now. The same holds true for antiquated videoconferencing tools born decades ago.

As Chapter 1 describes, the quality of Zoom's core technology and code base exceeds that of its predecessors on many levels. Yes, those legacy tools may still technically work on older devices running ancient operating systems. To claim that they are as powerful, user-friendly, and extensible as Zoom is ludicrous.

Zoom Is Fundamentally Insecure

When COVID-19 arrived in the United States in earnest, Zoom usage surged by an astonishing 2,000 percent over the course of three months. Consumers were using the enterprise communications tool in ways and at a scale for which Zoom had not prepared. Zoombombing became a thing, the FBI became involved, and the company faced severe public criticism. (Chapter 9 covers this subject in far more detail.)

When it comes to security and privacy, Zoom certainly hasn't batted 1.000. Make no mistake, though: Zoom's services have never been fundamentally unsafe to use. That's not to say, however, that Zoom could not have done better.

Faced with arguably its most significant challenge to date, Zoom responded well. The resulting backlash prompted the company to shore up its wares even more. Today, Zoom's tools are more secure than they were at the end of 2019. I suspect that the company will continue to make progress in this area. After all, as a company, Zoom has never been complacent.

If you're looking for a completely secure and hacker-proof application or software program, good luck with that. You're more likely to see a unicorn.

TIP

Zoom's Customers Use the Tools in a Uniform Way

There is no one right way to use and configure Zoom's suite of tools. This flexibility is a feature, not a bug. One of Zoom's primary strengths is the latitude that it affords a wide range of users. For example, a small group of friends will configure and use it differently than a 20,000-employee healthcare organization. You can say the same thing about schools, law firms, financial institutions such as banks, and plenty of other types of organizations.

Not every person, department, group, or organization will find Zoom's user interface and features as intuitive as others.

TIP

Zoom Ensures Flawless Business Communication

Hogwash. Zoom is no panacea for poor individual and group communication. As I wrote in my 2015 book *Message Not Received: Why Business Communication Is Broken and How to Fix It* (Wiley), no tool is.

Consider Hudsucker Industries, a fictitious company that has embraced Zoom. Employees can still engage in pernicious intra-office politics and backstabbing. Zoom doesn't preclude mansplaining, office gossip, or anything of the sort. Moreover, employees will sometimes misinterpret their colleagues' messages or motives, even when using Zoom. Some of those disconnects will be disastrous.

Zoom is just like any tool: You can use it constructively and destructively.

TIP

Zoom Decimates the Need for In-Person Communication

No, no, a thousand times no. Zoom's suite of tools doesn't replace the need for in-person communication.

Say that Geddy and Alex are colleagues who sit down the hall from each other. Both are in the office on Tuesday afternoon. Yes, they can discuss the quarterly sales numbers via Meetings & Chat from their desks. Still, they should probably just find a physical room and hold the meeting in person. If Gavin, Steven, and John are all on different continents, however, it's downright silly for them to board planes to hold a 15-minute meeting on a relatively unimportant subject.

Use your judgment.

Beyond that obvious example, a little humanity is in order. Sure, you could lay off longtime employees via a videoconferencing tool, such as Meetings & Chat. Anna Kendrick's character Natalie Keener attempts to do as much in the excellent 2009 movie *Up in the Air*. Alternatively, you could use it to break up with your significant other of six years. (I suppose that Zoom is marginally better than text here.) Just because you can, however, doesn't mean that you should.

Zoom Eliminates the Need for Email

Imagine that I sell widgets. You and I meet at a widget conference, and we exchange business cards. You're in the market for the very types of widgets that my company sells. You ask me to send you some more information. In this scenario, I'm an avid Zoom user, and you've never heard of it. What's more, you're old school and don't like trying new apps.

I could invite you to Zoom and insist that we use it as our primary or even exclusive communications medium. That move may not be wise, however. Remember that I'm introducing friction into the process — and possibly costing me a lucrative widget deal as well. If you refuse to use Zoom and I don't budge, then you'll go somewhere else for your widgets.

Brass tacks: Zoom does not eliminate the need for email. For certain types of communications, emailing someone a note or file may be easier, especially if that person works for another organization.

You Can't Overuse Zoom

I remember the first time that I visited Las Vegas. At the time, I was attending Cornell University and getting my master's degree. In March 1996, three of my friends and I descended upon Sin City during our spring break.

Trust me. I'm going somewhere with this little yarn.

Of course, we hit an all-you-can-buffet — a rite of passage for Vegas rookies. If my memory serves me correctly, we went to the Rio, waited in line for 90 minutes, and promptly gorged ourselves. Like all stubborn men, we paid our $20 each and were determined to get our money's worth. My friends and I weren't going to let the buffet win. To this end, why not try just about everything in sight? After all, whether you ate a little or way too much, the price was the same.

Pizza? Check. Chinese food? Check. Dessert? Check. I remember stuffing myself so much that I thought that I wouldn't eat again for the remainder of the trip. Homer Simpson would have been proud of me.

The same gluttonous mindset exists with new, overly exuberant Zoom users.

Perhaps Tom wants to hold a videoconference call with his colleagues to brainstorm over new product ideas. Maybe Verna wants to check in with her college friends during a global pandemic. To be sure, using Zoom in these scenarios makes sense.

In other instances, however, the logic for using Zoom is suspect. Consider the following:

>> Leo needs clarification on a simple instruction in a Slack message.

>> Johnny forgot to attach a file in his group email.

>> Bernie forgot to include the title slide in her PowerPoint presentation.

In these cases, scheduling a proper Zoom meeting to discuss the issue doesn't make a great deal of sense. It's best to use a different medium.

Zoom Is Too Expensive for Our Company

Any employee, group, department, and organization can begin using Meetings & Chat for free at any time. Should one of those entities decide to upgrade, Zoom requires minimal up-front cost. The same concept holds true for Zoom's webinar add-on. What's more, using Zoom isn't a binary. If it makes sense to purchase a limited subscription for only certain employees, have at it.

Rather than thinking exclusively about Zoom's out-of-pocket expenditures, though, contemplate the implicit costs of poor communication on the job. Do your subordinates, peers, or bosses tell you that your tone in emails is unnecessarily harsh? Wouldn't it be easier to convey difficult messages to others when they could see your face and hear the tone of your voice?

On a different level, say that you're experiencing a problem with your computer. Wouldn't a five-minute screen-sharing session with the IT help desk quickly identify — and possibly diagnose — the problem? Isn't that scenario better than exchanging 15 emails with the support folks and wasting valuable time?

Foolish is the soul who doesn't consider these legitimate business costs. Used properly, Zoom can more than pay for itself.

Zoom Won't Integrate with Our Key Enterprise Technologies

Say that your employer uses a customer relationship management (CRM) system that the IT folks cobbled together back in the mid-1990s. The clunky system runs off of a mainframe, and no one has updated it in years. In this case, then you're probably right: Zoom won't automatically connect to your legacy application. One-click calls to prospects or customers are pipe dreams.

Absent that, however, it's likely that Zoom's services play nicely with the productivity and communication tools that just about everyone at your organization currently uses. As Chapter 7 covers, Zoom's App Marketplace lets users easily connect with more than 200 different applications, such as Microsoft Outlook, Gmail, Slack, Microsoft Teams, Salesforce, and many others. For their part, teachers and professors who use Blackboard, Canvas, and other popular learning management systems (LMS) can integrate them with Zoom with a few mouse clicks.

Our Workers Don't Need a Tool like Zoom

I'm rolling my eyes. I hate to break it to you, but people who think that their colleagues effectively "collaborate" exclusively via email and old-school telephones are misguided or downright delusional. They just don't know the meaning of the word.

Even if everyone in your small company routinely shows up at work, what about when employees are traveling? What about video meetings with clients, prospects, and partners?

Only Hipsters at Tech-Savvy Startups Use Zoom

Folks who believe this statement are living in a world of make-believe As Chapter 1 discusses, Zoom's users and customers run the gamut. You can't pigeonhole them into a single company size, age, industry, or even geography.

Chapter **16**

Top Ten or So Zoom Resources

Zoom is a remarkably robust and dynamic suite of collaboration and communication tools. What's more, as the company has shown since its inception, it is anything but stagnant. It consistently releases exciting new features.

To this end, this chapter offers resources for you to expand your knowledge of Zoom beyond the scope of this book. Like most software companies these days, Zoom changes its features and adds new ones on a regular basis. As such, it's imperative to stay informed of new product developments. What's more, you'll have to deal with occasional issues when they pop up. It's folly to think that they never will.

I've placed the resources in this chapter into two natural buckets:

>> Resources for everyday users

>> Resources for developers

Resources for Everyday Users

It is impossible to know everything about all of Zoom's services. Fun fact: During the course of researching *Zoom For Dummies,* I connected with plenty of Zoomies. One of them conceded to me that maybe two people in the entire company know from memory how every feature works!

Brass tacks: The resources in this section

>> Help you get the most out of Zoom

>> Address issues as they manifest themselves

Zoom support

```
https://support.zoom.us
```

From time to time, you'll need to open a case with Zoom support. Perhaps you're experiencing a technical issue, or you're not sure about how something works. I haven't met too many people who enjoy the back and forth with tech support folks, but at least Zoom makes getting help easy.

To these ends, you're best off starting with Zoom's robust help center. The company has intelligently arranged support topics into the following buckets:

>> Getting Started

>> Audio, Video, Sharing

>> Meetings & Webinars

>> Zoom Phone

>> Account & Admin

>> Zoom Rooms

>> Messaging

>> Integration

>> On-Premises

TIP

If you're not sure about where to begin, just type your query into the search bar displayed prominently at the top of the page. Go nuts.

Zoom training

https://zoom.us/livetraining

Zoom wants its customers to be successful — and recommend more customers. After all, word of mouth remains the least expensive and most effective type of marketing. Along these lines, the company frequently hosts free, interactive, and informative webinars designed to introduce you to the product and get the most out of it. Whether you're a neophyte or an experienced user, you can easily find a session that piques your interest.

Even better, say that you missed a particularly interesting webinar. Fret not. Zoom records all training sessions and allows you to watch them at your leisure.

Also, I offer personal Zoom training.

Zoom on YouTube

https://www.youtube.com/user/ZoomMeetings

Zoom also publishes an extensive collection of videos on its YouTube channel. I find the customer stories especially useful: They allow you to get your arms around Zoom and learn from real-world customers.

REMEMBER

Zoom will often place the same video on multiple channels. That is, if a specific YouTube video looks eerily familiar, perhaps you saw it before somewhere else.

Zoom apps

https://marketplace.zoom.us

As Chapter 7 covers, Zoom understands the importance of letting its core products sync with other critical apps. Its App Marketplace provides links to a bevy of popular applications, including Slack, Gmail, Microsoft Outlook, and many more.

Zoom blog

https://blog.zoom.us

Just about every technology company these days provides a blog: a series of articles designed to inform current and prospective customers about its product(s). Zoom is no exception to this rule.

Zoom's blog could certainly use a fresh coat of paint. Aesthetics aside, however, it offers a wide array of articles and tips for all types of users. Interested in specific case studies, such as how schools are finding creative ways to use Zoom during the global COVID-19 pandemic? Check. Looking for insights on how Zoom lets managers keep tabs on their remote teams? You're in luck.

Zoomtopia

```
https://www.zoomtopia.com
```

Zoom's annual gala brings together users, developers, and partners from all over the globe. Oodles of speakers host dozens of sessions on a panoply of topics. What's more, the company offers regular updates and provides valuable glimpses of future product improvements. Oh, and if you're looking to pick the brain of a Zoom expert, you can sit at the Expert Bar for a one-on-one session.

Zoom virtual backgrounds

```
https://www.zoombackground.io
```

Mentioned in Chapter 4, virtual backgrounds let you add company branding to your meetings or just have some fun. No, it's not hard to create your own. (I use `canva.com` to do that very thing.) Still, `zoombackground.io` provides hundreds of interesting backgrounds. What's more, you can upload your own.

Zoom on social networks

Zoom makes it simple to follow product updates, announcements, and technical issues on different social networks. Table 16-1 displays the main ones.

TABLE 16-1 Pre-Zoom Video Conferencing Tools

Name	Description
LinkedIn	https://bit.ly/zoom-li
Twitter	https://twitter.com/zoom_us
Facebook	bit.ly/zoom-fb3

Resources for Software Developers

Technically inclined folks are a curious lot. In this case, perhaps they want to learn about how to extend Zoom's native functionality in new and innovative ways. Perhaps your company's IT department wants to stitch Zoom together with a custom-built system. (See Chapter 7 for more on this subject.)

Fortunately, Zoom provides no shortage of valuable resources for developers eager to flex their muscles. If you're not interested in developing apps for Zoom, then feel free to skip this section.

Zoom developer guides

```
https://marketplace.zoom.us/docs/guides
```

In this section of the Zoom App Marketplace, the company provides valuable technical documentation to help developers in their efforts to build custom apps and integrations.

Developer forums

```
https://devforum.zoom.us
```

Even highly skilled developers need to ask for help from time to time. Zoom's Developer Forums allow these folks to post technical questions.

Chapter **17**

Ten Ways to Socialize via Zoom

As I write these words in June 2020, the global pandemic is in full force. At some point, things will go back to normal — although most likely in dribbles. Zoom's suite of tools, however, will remain vital work and educational staples for the foreseeable future.

Make no mistake, though: As I cover throughout this book, hundreds of millions of people are using Zoom in remarkable and innovative ways every day. Weddings, bar and bat mitzvahs, birthday parties, dance parties, and poker games have all taken place on Zoom.

This final chapter presents some of them.

Cooking and Eating Meals

Restaurants typically run on slim profit margins — often along the lines of 5 percent. Operating at 25-percent capacity doesn't cut it. To this end, many have begun holding Zoom cooking classes and online tastings. For more on this subject, see https://bit.ly/zfd-cook.

Visiting Sick Friends and Family Members

Faced with travel restrictions, many people are "visiting" their loved ones confined to hospital beds in Zoom. No, it's not the same as the real thing, but checking in on a dear friend or family member via Zoom beats a simple phone call.

Dating

With so many bars, restaurants, and coffee shops closed, where do two people safely meet? How about on Zoom? See bit.ly/zfd-dating for more information on this subject.

Sharing a Few Drinks over Happy Hour

I'll cop to doing this a few times with my college friends. Again, I'd prefer to talk trash with them in person. Left with no in-person alternative, though, Zoom more than serves this purpose.

Playing Brick-and-Mortar Games

I asked a few of my former students if they used Zoom for social gatherings. Here's one particularly colorful response: I play trivia games with my family in England every Saturday via Zoom.

Sure, some games translate better than others, but you'd be surprised at how many games work reasonably well on Zoom. See bit.ly/zfd-games for more information.

Playing Video Games

You may not be able to use Twitch to play your favorite video game. If not, then give Zoom a shot. Visit bit.ly/zfd-games2 for more information here.

Watching Movies and TV Shows

As a kid, I would routinely watch *Jeopardy!* with my family. I'd sometimes go an entire show without answering a single question correctly.

Although I live across the country from my family, I can now relive that experience with them via Zoom. (At least now I can answer about 40 percent of the questions correctly.) In fact, plenty of folks use Meetings & Chat to view movies and binge-watch series. (See `bit.ly/zfd-netflix` for more information on this subject.)

Performing Stand-Up Comedy

Few things beat the feeling of laughing in unison with complete strangers as a comedian tears it up. In the midst of a pandemic, fans cannot see Gary Gulman or Neal Brennan live. Until then, however, I might watch some comedians perform via Zoom. Learn more at `bit.ly/zfd-com`.

Staying Fit

Since the age of 18, I have religiously gone to the gym. Broken fingers, the cold, and work-related commitments haven't stopped me from getting my sweat on. Yeah, I'm a gym rat — and plenty of people can relate.

Left without physical gyms, many people began working out over Zoom. For a quick video on this burgeoning trend, see `bit.ly/zfd-gym`.

Holding Miscellaneous Parties

A Zoomie told me that her in-laws held a weekly dance party on Zoom. Virtual graduations, birthday parties, and other formerly physical gatherings are taking place via the world's most popular videoconferencing tool.

Index

D

Daily, as type of usage report, 183

daily active users (DAUs), 15–16

dashboard
My Dashboard, 199, 200
reporting dashboard for Business and Education plans, 184
UI as, 59
Zoom account dashboard, 54
Zoom dashboard, 35
Zoom Phone dashboard, 44

data, Zoom's intelligent use of, 21

data sharing, as communication service, 11

data storage
staying within plan's limit of, 241
today's cheaper costs of, 20
viewing current level of, 119–120

dating, via Zoom, 356

Deep Work: Rules for Focused Success in a Distracted World (Newport), 132

Delete Contact, as Meetings & Chat contact action, 128

desktop client
defined, 55
downloading and installing, 54–56, 191
signing in to, 56–57
use of term, 55

desktop sharing, as communication service, 11

developer forums, 353

developer guides, for Zoom, 353

directory, Meetings & Chat directory, 122–128

distributed architecture, Zoom's use of, 21

Dogfight: How Apple and Google Went to War and Started a Revolution (Vogelstein), 250

do-not-disturb (DND), as Meetings & Chat status, 131–132

downgrades, 26, 52, 54, 67

Draw
as annotation option, 113
description of icon for host-annotation options (on webinar), 228

Drew University, use of Zoom Rooms by, 290–291

DTEN All-in-One Video Conferencing Device, 286, 287

Dunbar, Robin (anthropologist), 122

E

E2EE (end-to-end encryption), 253, 254

eBay, as benefitting from network effects, 317

Education Meetings & Chat plan, 35, 37, 39, 67, 77, 96, 117, 184, 268, 330

educators. *See* teachers/educators

Elgato Green Screen (virtual background), 99

email
as killer business app of last 25 years, 320
myth that Zoom eliminates need for, 346

emojis, adding of to messages, 144–145

empty white circle, as Meetings & Chat status icon, 129

Enable Waiting Room
as additional meeting option for hosts, 115
as security-related option, 252

encryption, enhancement of, 253–255

Encrypt.me, 255

End
description of icon for host (on webinars), 227
description of icon for (in meetings), 79

ending meeting, 115–116

endpoints, 289

end-to-end encryption (E2EE), 253, 254

end-user license agreements (EULAs), 41, 205

Enterprise Meetings & Chat plan, 35, 36, 67, 77, 96, 268, 330

Enterprise Plus Meetings & Chat plan, 35, 36–37, 39

Epic, as popular Zoom app, 203

Eraser
as annotation option, 113
description of icon for host-annotation options (on webinar), 229

Evans, Benedict (venture capitalist), 250

Eventbrite, as third-party app, 223

extensions, as diluted apps, 191

as supporting bevy of related collaboration tools, 18

uptime percentages with, 41

GoToMeeting, 18

graduations, via Zoom, 357

gray circular clock, as Meetings & Chat status icon, 129

green outlined rectangle, as Meetings & Chat status icon, 129

green solid circle, as Meetings & Chat status icon, 129

group chat
  comparing channels to, 164, 174
  inviting others to existing group chat, 128, 138–139
  leaving group chats, 137–138
  quickly setting notifications for, 176–177
  referencing a specific member in, 142–143
  setting specific notifications for, 174–177
  starting new group chat, 59, 136–167
  turning group chats into proper channels, 171–172

group meetings, taking them to the next level with Zoom Rooms, 279–292

growth, companies having to manage double-edged sword of sudden, massive growth, 247

H

H.323, 13, 289

hackers, 205, 246, 255, 257, 260, 264, 270, 332, 339

Hafner, Katie (author)
  Where Wizards Stay Up Late: The Origins of the Internet, 12

Halo Collaboration Center (HCC) (HP), 281

Halo Collaboration Studios (HCS) (HP), 281

Hanlon's Razro, 319

happy hour, via Zoom, 356

help center, 350

Hewlett-Packard (HP)
  Halo Collaboration Center (HCC), 281
  Halo Collaboration Studios (HCS), 281–282

Hold, description of icon for in-call options for Zoom Phone calls, 308

host
  annotation options for in webinars, 228–229
  managing and interacting with participants, 99–100
  mid-meeting actions of, 95–115
  other meeting options for, 114–115
  recording options, 95–97
  restricting who can attend meetings by, 264–265
  specifics of role of in meetings, 73
  specifics of role of in webinars, 217–218
  in-webinar controls for webinar hosts, 226–227

http (Hypertext Transfer Protocol), 13

HubSpot, as CRM and marketing automation tool, 223

huddle rooms, 284

I

IBM, on facial recognition, 333

iCal, using Zoom with, 33

icons
  in book, explained, 4–5
  Meetings & Chat status icons, 129–130
  Zoom In-Meeting menu icons, 79

IDs
  increasing length of, 255
  Personal Meeting ID (PMI), 35, 74–75, 86–87, 90–91, 268, 272
  removal of meeting ID from title toolbar as security-related measure, 252

IM (instant messaging), as communication service, 11

IM groups
  adding new group, 161
  adding users to, 161
  comparing channels to, 174
  types of, 161
  understanding need for, 160–162

immersive telepresence
  author's experience with, 282
  defined, 280
  early days of, 280–282

microphones, Yeti Blue, 94

Microsoft

  acquisition of Skype by, 18

  apps of as connecting with those of third-party, 204

  as benefitting from network effects, 317

  as encouraging third-party developers to create their own apps, 191

  on facial recognition, 333

  as fixated on cutting-edge technologies, 326

  Microsoft Access, 188

  Microsoft Authenticator, 262

  Microsoft Azure, 41

  Microsoft Cortana, 330

  Microsoft Excel, 188, 320

  Microsoft Exchange, 125

  Microsoft Office, 189, 321

  Microsoft Office 365, 57, 125

  Microsoft OneDrive, 146

  Microsoft Outlook, 27, 28, 33, 83, 193, 195, 348, 351

  Microsoft PowerBI, 188

  Microsoft Project, 321

  Microsoft Teams. *See* Microsoft Teams

  Microsoft Word, 107

  as serious player in cellphone market, 250

  as supporting bevy of related collaboration tools, 18

  Zoom Phone as competing with, 312

  Zoom's rise as carving out market share from, 22

Microsoft Teams

  as collaboration tool, 19, 128, 189, 221, 276, 302, 320, 321, 323

  cynics as dismissive of, 317

  as having functionality to create channels, 163

  as popular Zoom app, 203

  as supporting wildcards, 155

  Zoom as integrating with, 348

Minimize, description of icon for in-call options for Zoom Phone calls, 309

monetization, of webinars, 223

Mouse, description of icon for host-annotation options (on webinar), 228

movie watching, via Zoom, 357

multi-bitrate encoding, Zoom's use of, 21

multichanging, vs. multitasking, 132

multimedia routing, Zoom's use of, 21

Multipoint Control Unit (MCU), 21

Mute

  description of icon for host (on webinars), 226

  description of icon for (in meetings), 79

  description of icon for in-call options for Zoom Phone calls, 308

Mute Participants upon Entry, as additional meeting option for hosts, 115

myths, about Zoom, 343–348

N

Neat, Neat Bar, 286

Netflix, as benefitting from network effects, 317

network effect, Zoom as benefitting from, 317–318

Newport, Cal (author)

  Deep Work: Rules for Focused Success in a Distracted World, 132

nonverbal cues, how much they matter, 25

nonverbal overload, 342

notifications

  don't be a slave to, 132

  refining yours, 174–177-8

  setting keyword-specific ones, 177 178

  setting ones for all channels and group chats, 176–177

  setting specific ones for channels and group chats, 174–176

  staying current with, 133–134

Notify Me When Available, as Meetings & Chat contact action, 128

O

online tastings, via Zoom, 355

OpenText, videoconferencing backgrounds, 98

Operation Logs, as type of user-activity reports, 183

Otter.ai, as popular Zoom app, 203

Ovide, Shira (writer)

  "Zoom is easy. That's why it's dangerous.," 333

owner, as default user role, 67

P

packet switching, 12

panelist
  options for, 221
  specifics of role of in webinars, 218–219

Panopto, 223

The Paradox of Choice: Why More Is Less (Schwartz), 193

Pardot, as CRM and marketing automation tool, 223

participants
  adding internal contact to existing meeting, 126–127
  allowing them to chat, as security-related option, 252
  allowing them to rename themselves, as security-related option, 110, 115, 252
  description of icon for host (on webinars), 226
  description of icon for (in meetings), 79
  display of Participants panel, 99
  joining meeting using PMI, 90–91
  joining meeting via URL, 92
  letting meeting participants control your screen, 109–111
  looking your best in Zoom, 93
  managing and interacting with, 99–100
  notification to in Zoom Meetings desktop client, 90
  premeeting entry prompt, 92
  preventing removed ones from rejoining, 272–273
  putting your best foot forward, 93–95
  sharing content with, 105–114
  specifics of role of in meetings, 73–74
  waiting for hosts to begin meeting, 92

Participants tab, 99

parties, via Zoom, 357

partnerships and acquisitions, potential for in Zoom's future, 332

passwords
  enabling default passwords for all meetings, 255
  intelligent use of, 267–272
  100 worst ones from 2018, 270

requirement for, 338
  requiring more complex meeting and webinar passwords, 270–272
  setting one for individual upcoming meeting, 268
  setting other password-related options, 268–269
  use of, 91

PayPal, for monetization of webinars, 223

Performance Report, for webinars, 239

personal appearance, recommendations for, 94

personal information, locating your personal Zoom information, 74–75

Personal Meeting ID (PMI)
  creating and distributing of in Pro plan, 35
  joining a meeting using, 90–91
  keeping it private, 272
  as key to Personal Meeting Room (PMR), 74–75
  polls as tied to specific ones, 86–87
  requirement for, 268

Personal Meeting Room (PMR), 74

Phone System, as type of usage report, 183

Phone System Operation Logs, as type of user-activity reports, 183

phones
  cellphone market, 250
  ThinkingPhones, 19
  Zoom Phone. *See* Zoom Phone

plans
  adding Zoom Phone to your existing plan, 294–296
  Basic plan. *See* Basic plan
  Business Meetings & Chat plan. *See* Business Meetings & Chat plan
  canceling of, 52, 53–54, 67
  downgrading of, 26, 52, 54, 67
  Enterprise Meetings & Chat plan. *See* Enterprise Meetings & Chat plan
  Enterprise Plus Meetings & Chat plan. *See* Enterprise Plus Meetings & Chat plan
  modifying yours, 52–54
  Pro Meetings & Chat plan. *See* Pro Meetings & Chat plan
  upgrading of, 26, 34–35, 37, 52–53, 60, 67, 338

red circle with white exclamation point, as Meetings & Chat status icon, 129

red circle with white horizontal line in center, as Meetings & Chat status icon, 129

red telephone, as Meetings & Chat status icon, 129

red video camera, as Meetings & Chat status icon, 129

Redo
as annotation option, 113
description of icon for host-annotation options (on webinar), 229

Reeder Music Academy, adoption of Zoom by, 14

refactoring, 257

registration
for meetings, 87–89
registering for future meeting, 88
Registration Report for meetings, 183, 185
Registration Report for webinars, 239
requiring others to register for your meeting, 87
viewing registrant data, 88–89
for webinars, 210–212, 214–215

Registration Report
for meetings, 183, 185
for webinars, 239

Remote Support, as type of usage report, 183

Remove, as meeting participant action, 100

Rename/renaming, as meeting participant action, 100, 115, 252

Report, as meeting participant action, 100

reporting
customizing of, 186–188
exporting raw report data, 188
role-based reporting, 182–185
running simple report, 185–186
running webinar-related reports, 239–240
with Zoom, 38, 181–188

resources
for everyday users, 350–352
for software developers, 353

Restricted, as type of IM group, 161

RingCentral, 18

roles
meeting-specific roles, 72–73
user roles. *See* user roles

Running Engaging Online Events, 223

S

safeguards, 38, 246

Salesforce
as customer-relationship management (CRM) system, 27, 38, 217, 223
as encouraging third-party developers to create their own apps, 191
as enterprise system, 321
as popular Zoom app, 203
using Zoom with, 27, 38
Zoom as integrating with, 348

Save
as annotation option, 113
description of icon for host-annotation options (on webinar), 229

Sayre, Wallace Stanley (political scientist and professor), 328

Scheck, Justin (journalist), 281

Schumpeter, Joseph (economist), 246–247

Schwartz, Barry (author)
The Paradox of Choice: Why More Is Less, 193

screen captures, sending, 148–149

screen-sharing
allowing participants to share screen as security-related option, 252
basics of, 105–108
cautions with, 110
letting meeting participants control your screen, 109–111
limiting who can control main screen, 273
performing different tasks while, 109
regaining control of your computer, 111
requesting control of host's screen, 111
in webinars, 228–229
on Zoom Rooms, 283

TV watching, via Zoom, 357

Twitter

  as benefitting from network effects, 317

  as confronting security and privacy challenges, 274

  as encouraging third-party developers to create their own apps, 191

  as having to manage double-edged sword of sudden, massive growth, 247

  poll about individuals' preferred work-from-home (WFH) tools on, 22–23

  sharing webinar on, 214, 236

  use of 2FA for, 263

  Zoom on, 352

2019 Inc., Zoom's placement on 5000 list of America's fastest growing private companies, 16

two-factor authentication (2FA)

  activating it at organizational level, 261

  enabling of, 338

  overview, 260–261

  remaining vigilant, even with it enabled, 263–264

  turning it on for yourself, 261–263

U

UberConference, 19

UI (user interface)

  getting to know Zoom's, 58–59

  Zoom's changes to, 256

Undo

  as annotation option, 113

  description of icon for host-annotation options (on webinar), 229

Unified Communications (UC), 11

unified messaging, as communication service, 11

Upcoming Events, as type of usage report, 183

updates

  dealing with forced upgrades, 259

  importance of, 339

  locating your version of Meetings & Chat, 257

  process for updating, 258–259

  types of, 256

upgrades, 26, 34–35, 37, 52–53, 60, 67, 259, 338

Urben, Urben Immersive Datapresence (ID) product, 288, 289

Usage, as type of member report, 185

user authentication, 264–267

user groups

  applying different security options to different user groups, 269–270

  changing, 66–67

  comparing channels to, 174

  creating new user group, 65

  overview, 64

  populating, 65–66

user interface (UI)

  getting to know Zoom's, 58–59

  Zoom's changes to, 256

user management, 35

user roles

  changing an existing user's role, 69

  creating new ones, 68

  default user roles, 67

  importance of, 67–69

user status

  changing yours, 130–133

  understanding of, 128–134

users. *See also specific user groups*

  adding of to your Zoom account, 60–61

  deleting existing users, 62–63

  ensuring privacy of, 253

  managing of via IM groups, 160–162

  types of, 60

  unlinking of, 63–64

V

Valera, Richard (analyst), 16

vanity web addresses, creation of, 35

video

  pinning of in Zoom Rooms, 283

  spotlighting of in Zoom Rooms, 283

About the Author

Phil Simon is a dynamic keynote speaker, Slack and Zoom trainer, recognized technology authority, and college professor-for-hire. He is the award-winning author of nine previous books on communication, technology, strategy, and analytics, most recently *Slack For Dummies.*

Simon's contributions have appeared on The Harvard Business Review, *The New York Times,* CNBC, and many other media outlets. He holds degrees from Carnegie Mellon University and Cornell University.

To find out more about his work, watch his talks, and read additional tips on using Zoom, visit www.philsimon.com.

Dedication

In memory of George Floyd

— October 14, 1973 – May 25, 2020

Author's Acknowledgments

Kudos to Team Wiley: Steve Hayes, Paul Chen, Kristie Pyles, Prescott Perez-Fox, and my insanely talented editor Kelly Ewing.

My agent Matt Wagner helped seal the deal on this book. *Zoom For Dummies* wouldn't exist without his negotiation skills.

I am forever indebted to the following Zoomies for graciously sharing their time and knowledge with me throughout the writing process: Esther Yoon, Janelle Raney, Jeff Smith, Many Yeung Garby, Niel Levonius, Theresa Geis, and Wes Liu. Sebastian Thorpe, Jonny Entwistle, Jeff Fillbrandt, Shawn Spaventa, Gerald Abualy, David Flores, Kathy Katz, Michael Zihmer, Scott Krueckeberg, Luke Cocalis, Kerry Barrett, Rebekah Carter, and Melissa Turk let me pick their big brains as well.

A tip of the hat to the people who keep me grounded and listen to my rants: Alan Simon, Luke Fletcher, Terri Griffith, Mike Frutiger, Dalton Cervo, Rob Hornyak, Hina Arora, Steve Putnam, Emily and Seth Freeman, Chris Olsen, Greg Dawson, Steve Katz, Michael Viola, Joe Mirza, Dave Sandberg, Chris McGee, Scott Berkun, Josh Bernoff, Alan Berkson, Andrew Botwin, John Andrewski, Jennifer Zito, Thor Sandell, Rob Metting, Jason Horowitz, Marc Paolella, Peter and Hope Simon, Mark Cenicola, Jason Conigliari, JR Camillon, and Brian and Heather Morgan.

For decades of incredible music, a tip of the hat to the members of Rush (Geddy, Alex, and Neil), Marillion (h, Steve, Ian, Mark, and Pete), and Dream Theater (Jordan, John, John, Mike, and James). Your songs continue to inspire millions of discerning fans. I am proud to call myself one of them.

Vince Gilligan, Peter Gould, Bryan Cranston, Aaron Paul, Dean Norris, Anna Gunn, Bob Odenkirk, Betsy Brandt, Jonathan Banks, Giancarlo Esposito, RJ Mitte, Michael Mando, Rhea Seehorn, Michael McKean, and the rest of the *Breaking Bad* and *Better Call Saul* teams have made me want to do great work.

Finally, to my parents. I'm not here without you.

Publisher's Acknowledgments

Executive Editor: Steve Hayes

Project Editor: Kelly Ewing

Technical Editor: Prescott Perez-Fox

Sr. Editorial Assistant: Cherie Case

Proofreader: Debbye Butler

Production Editor: Siddique Shaik

Cover Image: © pixelfit/Getty Images

Take dummies with you everywhere you go!

Whether you are excited about e-books, want more from the web, must have your mobile apps, or are swept up in social media, dummies makes everything easier.

Find us online!

dummies.com

Leverage the power

Dummies is the global leader in the reference category and one of the most trusted and highly regarded brands in the world. No longer just focused on books, customers now have access to the dummies content they need in the format they want. Together we'll craft a solution that engages your customers, stands out from the competition, and helps you meet your goals.

Advertising & Sponsorships

Connect with an engaged audience on a powerful multimedia site, and position your message alongside expert how-to content. Dummies.com is a one-stop shop for free, online information and know-how curated by a team of experts.

- Targeted ads
- Video
- Email Marketing
- Microsites
- Sweepstakes sponsorship

20 MILLION PAGE VIEWS EVERY SINGLE MONTH

15 MILLION UNIQUE VISITORS PER MONTH

43% OF ALL VISITORS ACCESS THE SITE VIA THEIR MOBILE DEVICES

700,000 NEWSLETTER SUBSCRIPTIONS TO THE INBOXES OF *300,000* UNIQUE INDIVIDUALS EVERY WEEK

# of dummies

Custom Publishing

Reach a global audience in any language by creating a solution that will differentiate you from competitors, amplify your message, and encourage customers to make a buying decision.

- Apps
- Books
- eBooks
- Video
- Audio
- Webinars

Brand Licensing & Content

Leverage the strength of the world's most popular reference brand to reach new audiences and channels of distribution.

For more information, visit dummies.com/biz

PERSONAL ENRICHMENT

9781119187790	9781119179030	9781119293354	9781119293347	9781119310068	9781119235606
USA $26.00	USA $21.99	USA $24.99	USA $22.99	USA $22.99	USA $24.99
CAN $31.99	CAN $25.99	CAN $29.99	CAN $27.99	CAN $27.99	CAN $29.99
UK £19.99	UK £16.99	UK £17.99	UK £16.99	UK £16.99	UK £17.99

9781119251163	9781119235491	9781119279952	9781119283133	9781119287117	9781119130246
USA $24.99	USA $26.99	USA $24.99	USA $24.99	USA $24.99	USA $22.99
CAN $29.99	CAN $31.99	CAN $29.99	CAN $29.99	CAN $29.99	CAN $27.99
UK £17.99	UK £19.99	UK £17.99	UK £17.99	UK £16.99	UK £16.99

PROFESSIONAL DEVELOPMENT

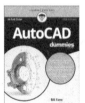

9781119311041	9781119255796	9781119293439	9781119281467	9781119280651	9781119251132	9781119310563
USA $24.99	USA $39.99	USA $26.99	USA $26.99	USA $29.99	USA $24.99	USA $34.00
CAN $29.99	CAN $47.99	CAN $31.99	CAN $31.99	CAN $35.99	CAN $29.99	CAN $41.99
UK £17.99	UK £27.99	UK £19.99	UK £19.99	UK £21.99	UK £17.99	UK £24.99

9781119181705	9781119263593	9781119257769	9781119293477	9781119265313	9781119239314	9781119293323
USA $29.99	USA $26.99	USA $29.99	USA $26.99	USA $24.99	USA $29.99	USA $29.99
CAN $35.99	CAN $31.99	CAN $35.99	CAN $31.99	CAN $29.99	CAN $35.99	CAN $35.99
UK £21.99	UK £19.99	UK £21.99	UK £19.99	UK £17.99	UK £21.99	UK £21.99

dummies.com

dummies®
A Wiley Brand

Learning Made Easy

ACADEMIC

9781119293576
USA $19.99
CAN $23.99
UK £15.99

9781119293637
USA $19.99
CAN $23.99
UK £15.99

9781119293491
USA $19.99
CAN $23.99
UK £15.99

9781119293460
USA $19.99
CAN $23.99
UK £15.99

9781119293590
USA $19.99
CAN $23.99
UK £15.99

9781119215844
USA $26.99
CAN $31.99
UK £19.99

9781119293378
USA $22.99
CAN $27.99
UK £16.99

9781119293521
USA $19.99
CAN $23.99
UK £15.99

9781119239178
USA $18.99
CAN $22.99
UK £14.99

9781119263883
USA $26.99
CAN $31.99
UK £19.99

Available Everywhere Books Are Sold

dummies.com

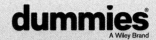

Small books for big imaginations

GETTING STARTED WITH Coding
Get Creative with Code!
Camille McCue, PhD

9781119177173
USA $9.99
CAN $9.99
UK £8.99

MODDING Minecraft
Build Your Own Minecraft Mods!
Sarah Guthals, PhD
Stephen Foster, PhD
Lindsey Handley, PhD

9781119177272
USA $9.99
CAN $9.99
UK £8.99

MAKING YouTube VIDEOS
Star in Your Own Video!
Nick Willoughby

9781119177241
USA $9.99
CAN $9.99
UK £8.99

DESIGNING Digital Games
Create Games with Scratch!
Derek Breen

9781119177210
USA $9.99
CAN $9.99
UK £8.99

GETTING STARTED WITH Raspberry Pi
Program Your Raspberry Pi!
Richard Wentk

9781119262657
USA $9.99
CAN $9.99
UK £6.99

EXPERIMENTING WITH Science
Think, Test and Learn!
Chris J. Mullins, PhD

9781119291336
USA $9.99
CAN $9.99
UK £6.99

CREATING Digital Animations
Animate Stories with Scratch!
Derek Breen

9781119233527
USA $9.99
CAN $9.99
UK £6.99

GETTING STARTED WITH Engineering
Think Like an Engineer!
Camille McCue, PhD

9781119291220
USA $9.99
CAN $9.99
UK £6.99

WRITING Computer Code
Learn the Language of Computers!
Chris Minnick and Eva Holland

9781119177302
USA $9.99
CAN $9.99
UK £8.99

Unleash Their Creativity

dummies.com